Oracle Information Integration, Migration, and Consolidation

The definitive guide to information integration and migration in a heterogeneous world

Use Oracle technologies and best practices to manage, maintain, migrate, and mobilize data

Tom Laszewski

Prakash Nauduri

Jason Williamson

[PACKT] enterprise ⚜
professional expertise distilled
PUBLISHING

BIRMINGHAM - MUMBAI

Oracle Information Integration, Migration, and Consolidation

The definitive guide to information integration and migration in a heterogeneous world

First published: September 2011

Production Reference: 4090112

Published by Packt Publishing Ltd.
Livery Place
35 Livery Street
Birmingham B3 2PB, UK

ISBN 978-1-849682-20-6

www.packtpub.com

Cover Image by Artie Ng (artherng@yahoo.com.au)

Credits

Authors
Tom Laszewski
Prakash Nauduri
Jason Williamson

Reviewers
Peter C. Boyd-Bowman
Martin A. Kendall
Asif Momen
Ronald Rood

Acquisition Editor
Stephanie Moss

Development Editor
Roger D'souza

Technical Editor
Shreerang Deshpande

Project Coordinator
Zainab Bagasrawala

Proofreader
Kelly Hutchinson

Indexer
Monica Ajmera Mehta

Graphics
Geetanjali Sawant
Valentina Dsilva

Production Coordinator
Alwin Roy

Cover Work
Alwin Roy

About the Authors

Tom Laszewski has over 20 years experience in databases, middleware, software development, management, and building strong technical partnerships. He is currently the Director of Cloud Migrations in the Oracle Platform Migrations Group. He has established the initial business and technical relationships with Oracle's migration SIs and tools partners. His main responsibility is the successful completion of migration projects initiated through the Oracle partner ecosystem and Oracle Sales. These migration projects involve mainframe service enablement and integration, mainframe re-host and re-architecture, and Sybase, DB2, SQL Server, Informix, and other relational database migrations. Tom works on a daily basis with TCS, Infosys, and niche migration systems integrators, customer technical architectures, CTOs and CIOs, and Oracle account managers to ensure the success of migration projects. He is the sole Oracle person responsible for third-party migration services and tools partners. He provides customer feedback, tools direction, and design feedback to Oracle product development, management, and executive teams regarding Oracle migration and integration tools. Tom also works with cloud service providers to assist in their migration of current non-Oracle based offerings to an Oracle-based platform. This work involves solution architecture of Oracle based cloud solutions utilizing Oracle Exadata, Oracle Virtual Server, and Oracle Enterprise Linux.

Before Oracle, Tom held technical and project management positions at Sybase and EDS. He has provided strategic and technical advice to several startup companies in the Database, Blade, XML, and storage areas. Tom holds a Master of Science degree in Computer Information Systems from Boston University.

He has authored *Oracle Modernization Solutions*, Packt Publishing, and co-authored *Information Systems Transformation*, Morgan Kaufmann.

My two sons, Slade and Logan, are the greatest as they understood the importance of "daddy's book writing", but also kept the task from consuming my life. I would also like to thank both my co-authors, Prakash and Jason, as they have been instrumental in moving my career and life in a positive direction. A special thanks to Prakash as he has been a direct contributor to my career growth while working for me this past decade. His problem solving and technical skills depth and breath are unparalleled in this ever-changing world of technology. I would also like to thank my dad, Eugene Laszewski, for teaching me the merit of hard work and integrity.

Prakash Nauduri has over 19 years of experience working with databases, middleware, development tools/technologies, software design, development, and training. In his current role as Technical Director of the Oracle Platform Migrations Group, he is responsible for evaluating/evangelizing Oracle technologies that serve the customer's needs for platform migrations, consolidation, and optimization efforts. He is also responsible for assisting Oracle customers/partners in developing migration methodologies, strategies, and best practices, as well as engaging with the customers/partners in executing PoCs, Pilots, Workshops, and Migration Projects to ensure successful completion of the migration projects.

Prakash has been working with Oracle Partners for over 12 years focusing on the successful adoption of the latest Oracle technologies. He has participated in numerous competitive performance benchmarks while customers/partners evaluated Oracle as the platform of choice against competition.

Before joining Oracle, Prakash worked with automotive industries in India, namely Hero Group and Eicher Tractors Ltd. as Developer/DBA/Systems Analyst. He holds a Bachelor's Degree in Science from Berhampur University, Orissa, India.

I would like to thank my wife Kavita and daughter Sriya for their endless love, patience, and support; and allowing me to write this book over many late evenings and weekends. I would also like to thank Tom Laszewski and Jason Williamson for their valuable input and guidance. Many thanks to my management team, Lance Knowlton and John Gawkowski for encouraging me to pursue opportunities like this to broaden my horizons.

Jason Williamson is an experienced business and IT executive and a recognized innovator of technology and business transformation. As an expert in modernization and business transformation, he has worked with G1000 organizations developing IT and business modernization strategies. He has also been responsible for executing Oracle's modernization program.

He currently serves as Executive Client Advisor for Oracle. As a client advisor, he works directly with the most senior-level executives (C-level) in Oracle's most marquee accounts, advising senior executives on business and technology strategy and alignment, increasing returns on previous investments and identifying innovative, strategic solutions to solve challenging business problems.

Prior to joining Oracle, he had experience in technology and business leadership. Jason was the founder and CTO for the construction industry's first SaaS/CRM offering. He led BuildLinks from a concept to a multi-million dollar company and forged key financial and business partnerships with Sprint/Nextel and Intuit, helping to create innovative products. His creative thinking and vision opened the door for him to establish a non-profit NGO dedicated to entrepreneurial and technology education in developing nations, which enabled the establishment of multiple self-sustaining companies in Latin America.

Beyond his entrepreneurial efforts, he has served in key positions within Fortune 500 professional services and financial services firms including Capital One and GE Capital. His background includes experience in financial services, construction, public sector, defense, and healthcare. He also served his country in the United States Marine Corps.

Mr. Williamson obtained his B.S. degree in MIS from Virginia Commonwealth University, and is completing his M.S. in Management of IT Strategy from the University of Virginia.

Mr. Williamson also co-authored *Oracle Modernization Solutions*, Packt Publishing.

Thanks to my friends and colleagues at Oracle for providing collaboration and support. Thanks to Prakash and Tom for letting me rope them into yet another project. Tom, you are welcome. Thanks to Solix and Raghu Kodali for their gracious contribution to this work. I want to give a final thank you to my wife, Susan, for always supporting and encouraging me on my endeavors. You are a gift.

Acknowledgements

The authors would like to thank Estuate, Inc. for a significant contribution to Chapter 8, including two customer case studies. Estuate, Inc. is a Silicon Valley-based IT services firm founded in 2004 by two ex-Oracle executives — Prakash Balebail and Nagaraja Kini. Together they created and managed the Oracle Cooperative Applications Initiative for many years, and so have deep Oracle-based application integration experience. Since its inception, Estuate has executed 20+ application integration projects, many for ISVs who build out-of-the-box integration between their products and Oracle Applications — including Oracle E-Business Suite, Siebel, PeopleSoft, and JD Edwards.

We would also like to thank another contributer, Raghu Kodali of Solix. Raghu's work on chapter 9 and Information Lifecycle Management brought forth some important ideas and strategies to the book. Raghu is also a former Oracle employee and works for Solix, a Silicon Valley-based company focusing on ILM solutions.

About the Reviewers

Peter C. Boyd-Bowman is a Technical Manager and Consultant with the Oracle Corporation. He has over 30 years of software engineering and database management experience, including 12 years of focused interest in data warehousing and business intelligence. Capitalizing on his extensive background in Oracle database technologies dating back to 1985, he has spent recent years specializing in data migration. After many successful project implementations using Oracle Warehouse Builder and shortly after Oracle's acquisition of the Sunopsis Corporation, he switched his area of focus over to Oracle's flagship ETL product: Oracle Data Integrator. He holds a BS degree in Industrial Management and Computer Science from Purdue University and currently resides in North Carolina.

Martin A. Kendall has been working with IT systems since the mid 1980s. He has a deep understanding of application infrastructure, system engineering, and database architecture. He specializes in Oracle RAC and Oracle Identity Management solutions, along with object-oriented software engineering through the use of the Unified Process.

Martin consults through two distinct organizations to deliver Oracle integration services through sysnetica.com and to provide private cloud infrastructure adoption consultancy through dicedcloud.com.

Respect to my wife in understanding my interest in helping review this book among all the other 1001 things that life is waiting for me to do.

Asif Momen has been working with Oracle technologies for over 12 years and has expertise in performance tuning and high availability. He has a Master's degree in Software Systems from Birla Institute of Technology and Science (BITS), Pilani.

He is an Oracle ACE and is an OCP certified DBA, Forms Developer, and RAC Expert. He is a speaker at Oracle OpenWorld and All India Oracle User Group (AIOUG). In addition, he is the Editor of *Oracle Connect*—the quarterly publication of AIOUG. His particular interests are database tuning, Oracle RAC, Oracle Data Guard, and backup and recovery.

Asif posts his ideas and opinions on *The Momen Blog* (`http://momendba.blogspot.com`). He can be reached at `asif.momen@gmail.com`.

Ronald Rood is an innovating Oracle DBA, an ACE with over 20 years of IT experience. He has built and managed cluster databases on about each and every platform that Oracle ever supported from the famous OPS databases in version 7, until the latest RAC releases, currently being 11*g*. Ronald is constantly looking for ways to get the most value out of the database to make investment for his customers even more valuable. He knows how to the handle the power of the rich Unix environment very well, making him a first class trouble-shooter and solution architect. Next to the spoken languages like Dutch, English, German, and French, he also writes fluently in many scripting languages.

Currently, he is a principal consultant working for Ciber (CBR) in The Netherlands, where he cooperates in many complex projects for large companies where downtime is not an option. Ciber CBR is an Oracle Platinum Partner and committed to the limit.

He can often be found replying in the Oracle forums where he is an active member, writes his own blog (`http://ronr.blogspot.com`) called *From errors we learn*, and writes for various Oracle-related magazines. He is also the author of Packt Publishing's *Mastering Oracle Scheduler in Oracle 11g Databases*, where he fills the gap between the Oracle documentation and the customer questions. As well as reviewing this book, he was also part of the technical reviewing team for Packt Publishing's *Oracle 11g R1/R2 Real Application Clusters Essentials*.

Ronald has lots of certifications, among them:

- Oracle Certified Master
- Oracle RAC ACE
- Oracle Certified Professional
- Oracle Database 11*g* Tuning Specialist
- Oracle Database 11*g* Data Warehouse Certified Implementation Specialist

Ronald fills his time with Oracle, his family, sky-diving, radio controlled model airplane flying, running a scouting group, and having a lot of fun.

His quote: "*A problem is merely a challenge that might take a little time to solve.*"

www.PacktPub.com

Support files, eBooks, discount offers and more

You might want to visit www.PacktPub.com for support files and downloads related to your book.

Did you know that Packt offers eBook versions of every book published, with PDF and ePub files available? You can upgrade to the eBook version at www.PacktPub.com and as a print book customer, you are entitled to a discount on the eBook copy. Get in touch with us at service@packtpub.com for more details.

At www.PacktPub.com, you can also read a collection of free technical articles, sign up for a range of free newsletters and receive exclusive discounts and offers on Packt books and eBooks.

PACKTLiB

http://PacktLib.PacktPub.com

Do you need instant solutions to your IT questions? PacktLib is Packt's online digital book library. Here, you can access, read and search across Packt's entire library of books.

Why Subscribe?

- Fully searchable across every book published by Packt
- Copy and paste, print and bookmark content
- On demand and accessible via web browser

Free Access for Packt account holders

If you have an account with Packt at www.PacktPub.com, you can use this to access PacktLib today and view nine entirely free books. Simply use your login credentials for immediate access.

Instant Updates on New Packt Books

Get notified! Find out when new books are published by following @PacktEnterprise on Twitter, or the *Packt Enterprise* Facebook page.

Table of Contents

Preface

Information integration and migration in most organizations is a critical function and takes place every day. This is usually accomplished through home-grown Extraction Transformation and Load (ETL) processes, File Transfer Protocol (FTP), and bulk file loads. This is even the case in Oracle shops. What has been created in the industry is an inefficient, cumbersome process that is not rationalized, full of errors, and is costly to maintain. To further complicate matters, this has to be accomplished with disported data sources and platforms.

Today, Oracle information integration still takes place this way, even though Oracle offers an extensive and rich set of information integration products and technologies. Oracle Information Integration architectures contain solutions and tools that leverage things like PL/SQL stored procedures, SQL Perl scripts, SQL Loader Korn Shells, and custom C and Java code. This book will allow you to drive more business value from IT by enabling more efficient solutions at a lower cost and with fewer errors. This will increase transparency for the business, improve data quality, and provide accurate market intelligence for executives. We will help you by showing you when, where, and how to use Oracle GoldenGate, Oracle Data Integrator, Oracle Stand-by Database, Oracle SOA Suite, Oracle Data Hub, Oracle Application Integration Architecture, Oracle SQL Developer, and more.

This book will provide you with valuable information and hands-on resources to be successful with information integration and migration with Oracle. If you are already an Oracle shop and want to learn the latest on Oracle's information integration platform, or you are migrating or consolidating to an Oracle Database platform, this book is for you.

What this book covers

Chapter 1, Getting Started With Information Integration, we present the overview of the information integration, data migration, and consolidation topic. You will learn the key concepts and build the foundations for the hands-on application of these concepts for your organization's needs in the remainder of the book.

Chapter 2, Oracle Tools and Products, covers all the key Oracle products, tools, and technologies for you to consider when planning to implement integration, consolidation, and migration projects. The Oracle products, tools, and technologies are discussed separately and also compared and contrasted to provide you with the information needed to decide the product or products for your unique use cases.

Chapter 3, Application and Data Integration Case Study, provides the readers with the experience of a real world end-to-end application and process integration. In this chapter, we will look at the products and tools used, and even the work plan and design documents that were used. This is an excellent blueprint for your current or future projects.

Chapter 4, Oracle Database Migrations is a hands-on guide on how to migrate non-Oracle relational database sources to the Oracle Database. Oracle SQL Developer, a relational database modeling and migration tool, is covered in detail along with Oracle Data Integrator and GoldenGate.

Chapter 5, Database Migration Challenges and Solutions, covers database migration challenges and solutions. Schema and data migration are covered, along with specific issues like globalization. Some customer migration case studies are also covered.

Chapter 6, Data Consolidation and Management, investigates the key concepts and infrastructure needed for producing a consolidated view of data for the whole organization. We will look at Oracle Data Hub, Coherence, TimesTen products and Oracle Exadata, a database machine which is a consolidated software, hardware, and storage solution for your consolidation efforts.

Chapter 7, Database-centric Data Integration, focuses on the data-centric integration and data interchange between different databases either in near real-time, on-demand in the context of active transaction or bulk data merges between source and target databases. Oracle GoldenGate, Oracle Data Integrator, and Oracle Gateways are all covered in detail. We look at a case study for `Overstock.com` and their usage of Oracle Golden Gate and Oracle Data Integrator for highly available and integrated solutions.

Chapter 8, Application and Process Integration examines Oracle SOA Suite integration products like Oracle BPEL, Oracle Service Bus, Oracle SOA Adapters, and Oracle Application Integration Architecture. At the end of the chapter, you will have a clear understanding of what Oracle products to use for each specific application integration project you have.

Chapter 9, Information Lifecycle Management for Transactional Applications is the final installment of data integration. In this chapter we look at how to manage the entire lifecycle of data. We will look at Oracle ILM and how to manage and archive non-Oracle data sources.

The *Appendix* explores emerging cloud trends such as integration in the cloud, and data application and process integration convergence. It also contains the merits and drawbacks to some of these emerging trends and technologies, such as web services for all integration. By the end of the appendix, you will have an understanding on whether web services for all your integration needs is the best approach for your company.

Who this book is written for

If you are a DBA, architect or data integration specialist who is running an Oracle Database and want to learn the latest on Oracle's information integration platform, then this book is for you. Middleware application integration specialists, architects or even developers that are dealing with application integration systems can find this book useful. It will also be incredibly beneficial for anyone who is migrating or consolidating to an Oracle Database platform.

Having a working knowledge of Oracle Database, data integration, consolidation and migration, as well as some familiarity with integration middleware products and information service buses will be helpful in understanding the concepts in this book.

Conventions

In this book, you will find a number of styles of text that distinguish between different kinds of information. Here are some examples of these styles, and an explanation of their meaning.

New terms and **important words** are shown in bold. Words that you see on the screen, in menus or dialog boxes for example, appear in the text like this:

"JDBC Drivers can also be added in the **Migration Wizard** during the migration process, which is discussed later in this chapter, by clicking on the **Add Platform** link on the Source Database selection window, as shown in the following screenshot:"

[📝 Warnings or important notes appear in a box like this.]

[💡 Tips and tricks appear like this.]

Reader feedback

Feedback from our readers is always welcome. Let us know what you think about this book—what you liked or may have disliked. Reader feedback is important for us to develop titles that you really get the most out of.

To send us general feedback, simply send an e-mail to feedback@packtpub.com, and mention the book title via the subject of your message.

If there is a book that you need and would like to see us publish, please send us a note in the **SUGGEST A TITLE** form on www.packtpub.com or e-mail suggest@packtpub.com.

If there is a topic that you have expertise in and you are interested in either writing or contributing to a book, see our author guide on www.packtpub.com/authors.

Customer support

Now that you are the proud owner of a Packt book, we have a number of things to help you to get the most from your purchase.

Errata

Although we have taken every care to ensure the accuracy of our content, mistakes do happen. If you find a mistake in one of our books—maybe a mistake in the text or the code—we would be grateful if you would report this to us. By doing so, you can save other readers from frustration and help us improve subsequent versions of this book. If you find any errata, please report them by visiting http://www.packtpub.com/support, selecting your book, clicking on the **errata submission form** link, and entering the details of your errata. Once your errata are verified, your submission will be accepted and the errata will be uploaded on our website, or added to any list of existing errata, under the Errata section of that title. Any existing errata can be viewed by selecting your title from http://www.packtpub.com/support.

Piracy

Piracy of copyright material on the Internet is an ongoing problem across all media. At Packt, we take the protection of our copyright and licenses very seriously. If you come across any illegal copies of our works, in any form, on the Internet, please provide us with the location address or website name immediately so that we can pursue a remedy.

Please contact us at copyright@packtpub.com with a link to the suspected pirated material.

We appreciate your help in protecting our authors, and our ability to bring you valuable content.

Questions

You can contact us at questions@packtpub.com if you are having a problem with any aspect of the book, and we will do our best to address it.

1
Getting Started with Information Integration

Business change is a constant necessity as a result of increased competition, improved technology, and shifts in consumer patterns. As a result, an enterprise will reorganize, acquire other businesses, create new applications, and downsize others. Throughout these changes, companies are faced with the challenge of efficiently provisioning their resources in response to their business priorities. To deliver data where it is needed, when it is needed, requires sophisticated information integration technologies.

This chapter discusses the basic concepts of information integration and reviews historical approaches to information integration. We will compare data-level integration with process and application integration. This will provide some solid examples for real world decisions, when trying to understand information integration and how this relates to your business and technical initiatives.

This point is often the hard part of any heterogeneous situation. In the latter part of the chapter, you will understand how information integration is used in a **Service Oriented Architecture (SOA)** and the impact to a SOA-based system.

Why consider information integration?

The useful life of pre-relational mainframe database management system engines is coming to an end because of a diminishing application and skills base, and increasing costs. – Gartner Group

During the last 30 years, many companies have deployed mission critical applications running various aspects of their business on the legacy systems. Most of these environments have been built around a proprietary database management system running on the mainframe. According to Gartner Group, the installed base of mainframe, Sybase, and some open source databases has been shrinking. There is vendor sponsored market research that shows mainframe database management systems are growing, which, according to Gartner, is due primarily to increased prices from the vendors, currency conversions, and mainframe CPU replacements.

Over the last few years, many companies have been migrating mission critical applications off the mainframe onto open standard **Relational Database Management Systems (RDBMS)** such as Oracle for the following reasons:

- **Reducing skill base**: Students and new entrants to the job market are being trained on RDBMS like Oracle and not on the legacy database management systems. Legacy personnel are retiring, and those that are not are moving into expensive consulting positions to arbitrage the demand.

- **Lack of flexibility to meet business requirements**: The world of business is constantly changing and new business requirements like compliance and outsourcing require application changes. Changing the behavior, structure, access, interface or size of old databases is very hard and often not possible, limiting the ability of the IT department to meet the needs of the business. Most applications on the aging platforms are 10 to 30 years old and are long past their original usable lifetime.

- **Lack of Independent Software Vendor (ISV)applications**: With most ISVs focusing on the larger market, it is very difficult to find applications, infrastructure, and tools for legacy platforms. This requires every application to be custom coded on the closed environment by scarce in-house experts or by expensive outside consultants.

- **Total Cost of Ownership (TCO)**: As the user base for proprietary systems decreases, hardware, spare parts, and vendor support costs have been increasing. Adding to this are the high costs of changing legacy applications, paid either as consulting fees for a replacement for diminishing numbers of mainframe trained experts or increased salaries for existing personnel. All leading to a very high TCO which doesn't even take into account the opportunity cost to the business of having inflexible systems.

Business challenges in data integration and migration

Once the decision has been taken to migrate away from a legacy environment, the primary business challenge is **business continuity**. Since many of these applications are mission critical, running various aspects of the business, the migration strategy has to ensure continuity to the new application—and in the event of failure, rollback to the mainframe application. This approach requires data in the existing application to be synchronized with data on the new application.

Making the challenge of data migration more complicated is the fact that legacy applications tend to be interdependent, but the need from a risk mitigation standpoint is to move applications one at a time. A follow-on challenge is prioritizing the order in which applications are to be moved off the mainframe, and ensuring that the order meets both the business needs and minimizes the risk in the migration process.

Once a specific application is being migrated, the next challenge is to decide which business processes will be migrated to the new application. Many companies have business processes that are present, because that's the way their systems work. When migrating an application off the mainframe, many business processes do not need to migrate. Even among the business processes that need to be migrated, some of these business processes will need to be moved as-is and some of them will have to be changed. Many companies utilize the opportunity afforded by a migration to redo the business processes they have had to live with for many years.

Data is the foundation of the modernization process. You can move the application, business logic, and work flow, but without a clean migration of the data the business requirements will not be met. A clean data migration involves:

- Data that is organized in a usable format by all modern tools
- Data that is optimized for an Oracle database
- Data that is easy to maintain

Technical challenges of information integration

The technical challenges with any information integration all stem from the fact that the application accesses heterogeneous data (VSAM, IMS, IDMS, ADABAS, DB2, MSSQL, and so on) that can even be in a non-relational hierarchical format. Some of the technical problems include:

- The flexible file definition feature used in COBOL applications in the existing system will have data files with multi-record formats and multi-record types in the same dataset—neither of which exist in RDBMS. Looping data structure and substructure or relative offset record organization such as a linked list, which are difficult to map into a relational table.

- Data and referential integrity is managed by the Oracle database engine. However, legacy applications already have this integrity built in. One question is whether to use Oracle to handle this integrity and remove the logic from the application.

- Finally, creating an Oracle schema to maximize performance, which includes mapping non-oracle keys to Oracle primary and secondary keys; especially when legacy data is organized in order of key value which can affect the performance on an Oracle RDBMS. There are also differences in how some engines process transactions, rollbacks, and record locking.

General approaches to information integration and migration

There are several technical approaches to consider when doing any kind of integration or migration activity. In this section, we will look at a methodology or approach for both data integration and data migration.

Data integration

Clearly, given this range of requirements, there are a variety of different integration strategies, including the following:

- **Consolidated**: A consolidated data integration solution moves all data into a single database and manages it in a central location. There are some considerations that need to be known regarding the differences between non-Oracle and Oracle mechanics. Transaction processing is an example. Some engines use implicit commits and some manage character sets differently than Oracle does, this has an impact on sort order.

- **Federated**: A federated data integration solution leaves data in the individual data source where it is normally maintained and updated, and simply consolidates it on the fly as needed. In this case, multiple data sources will appear to be integrated into a single virtual database, masking the number and different kinds of databases behind the consolidated view. These solutions can work bidirectionally.

- **Shared**: A shared data integration solution actually moves data and events from one or more source databases to a consolidated resource, or queue, created to serve one or more new applications. Data can be maintained and exchanged using technologies such as replication, message queuing, transportable table spaces, and FTP.

Oracle has extensive support for consolidated data integration and while there are many obvious benefits to the consolidated solution, it is not practical for any organization that must deal with legacy systems or integrate with data it does not own. Therefore, we will not discuss this type any further, but instead concentrate on federated and shared solutions.

Data migration

Over 80 percent of migration projects fail or overrun their original budgets/ timelines, according to a study by the Standish Group. In most cases, this is because of a lack of understanding of some of the unique challenges of a migration project. The top five challenges of a migration project are:

- **Little migration expertise to draw from**: Migration is not an industry-recognized area of expertise with an established body of knowledge and practices, nor have most companies built up any internal competency to draw from.

- **Insufficient understanding of data and source systems**: The required data is spread across multiple source systems, not in the right format, of poor quality, only accessible through vaguely understood interfaces, and sometimes missing altogether.

- **Continuously evolving target system**: The target system is often under development at the time of data migration, and the requirements often change during the project.

- **Complex target data validations**: Many target systems have restrictions, constraints, and thresholds on the validity, integrity, and quality of the data to be loaded.

- **Repeated synchronization after the initial migration**: Migration is not a one-time effort. Old systems are usually kept alive after new systems launch and synchronization is required between the old and new systems during this handoff period. Also, long after the migration is completed, companies often have to prove the migration was complete and accurate to various government, judicial, and regulatory bodies.

Most migration projects fail because of an inappropriate migration methodology, because the migration problem is thought of as a four stage process:

- Analyze the source data
- Extract/transform the data into the target formats
- Validate and cleanse the data
- Load the data into the target

However, because of the migration challenges discussed previously, this four stage project methodology often fails miserably.

The challenge begins during the initial analysis of the source data when most of the assumptions about the data are proved wrong. Since there is never enough time planned for analysis, any mapping specification from the mainframe to Oracle is effectively an intelligent guess. Based on the initial mapping specification, extractions, and transformations developed run into changing target data requirements, requiring additional analysis and changes to the mapping specification. Validating the data according to various integrity and quality constraints will typically pose a challenge. If the validation fails, the project goes back to further analysis and then further rounds of extractions and transformations. When the data is finally ready to be loaded into Oracle, unexpected data scenarios will often break the loading process and send the project back for more analysis, more extractions and transformations, and more validations. Approaching migration as a four stage process means continually going back to earlier stages due to the five challenges of data migration.

The biggest problem with migration project methodology is that it does not support the iterative nature of migrations. Further complicating the issue is that the technology used for data migration often consists of general-purpose tools repurposed for each of the four project stages. These tools are usually non-integrated and only serve to make difficult processes more difficult on top of a poor methodology.

The ideal model for successfully managing a data migration project is not based on multiple independent tools. Thus, a cohesive method enables you to cycle or spiral your way through the migration process — analyzing the data, extracting and transforming the data, validating the data, and loading it into targets, and repeating the same process until the migration is successfully completed. This approach enables target-driven analysis, validating assumptions, refining designs, and applying best practices as the project progresses. This agile methodology uses the same four stages of analyze, extract/transform, validate and load. However, the four stages are not only iterated, but also interconnected with one another.

An iterative approach is best achieved through a unified toolset, or platform, that leverages automation and provides functionality which spans all four stages. In an iterative process, there is a big difference between using a different tool for each stage and one unified toolset across all four stages. In one unified toolset, the results of one stage can be easily carried into the next, enabling faster, more frequent and ultimately less iteration which is the key to success in a migration project. A single platform not only unifies the development team across the project phases, but also unifies the separate teams that may be handling each different source system in a multi-source migration project. We'll explore a few of these methods in the coming chapters and see where the tools line up.

Architectures: federated versus shared

Federated data integration can be very complicated. This is especially the case for distributed environments where several heterogeneous remote databases are to be synchronized using two-phase commit. Solutions that provide federated data integration access and maintain the data in the place wherever it resides (such as in a mainframe data store associated with legacy applications). Data access is done 'transparently' for example, the user (or application) interacts with a single virtual or federated relational database under the control of the primary RDBMS, such as Oracle. This data integration software is working with the primary RDBMS 'under the covers' to transform and translate schemas, data dictionaries, and dialects of SQL; ensure transactional consistency across remote foreign databases (using two-phase commit); and make the collection of disparate, heterogeneous, distributed data sources appear as one unified database. The integration software carrying out these complex tasks needs to be tightly integrated with the primary RDBMS in order to benefit from built-in functions and effective query optimization. The RDBMS must also provide all the other important RDBMS functions, including effective query optimization.

Data sharing integration

Data sharing-based integration involves the sharing of data, transactions, and events among various applications in an organization. It can be accomplished within seconds or overnight, depending on the requirement. It may be done in incremental steps, over time, as individual one-off implementations are required. If one-off tools are used to implement data sharing, eventually the variety of data-sharing approaches employed begin to conflict, and the IT department becomes overwhelmed with an unmanageable maintenance, which increases the total cost of ownership.

What is needed is a comprehensive, unified approach that relies on a standard set of services to capture, stage, and consume the information being shared. Such an environment needs to include a rules-based engine, support for popular development languages, and comply with open standards. GUI-based tools should be available for ease of development and the inherent capabilities should be modular enough to satisfy a wide variety of possible implementation scenarios.

The data-sharing form of data integration can be applied to achieve near real-time data sharing. While it does not guarantee the level of synchronization inherent with a federated data integration approach (for example, if updates are performed using two-phase commit), it also doesn't incur the corresponding performance overhead. Availability is improved because there are multiple copies of the data.

Considerations when choosing an integration approach

There is a range in the complexity of data integration projects from relatively straightforward (for example, integrating data from two merging companies that used the same Oracle applications) to extremely complex projects such as long-range geographical data replication and multiple database platforms. For each project, the following factors can be assessed to estimate the complexity level. Pretend you are a systems integrator such as EDS trying to size a data integration effort as you prepare a project proposal.

- **Potential for conflicts**: Is the data source updated by more than one application? If so, the potential exists for each application to simultaneously update the same data.

- **Latency**: What is the required synchronization level for the data integration process? Can it be an overnight batch operation like a typical data warehouse? Must it be synchronous, and with two-phase commit? Or, can it be quasi-real-time, where a two or three second lag is tolerable, permitting an asynchronous solution?

- **Transaction volumes and data growth trajectory**: What are the expected average and peak transaction rates and data processing throughput that will be required?

- **Access patterns**: How frequently is the data accessed and from where?

- **Data source size**: Some data sources of such volume that back up, and unavailability becomes extremely important.

- **Application and data source variety**: Are we trying to integrate two ostensibly similar databases following the merger of two companies that both use the same application, or did they each have different applications? Are there multiple data sources that are all relational databases? Or are we integrating data from legacy system files with relational databases and real-time external data feeds?

- **Data quality**: The probability that data quality adds to overall project complexity increases as the variety of data sources increases.

One point of this discussion is that the requirements of data integration projects will vary widely. Therefore, the platform used to address these issues must be a rich superset of the features and functions that will be applied to any one project.

Integration and SOA, bringing it together

We hear from customers over and over again about how difficult it is to add a new interface, support a new customer file, and about the amount of custom code, scripts, and JCL dedicated to simple integration solutions. The outdated proprietary methods of FTP-ing flat files, or calling CICS transactions on another mainframe are replaced by **Enterprise Information Integration** (EII) and **Enterprise Application Integration** (EAI) products that are based on standards. EII and EAI tools and technologies give you the capability to create new application interfaces in days instead of months. The following chart shows an example of a reference architecture where integration products are used to bring it all together. Here we will look at the advantages of such an end state.

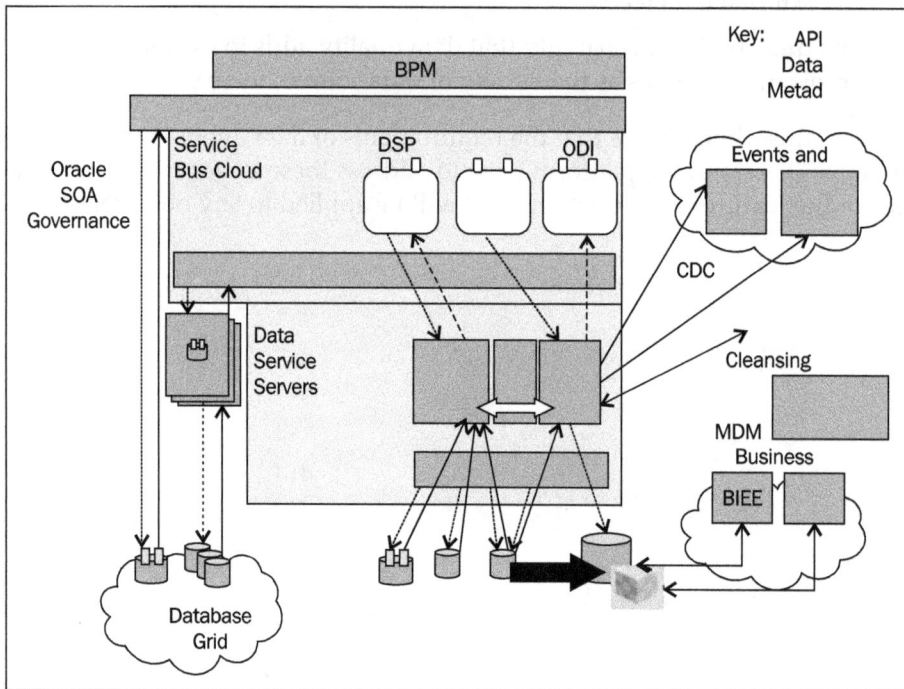

Architected for the Internet

Technologies used in Legacy SOA Integration can get you on the web, but this does not mean the core of your application is built for the Internet. In an integrated solution, the architecture is built to support the Internet and SOA technologies. Your application architecture inherently includes HTTP, SOAP, web services, HTML-based reporting, business process flows, portals, and business activity monitoring. In other words, your new open-systems application is built to be truly web-enabled.

Scalability

Scalability is not all about being able to handle additional workload without significant degradation in response time. It is also about the ability to handle periodic workload changes such as end-of-year processing, sales traffic, or the retailer's experience during the holidays. Database and application server grids are the perfect match for scalability. Not only can you scale out (add more databases, application server processes, storage, and hardware), but you can also provision your workload to utilize your hardware and software based on the current environment. So for the month of December, when your retail sales are higher, more machines can be dynamically configured to handle sales transactions. When December 31 rolls around and you need to close your books for the year, your infrastructure can be changed to handle financial and accounting transactions.

Availability

Legacy systems can certainly be called reliable, but availability is a whole new subject. In the age of the Internet, clients expect your systems to be up '24/7', throughout the year. Legacy systems are typically down anywhere from two to twelve hours a night for batch processing. Much of this has to do with the lack of concurrency built into legacy databases. When the legacy applications were developed, applications were not expected to be available all day. Businesses did not operate on a global scale in what is often a 24 hour day. IT systems were architectured to match the business requirements at the time. These systems, however, do not match the business requirements of today.

With the advent of grid computing, open systems infrastructure, and the application and database software that runs on top of it are built to operate 24/7, 365 days a year. Maximum Availability Architectures are commonplace in open systems as businesses expect the system to be 'Always on'.

Greater software options

The major software vendors' product strategies are focused on relational database, SQL, Java, .NET, and open systems hardware platforms. Therefore, the entire ecosystem that exists in software development tools, database and application management tools, ISV applications, commercial of-the-shelf (COTS) applications, and hardware and storage support is in the thousands, rather than dozens or perhaps hundreds. The combination of more options, more competition, and more standards-based technologies lower the acquisition cost, support and maintenance costs, and increase customer service. It is only logical that the open market creates more choices for you at a lower cost with better service.

On-demand reporting

One of the main reasons for the proliferation of spreadsheets, Microsoft Access applications, departmental level systems, and 'the guy in accounting who took a night class on Crystal Reports' creating dozens of reports which potentially have queries that run for hours, is that in the legacy world it took way too long for the IT department to respond to new reporting and business intelligence requests. So the user community took it upon themselves to solve the problem. Departmental databases and spreadsheet-driven applications became part of the corporate fabric, and many companies rely on these systems for mission critical processing such as sales forecasting, inventory control, budgeting, and purchasing. The information is in the legacy system, but it is too difficult to get to, manipulate, and report on. With hundreds of open systems reporting, querying, data mining, and BI tools in the market place, users can access the re-architected relational database themselves. Or the IT department can easily create the reports or the BI system that the user community is asking for.

Security

Security is often seen as the domain of the legacy environment, especially in a mainframe. We hear, "My mainframe is so secure that I am never going to move off". On the other hand, we also hear of companies getting off the mainframe because there is no way to encrypt the data. Relational databases on open systems have built-in security, so IT personnel cannot access data that is not part of their daily job. They also offer transparent data encryption. Remember, most security breaches are made by your own people. This is security of data at rest. Then, there is the security of data on the network, and application-based security. This is where open system options such as network encryption, single sign-on, user ID provisioning, federated identity management, and virtual directories, all make sure open systems are more secure than your legacy environment.

Overcoming barriers to change

You can always tell the folks in the room who are just waiting for retirement and don't want the legacy system to retire before they do. Often, we can hear them say, *"This can't be done, our system is way too complicated, only a mainframe can handle this workload, we have tried this before and it failed"*. Then you find out that they are running a 300 MIP mainframe with about one million lines of code and about two gigabytes of data. In some cases, you can handle this processing on a two node dual core processor! Or, you may find out that the system is really just a bunch of flat file interfaces that apply 300 business rules and send transactions out to third parties. This can be re-architected to a modern platform, using technologies such as Extract, Transform, and Load (ETL) that did not exist 20 years ago.

You also have to be careful when re-architecting a legacy system, as the business processes and data entry screens, as well as the people who use them, have been around for decades. You have to balance the amount of technology change with the amount of change your business community can digest. You would think that all companies would want an Internet-based web interface to a re-architected system. However, there was one occasion wherein a re-architecture System Integrator (SI) had to include a third-party screen emulation vendor that actually turned HTML into 3270 'green screens'. This was so the users could have the same look and feel, including PF keys, on the web as they did on their character-based dumb terminals.

One of the most discouraging aspects of my role as a modernization architect is that many companies re-architect legacy systems but continue to custom code application features that can be found in 'off-the-shelf' technology products. This happens often, because they don't know the new technologies properly (or even that they exist), developers still like to code, or they cannot change their mindset from 'not invented here' (meaning that we know the best way to do this).

Custom integration applications and utilities

With all the EII and EAI technologies in the market place, we still see modern-day architects decide that they can write their own integration software or write it better than a vendor who has spent years developing the solution. Initial cost (or sticker shock, some may say) is another reason. The client looks at the initial cost only, and not at the cost of maintenance, adding new interfaces, and of supporting another in-house software application. Looking at the total cost of ownership, in most cases, the advantages of using an EII or EAI product will outweigh the use of FTP and flat files, or some variant of this typical homegrown integration application.

Custom workflow

As indicated previously, workflow in legacy applications is often built into the user interface module or is implicitly part of the existing batch system. You would think companies that run legacy systems would have learned their lesson that this makes maintenance a nightmare and ends up costing large amounts of money, since changes to the legacy code or batch systems disrupt the workflow, and vice versa. These new open systems will then have the same problem that exists in legacy code today — the code cannot be changed, as no one knows what impact the change will have on processing.

The real world: studies in integration

In the following sections, we will take a look at several businesses and their challenges for integration. Such solutions as replication, integration with non-Oracle sources, and queuing will be discussed.

Banking case

Gruppo Sanpaolo d'Intermediazione Mobiliare is Italy's second largest bank and among the top 50 banks worldwide. The investment banking arm of the group is Banca d'Intermediazione Mobiliare (Banca IMI). In addition to servicing the other parts of the Sanpaolo Group, Banca IMI provides investment banking services to a wide range of institutions, including other banks, asset managers for major global corporations, and other financial institutions. In the process of buying and selling a variety of financial instruments, Banca IMI must communicate with all of the major exchanges (for example, the New York Stock Exchange). The volume of its daily trades can frequently scale up to hundreds of thousands.

Because its business operations are global, its IT systems must operate 24/7, and transactions with both internal application systems and external trading centers must be processed with minimum error and as close to real time as possible. This is a very demanding business application and a complex example of data integration. The main applications with which Banca IMI must communicate include its own backend administrative systems and legacy applications, the financial exchanges, domestic and international customers, and financial networks. Not only do all of these have different protocols and formats, but there are also differences just within the financial exchanges themselves. The latter is handled through a marketing interface layer with custom software for each exchange. Domestic customers are connected through open standard protocols (financial information exchange standards, FIX) and are used with international customers and other financial institutions.

Banca IMI uses **Oracle Streams** (**Advanced Queuing**) to coordinate transactions across all these stakeholders. Streams is a fully integrated feature of the Oracle database, and takes full advantage of Oracle's security, optimization, performance, and scalability. Streams can accommodate Banca IMI's very high level of transactions close to real time and still perform all the transformations required to communicate in the various protocols needed. Scalability is very important to Banca IMI and the primary reason why it moved to Oracle Streams from a previous solution that relied on another vendor's product. *"We're happy about what Advanced Queuing offers us"*, says Domenico Betunio, Banca IMI's manager of electronic trading. *"Besides speed and scalability, we're impressed by messaging reliability, and especially auditing"*.

Education case

The Hong Kong Institute of Education (HKIEd) is a leading teacher education institution in the Hong Kong Special Administrative Region (HKSAR). The institute was formally established by statute in April 1994 by uniting the former Northcote College of Education, Grantham College of Education, Sir Robert Black College of Education, the Hong Kong Technical Teachers' College, and the Institute of Languages in Education, the earliest of which was started in 1939. The Institute plays a key role in helping the Hong Kong government fulfill its commitments: to develop new curriculum; to achieve its goal of an 'all graduate all trained' teaching profession; and to provide for the continuous professional development of all serving teachers. The Institute is organized around four schools with a current enrollment of nearly 7,000 students in a variety of daytime and evening degree programs. The Institute staff exceeds 1,000, almost 400 of whom are teaching staff. Across the Institute, more than 200 funded research and development projects are being actively pursued. The two main languages the Institute must accommodate are English and Traditional Chinese.

Soon after its founding, HKIEd began in-house development of several administrative applications, all running in conjunction with Sybase databases. These applications included student admission, enrollment and profiling, human resources and payroll, smart card management, and a library interface. In 2002, HKIEd purchased a set of packaged applications: Banner, from SCT. SCT's Banner system runs on Oracle and is analogous to an enterprise resource planning system. It supports student services, admission, enrollment, and finance functions, some of which it took over from the in house Sybase applications. The Sybase in-house applications still account for roughly 50 percent of the Institute's administrative applications, including classroom booking, HR, payroll, JUPAS student selection, smart card management, and the library INNOPAC system.

As these vital Institute administrative systems are on two platforms, Sybase and Oracle, there is a requirement to keep the data consistent in more than ten common data fields. They account for less than 5 percent of the total number of fields, which is still significant. Each database contains more than 10,000 records. The number of daily transactions affecting these data fields ranges from 200 to 5,000.

After experimenting with SQL Loader scripts to update the common fields using a batch upload process, HKIEd switched to using the Oracle Transparent Gateway. Since January 2003, HKIEd has been using the gateway to access and update the Sybase database from Oracle to keep the common data fields in sync in real-time. HKIEd has created views in the Oracle database based on a distributed join of tables from the Oracle and Sybase databases. This enables SCT's Banner system to transparently access and update fields in the Oracle and Sybase databases. The system automatically performs a two-phase commit to preserve transactional consistency across the two databases. The Transparent Gateway has NLS support, enabling access to Sybase data in any character set.

High technology case

This case illustrates the use of Oracle Streams for information integration, load balancing, and consolidation.

Internet Securities, Inc. (ISI), a Euromoney Institutional Investor Company is the pioneering publisher of Internet-delivered emerging market news and information. Internet Securities (www.securities.com) provides hard-to-get information through its network of 20 offices in 19 countries, covering 45 national markets in Asia, Central and Eastern Europe, and Latin America. Its flagship product, the Emerging Markets Information Service aggregates and produces unique company and industry information including financial, economic and political news, for delivery to professionals over the Internet. The subscription-based service enables users to access and search through a comprehensive range of unique business information derived directly from over 6,800 leading local and international sources. Primarily because of its international clientele, the operations of ISI are run on a 24/7 basis. ISI has offices in 18 locales around the globe, with clients in each locale. Its provisioning operations are centralized and located, along with its headquarters, in New York City.

ISI's content is also global and emphasizes information about emerging markets, which in this context means markets in countries like Romania, Brazil, or China. The content being aggregated arrives in automated feeds of various forms at an average rate of 50,000 documents a day, with hourly arrival rates ranging from 100 to several thousand per hour. All documents, regardless of the source language, are converted to a single encoding standard (UTF8) when being loaded into the ISI document base.

One of ISI's competitive differentiators is that information is retained regardless of age. The size of the ISI content base has grown rapidly to over one terabyte and, in tandem, the level of query activity has grown as well. Until recently, daily operations were run on NT-based systems using Oracle. The need for high scalability and availability while superseding performance prompted ISI to migrate its database operations onto Solaris using Oracle9. Oracle Streams was selected to achieve a major increase in availability and performance. Higher availability is obtained by fully replicating to a secondary server and by being able to perform much faster backups. The performance improvements come from load balancing between the servers and the upgraded hardware.

Overall, Oracle Streams is used for three databases supporting ISI operations. Each database is replicated to a secondary server. The three are:

- **Back-office database (100 GB)**: This database supports the company's proprietary CRM and authentication systems.
- **Document database (50 GB)**: This contains metadata about documents and true paths to the physical location of documents.
- **Search database (1 TB)**: This is the database in which the documents are loaded and where the client queries are executed. Documents are stored as BLOBS. Each record is one document.

The replication for each database is such that either replica can service the functions of both, but for performance (load balancing) and administrative reasons, both are typically serving different operational needs. For example, ISI call center agents primarily use 'Backoffice A' while 'Backoffice B' services all of the client activity monitoring. In the context of the Document database, 'Documents A' is the production machine, and 'Documents B' is the standby. In the case of the huge Search database, 'Search A' is used to perform the document loading that occurs in hourly batches, and 'Search B' is used to receive the users' queries that can be executed on either Search database server.

ISI expected to obtain benefits in two ways: performance and availability. It had evaluated other possible solutions, but these fell short in the performance dimension. Oracle Streams did not. With the Streams-based solution, queries are executing in half the time or better. With respect to availability, switchover in case of a failure is now instantaneous. With NT, ISI was using a physical standby that could be switched over in the best case in 7 to 8 minutes for read-only, and 10 to 15 minutes for read/write transactions.

Summary

In this chapter, we have opened the book, as it were, on many topics in the sphere of integration and migration of data. We began the chapter laying the foundation by addressing some of the reasons that propel an organization to tackle this problem, while addressing some of the unique challenges that one will face both from a technical and business perspective. Next, we began to unpack the concepts and approaches to integration, which will provide the foundation in the coming chapters, when we get more hands-on examples. Finally, we explored several real world examples in multiple industries that have dealt with migration and integration issues. In the coming chapters, we will begin to get more hands-on and take a deeper dive into specific tools and techniques, as well as more case studies throughout to illustrate the problems and solutions that other firms have experienced.

2
Oracle Tools and Products

In early 2010, when you went to the **Oracle Technology Network** (OTN) website, it had just one link called **Information Integration**. This link led you to a simple web page that had information on Oracle-to-Oracle database-centric migration and integration tools such as SQL Loader, Data Pump, Oracle Streams, and Oracle Data Guard. The OTN website has been updated, but still lacks comprehensive coverage of the Oracle Information Integration stack. In this chapter, we will provide you with the relevant information, so that you can use the right Oracle **Enterprise Information Integration** (EII) or data migration product for your data migration, consolidation, and information integration projects.

Oracle has always had a robust set of database-centric data integration tools. The products include **Oracle Warehouse Builder** (OWB) and **Oracle Gateways** to access other relational databases. Oracle has also offered middle tier products such as an enterprise service bus, messaging technologies, and a Business Process Execution Language Engine. One of the problems is that Oracle has offered a host of middleware solutions that have changed over the years. In addition, there was no cohesive strategy and these products were not well understood by Oracle developers, architects, and Database Administrators (DBAs). This made it difficult for customers to build a sustainable EII solution based on Oracle technology across both the database and middle tier stack. The middleware and database enterprise information integration product set did not consolidate, stabilize, or become well-defined until the acquisition of BEA in 2008.

Oracle has almost been 'forced' to embrace heterogeneous data and application integration due to all the vertical applications it has acquired. JD Edwards World only runs on DB2 on the IBM iSeries. Oracle PeopleSoft and Siebel have hundreds of installations on Sybase, SQL Server, and DB2. The i-flex Financial Services package runs on DB2 and Sybase. Other products are based on .NET and use information integration products which are as diverse as Information PowerCenter and IBM Data Stage. Oracle has changed from a company where everyone runs on the Oracle database and application server, to a company that embraces a heterogeneous IT infrastructure. Whether by choice, or as an outcome of hundreds of acquisitions, Oracle is a company that supports multiple databases, application languages and has a solid information integration platform.

However, we see too many customers and partners reinventing the wheel by using a combination of PL/SQL stored procedures, SQL Perl scripts, SQL Loader, Korn Shells, and custom C, Ruby, JPython, and Java code to meet both simple and enterprise level integration and data migration needs. This chapter will provide you with the knowledge to move away from your bulk FTP SQL Loader-based database-centric approach to migrations and integration with Oracle products, thus preventing a do it yourself (DIY) solution that in the end costs you more money and much more development effort then an out-of-the-box Oracle solution.

This InformationWeek survey confirms that the process of moving from manual legacy data integration, to automated, out of the box solutions, has a long way to go before it becomes mainstream; the Oracle customer preference for new integration is:

- 39 percent: Custom code directly into main system
- 34 percent: Server-based feed (Oracle XML, MarkLogic,and so on.)
- 12 percent: Appliance
- 12 percent: Cloud-based portal
- 4 percent: Other

So, 73 percent of Oracle customers still use custom code or base technologies instead of products for new integration. This InformationWeek article (*Oracle Focuses On Real-Time Data Integration*, based upon InformationWeek Analytics survey of 281 business technology professionals) on September 13, 2010, validates the customer opinion that Oracle does have a well understood data integration message, and that Oracle customers still tend to code DIY solutions.

This chapter covers the Oracle integration, migration, and consolidation products, tools and technologies in terms of the following taxonomies: data migration, physical federation, virtual federation, data services, data consolidation, data grid, Oracle-to-Oracle integration, Information Lifecycle Management, and application integration. The focus of this chapter is to cover the great breadth and depth of Oracle products, not all the finer details. The remaining chapters in this book will cover in detail the products, technologies, and tools that are most commonly used or are strategic to Oracle:

- Oracle SQL Loader
- Oracle SQL Developer Migration Workbench
- Oracle BPEL
- Oracle SOA Adapters
- Oracle Data Integrator (ODI)
- Oracle GoldenGate
- Oracle Gateways
- Oracle Application Integration Architecture (AIA)
- Oracle Master Data Management (MDM)

Readers in a DBA or database development role will most likely be familiar with SQL Loader, Oracle database external tables, Oracle GoldenGate, and Oracle Warehouse Builder. Application developers and architects will mostly likely be familiar with Oracle BPEL and the Oracle Service Bus. Whatever your role or knowledge of Oracle, at the end of this chapter you will be familiar with the Oracle Enterprise Application Integration (EAI), data consolidation, data management, and data migration products, tools and technologies. You will also understand which Oracle tools, technologies, or products are most appropriate for your company's projects.

Database migration products and tools

Data migration is the first step when moving your mission critical data to an Oracle database. The initial data loading is traditionally done using Oracle SQL Loader. As data volumes have increased and data quality has become an issue, Oracle Data Warehouse and Oracle Data Integrator have become more important, because of their capabilities to connect directly to source data stores, provide data cleansing and profiling support, and graphical drag and drop development. Now, the base addition of Oracle Data Warehouse Builder is a free, built-in feature of the Oracle 11*g* database, and price is no longer an issue.

Oracle Warehouse Builder and Oracle Data Integrator have gained adoption as they are repository based, have built-in transformation functions, are multi-user, and avoid a proliferation of scripts throughout the enterprise that do the same or simpler data movement activity. These platforms provide a more repeatable, scalable, reusable, and model-based enterprise data migration architecture.

SQL Loader

SQL Loader is the primary method for quickly populating Oracle tables with data from external files. It has a powerful data parsing engine that puts little limitation on the format of the data in the data file. The tool is invoked, when you specify the `sqlldr` command or use the Oracle Enterprise Manager interface.

SQL Loader has been around as long as the Oracle Database logon "scott/tiger" and is an integral feature of the Oracle database. It works the same on any hardware or software platform that Oracle supports. Therefore, it has become the de facto data migration and information integration tool for most Oracle partners and customers. This also makes it an Oracle legacy data migration and integration solution with all the issues associated with legacy tools, such as:

- Difficult to move away from as the solution is embedded in the enterprise.
- The current solution has a lot of duplicated code, because it was written by many different developers before the use of structured programming and shared modules.
- The current solution is not built to support object-orientated development, Service Orientated Architecture products, or other new technologies such as web services and XML.
- The current solution is difficult and costly to maintain because the code is not structured, the application is not well documented, the original developers are no longer with the company, and any changes to the code cause other pieces of the application to either stop working or fail.

SQL Loader is typically used in 'flat file' mode. This means the data is exported into a command-delimited flat file from the source database or arrives in an ASCII flat file. With the growth of data volumes, using SQL Loader with named pipes has become common practice. Named pipes eliminate the need to have temporary data storage mechanisms—instead data is moved in memory.

It is interesting that Oracle does not have an SQL unload facility, as Sybase and SQL Server have the Bulk Copy Program (BCP). There are C, Perl, PL/SQL, and other SQL-based scripts to do this, but nothing official from Oracle. The SQL Loader source and target data sources along with development languages and tools supported are as follows:

Data source	Data target	Development languages and tools
Any data source that can produce flat files. XML files can also be loaded using the Oracle XMLtype data type	Oracle	Proprietary SQL Loader control files and SQL Loader Command Line Interface (CLI)

The most likely instances or use cases when Oracle SQL Loader would be the Oracle product or tool selected are:

- Bulk loading data into Oracle from any data source from mainframe to distributed systems.
- Quick, easy, one-time data migration using a free tool.

Oracle external tables

The external tables feature is a complement to the existing SQL Loader functionality. It enables you to access data in external sources as if it were in a table in the database. Therefore, standard SQL or Oracle PL/SQL can be used to load the external file (defined as an external table) into an Oracle database table.

Customer benchmarks and performance tests have determined that in some cases the external tables are faster than the SQL Loader direct path load. In addition, if you know SQL well, then it is easier to code the external table load SQL than SQL Loader control files and load scripts. The external table source and target data sources along with development languages and tools supported are:

Data source	Data target	Development languages and tools
Any data source that can produce flat files	Oracle	SQL, PL/SQL, Command Line Interface (CLI)

The most likely instances or use cases when Oracle external tables would be the Oracle product or tool selected are:

- Migration of data from non-Oracle databases to the Oracle database.
- Fast loading of data into Oracle using SQL.

Oracle Warehouse Builder

Oracle Warehouse Builder (OWB) allows users to extract data from both Oracle and non-Oracle data sources and transform/load into a Data Warehouse, Operational Data Store (ODS) or simply to be used to migrate data to an Oracle database. It is part of the Oracle Business Intelligence suite and is the embedded Oracle Extract-Load-Transform (ELT) tool in this BI suite. With the usage of platform/product specific adapters it can extract data from mainframe/legacy data sources as well.

Starting with Oracle Database 11*g*, the core OWB product is a free feature of the database. In a way, this is an attempt to address the free Microsoft entry level ELT tools like Microsoft Data Transformation Services (DTS) and SQL Server Integration Services (SSIS) from becoming de facto ELT standards, because they are easy to use and are cheap (free). The Oracle Warehouse Builder source and target data sources along with development languages and tools supported are:

Data source	Data target	Development languages and tools
Any data source that can produce flat files Any databases from mainframe to open systems that has ODBC or JDBC connectivity Can be used with the Oracle Gateways, so any data source that the Gateway supports	Oracle, ODBC compliant data stores, and any data source accessible through Oracle Gateways, flat files, XML	OWB GUI development tool, PL/SQL, SQL, CLI

The most likely instances or use cases when OWB would be the Oracle product or tool selected are:

- Bulk loading data on a continuous, daily, monthly or yearly basis.
- Direct connection to ODBC compliant databases for data migration, consolidation and physical federation, including data warehouses and operational data stores.
- Low cost (free) data migration that offers a graphical interface, scheduled data movement, data quality, and cleansing.

SQL Developer Migration Workbench

Oracle SQL Developer Migration Workbench is a tool that enables you to migrate a database, including the schema objects, data, triggers, and stored procedures, to an Oracle Database 11*g* using a simple point-and-click process. It also generates scripts necessary to perform the migration in batch mode. Its tight integration into SQL Developer (an Oracle database development tool) provides the user with a single-stop tool to explore third-party databases, carry out migrations, and to manipulate the generated schema objects and migrated data. Oracle SQL Developer is provided free of charge and is the first tool used by Oracle employees to migrate Sybase, DB2, MySQL and SQL Server databases to Oracle.

SQL Developer Migration Workbench 3.0 was released 2011 and includes support for C application code migration from Sybase and SQL Server DB-Library and CT-Library, a Command Line Interface (CLI), a host of reports that can be used for fixing items that did not migrate, estimating and scoping, and database analysis, and a pluggable framework to support identification and changes to SQL in Java, Powerbuilder, Visual Basic, Perl, or any programming language.

SQL Developer Migration Workbench actually started off as a set of Unix scripts and a crude database procedural language parser based on SED and AWK. This solution was first made an official Oracle product in 1996. Since then, the parser has been totally rewritten in Java and the user interface integrated with SQL Developer. SQL Developer Migration Workbench source and target data sources along with development languages and tools supported are:

Data source	Data target	Development languages and tools
DB2 LUW, MySQL, Informix, SQL Server, Sybase	Oracle	SQL Developer GUI development tool, Command Line Interface (CLI)

The most likely instances or use cases when SQL Developer Migration Workbench would be the Oracle product or tool selected are:

- Data migration from popular LUW RDBMS systems to Oracle using flat files or JDBC connectivity.
- RDBMS object (stored procedures, triggers, views) translation from popular LUW RDBMS to Oracle.

Oracle Data Integrator

Oracle Data Integrator (ODI) is a product that Oracle acquired from Sunopsis SA in 2006. This acquisition may have seemed unnecessary at the time as Oracle already had OWB for data migration and integration. However, the complaint from customers was that OWB required an Oracle database and the OWB engine was based on PL/SQL. Therefore, it was a very database-centric product, and at the time did not support target databases other then Oracle.

ODI is a data migration and integration software product, providing a declarative design approach to defining data transformation and integration processes, resulting in faster and simpler development and maintenance. Based on an Extract-Load-Transform (E-L-T) architecture, Oracle Data Integrator, unlike traditional Extract-Transform-Load (E-T-L) products, loads the data into the target database and then does the transformation processing. The ELT approach is important for a number of reasons:

- The underlying target database SQL and database languages (such as PL/SQL, T-SQL, and DB2 SQL PL) are used to perform the transformations and not a proprietary ETL language.
- The RASP (Reliability, Availability, Scalability, Performance) of the underlying database can be used instead of a proprietary engine that is external to where the data resides.
- In most cases, getting the data into the database and then transforming it is faster than the way most IT developers and DBAs use ETL products.

By combining data, event-based, and service-based integration, ODI is able to address varying needs from legacy data migration, data warehousing, and business intelligence to Master Data Management, Service Oriented Architecture, and others (such as cloud computing). Oracle Data Integrator provides a unified infrastructure to streamline data migration and integration projects. A white paper on ODI and legacy modernization using ODI can be found at http://www.oracle.com/us/products/middleware/059481. The ODI source and target data sources along with development languages and tools supported are:

Data source	Data target	Development languages and tools
Flat files, JDBC, ODBC, web services, XML	Any ODBC or JDBC compliant database, JMS, flat files, XML, web services	ODI GUI development tool, SQL, PL/SQL, T-SQL, DB2 SQL PL, Java, CLI

The most likely instances or use cases when ODI would be the Oracle product or tool selected are:

- Bulk loading data on a continuous, daily, monthly, or yearly basis.
- Direct connection to ODBC and JDBC compliant databases for data modernization, migration, consolidation, and physical federation (data mart, data hub, and data warehouses).
- Web services-based data migration.
- Data migration or Change Data Capture (CDC) that offers a graphical interface, scheduled data movement, data quality and cleansing, and data profiling.

Oracle Enterprise Manager tuning and diagnostic packs

Oracle Enterprise Manager (OEM) 11*g* provides a single, integrated solution for testing, deploying, operating, monitoring, diagnosing, and resolving performance problems. It delivers manageability and automation for your grid across both Oracle and non-Oracle technologies. This means that Oracle Enterprise Manager (OEM) can be used to diagnose data migration issues across Oracle databases, non-Oracle databases, and the application tiers.

OEM was at one point a thick client-based solution that had both a slow response time and limited graphical capabilities. OEM also lacked support for other databases or even the Oracle Application Server. In the last few years, OEM has been upgraded to support other databases (Sybase, SQL Server, DB2, and others), and includes support for the Oracle Application Server and other application servers such as IBM Websphere. OEM now has browser-to-database support; support for the web-to-application server tier to database level tracing and diagnostics.

The OEM tuning and diagnostic packs can be used in place of Oracle UTLBSTAT/ UTLESTAT or the Oracle Stats Pack. The **Oracle Stats Pack** was introduced in Oracle 8*i* and replaced UTLBSTAT/UTLESTAT – which are still in use today. Oracle Stats Pack has been the typical method of diagnosing Oracle performance concerns. It is a great tool, but a lot like coding in Unix VI, and really requires an expert to determine the root cause. OEM tuning and diagnostic packs make the process more of a science than an art. OEM tuning and diagnostic packs, unlike the Oracle Stats Pack, are an OEM option which means that there are license fees associated with their usage. The source and target data sources of OEM tuning and diagnostic packs along with development languages and tools supported are:

Data source	Data target	Development languages and tools
DB2 LUW, MySQL, Informix, SQL Server, Sybase Any databases from mainframe to open systems that have ODBC or JDBC connectivity	Oracle	Oracle Enterprise Manager web UI, SQL, PL/SQL, CLI

The most likely instances or use cases when the OEM tuning and diagnostic packs would be the Oracle product or tool selected are:

- Database migration, consolidation, performance, and tuning.
- Information integration, data consolidation, and data grid deployments.

You get what you pay for. Using free tools like SQL Loader, SQL Developer Migration Workbench and, to a lesser degree, Oracle Warehouse Builder all seem like the logical choice because of their perceived cost advantage. This is only a perceived cost as the actual cost to build high speed data migration solutions, sophisticated data mapping, or data quality functionality on top of these free tools far outweigh the initial no cost solution. Certainly, for quick, one-time data migration involving less than 500 tables and 100 gigabytes of data, the 'free' solutions will work just fine. In these cases, SQL Loader or SQL Developer Migration Workbench may be 'enough tool'.

Physical federation products

Physical federation, as the name implies, involves physically moving data from its target data source into an Oracle **Online Transaction Processing (OLTP)** system, **Data Warehouse (DW)** or **Operational Data Store (ODS)**. The data movement may take place using bulk file transport, data streaming through ODBC or JDBC, a messaging system, reading of database log files or any information integration mechanism.

Traditionally, physical federation has been associated with enterprise data warehousing. Master Data Management and data hubs have moved physical federation from being a read-only database (such as a data warehouse or data mart) to a component of a company's OLTP infrastructure. This complicates the situation as solutions like Change Data Capture (CDC), bi-directional replication, and data write back to the source may be required.

Since we are pulling data in many cases from legacy environments, non-Oracle databases, or consolidating information that may have duplicate data, solutions such as data quality, cleaning, and profiling are often a component of physical federation architectures. Oracle offers products that not only move the data, read the changes from the source (CDC), and replicate the data in a bidirectional fashion, but also cleanse the data and provide detailed analysis and a profile of your various data sources.

Oracle Data Integrator

Oracle Data Integrator (ODI) can be used for initial data migration and can be used for physical federation. This is the case as ODI offers both bulk load and CDC capabilities. Therefore, ODI could be used to do the initial load of your federated database and then keep the federated database in sync with the online source databases. ODI CDC capabilities are provided through Knowledge Modules. ODI comes with a large set of out of the box **Knowledge Models (KM)** or you can develop your own.

Knowledge Modules are code templates. Each KM is dedicated to a specialized task or set of tasks in the overall data integration process. The code in the KMs appears in the form that it will be executed except that it includes ODI substitution methods, enabling it to be used generically by many different integration jobs.

The code that is generated and executed is derived from the declarative rules and metadata defined in the ODI Designer module. The ODI physical federation source and target data sources along with development languages and tools supported are:

Data source	Data target	Development languages and tools
Flat files, JDBC, ODBC, XML, web services, custom developed KDM to support any data source or source application system	Any ODBC or JDBC compliant database, JMS, flat files, XML, web services, custom developed KDM to support a target data source or application	ODI GUI development tool, SQL, PL/SQL, T-SQL, DB2 SQL PL, Java, CLI

The most likely instances or use cases when ODI would be the Oracle product or tool selected are:

- Physical federation where sophisticated data transformations, data cleansing, and data profiling is required
- Data sources or target not supported by Oracle GoldenGate

Oracle GoldenGate

Oracle GoldenGate software was acquired from the software company GoldenGate in 2009. Prior to GoldenGate, Oracle did not offer a heterogeneous bidirectional data replication solution. Oracle did offer Oracle Streams at the time of the acquisition, but this product only supported Oracle-to-Oracle replication; replication to non-Oracle databases could be done but required custom development. GoldenGate was clearly the leader in the marketplace for heterogeneous replication; so the acquisition jumped Oracle to the forefront in the software space of log-based heterogeneous data replication solutions.

GoldenGate's zero-downtime solution allows new systems to be continuously updated with the changes committed in source databases, so that applications and/or users can continue to use the source and target databases without any downtime. To support this approach, GoldenGate's core software platform captures, transforms, routes, and delivers transactional data in real-time across heterogeneous databases and operating systems. The platform consists of decoupled modules that can be combined across the enterprise to provide maximum flexibility, availability, and performance.

The bidirectional capabilities of GoldenGate provide for multi-master database configurations in a federated databases environment. A GoldenGate Capture module resides on the source system, and a GoldenGate delivery module resides on the target system. In some cases, Oracle customers have used GoldenGate in addition to, or as an alternative to, Oracle DataGuard as an Oracle standby database solution. The Oracle GoldenGate source and target data sources along with development languages and tools that are supported are:

Data source	Data target	Development languages and tools
Oracle, DB2 z/OS, JMS-based systems, DB2 LUW, Sybase, SQL Server, Enscribe, SQL/ MX, MySQL	Oracle, SQL Server, Sybase, Enscribe, SQL/MX, Teradata, Oracle TimesTen, DB2 iSeries, DB2 LUW , Oracle E-Business Suite, Oracle PeopleSoft, Oracle JD Edwards	SQL, Unix Shell, DOS BAT

The most likely instances or use cases when Oracle GoldenGate would be the Oracle product or tool selected are:

- Physical federation with limited data transformation, data quality, and data cleansing
- Log-based CDC solution for performance and minimal impact to source database that may be incurred using trigger-based CDC
- Near real-time data replication

Oracle CDC adapters

Oracle CDC offers log-based, non-intrusive database-based change data capture. The product offers change record filtering by operation, column, and content. The solution offers flexible delivery models including batch, micro-batch, and events. It also includes reliable delivery and recovery, and seamless integration with Service Orientated Architecture (SOA) Suite, and ODI. The Oracle CDC JCA-based adapters are configured using Oracle JDeveloper.

Development of applications that use the CDC adapters is done using a model-driven wizard approach in Oracle JDeveloper. The CDC adapters are JCA-based, there is a roadmap in place for JMS-based events support. The Oracle CDC adapters are Original Equipment Manufacturer (OEM) from Attunity Software. Except for the SQL Server adapter, there is no overlap with the GoldenGate solution. They are both log-based solutions, so the future merger of these two products does seem to make sense; but nothing has been announced. The Oracle CDC source and target data sources along with development languages and tools supported are:

Data source	Data target	Development languages and tools
Mainframe DB2, IMS, VSAM, Adabas, and SQL Server	Oracle	Oracle Legacy Studio GIU, proprietary control files

The most likely instances or use cases when Oracle CDC would be the Oracle product or tool selected are:

- Mainframe data sources are involved in the solution
- CDC where tight integration with ODI is required

Oracle Master Data Management

Oracle's **Master Data Management** (**MDM**) solution is a set of applications (MDM data hubs) designed to consolidate, cleanse, govern, and share business data objects across the enterprise and across time. The business data objects are basically consolidated data that resides in different databases across the enterprise. It includes pre-defined extensible data models and access methods with applications to centrally manage the quality and lifecycle of master business data.

The first data hub solution Oracle offered was the customer data hub. This customer data hub was introduced in 2004 and it was a year later when the product data hub was introduced. One of the interesting aspects of all the data hub solutions is that there is no data integration or CDC solution embedded in the offerings. You are free to use any of the Oracle-based solutions or a third-party solution to collect the data from it's source database.

In the event that all customer systems can't be modernized and migrated at the same time, the Oracle MDM solution can be used to provide a single customer view across the organization. The Oracle Customer Hub is a **Customer Data Integration (CDI)** solution that enables organizations to centralize information from heterogeneous systems, creating a single view of customer information that can be leveraged across all functional departments and analytical systems.

The Oracle Customer Hub is the most mature of the Oracle data hub products. Oracle also offers product, supplier, site, and financial data hubs. I am sure the list of these data hubs will grow. These data hubs along with other Oracle solutions such as Oracle Portal, Oracle Gateways, SOA adapters and BI Suite make up a complete federation solution. A complete federation solution is an end-to-end solution that has a web portal frontend (Oracle Portal), Oracle Gateways for virtually federated data access, SOA adapters to access legacy data stores, and non-data centric sources like web services, and a BI Suite to provide data analysis and ad hoc reporting. Oracle MDM source and target data sources along with development languages and tools supported are:

Data source	Data target	Development languages and tools
Any data source	Oracle	Java, SQL, web services

The most likely instances or use cases when Oracle MDM would be the Oracle product or tool selected are:

- Out of the box customer, product, and other data hubs
- An enterprise view of customers, products, suppliers, sites, and financial data

Oracle Data Quality and Profiling

The Oracle Data Quality and Profiling solutions are OEM'd from Trillium. Trillium offers industry leading data quality and profiling solutions. Thus, it was an Oracle decision not to build a solution, but rather to use the best of the breed.

The Oracle Data Quality and Profiling products are offered as part of ODI. The data quality and profiling product includes functionality for data rule derivation and data rule profiling, and provides support for custom and predefined data rules. This includes the ability to apply the data rules to data objects. The following is a list of the key features of Oracle Data Profiling:

- Automatically searches for relationships across sources; all the data can be collected and compared to data from other sources

- Provides data standard definition rules that can validate user-specified patterns or data rules
- Loads and analyzes the data in one single pass without impacting the source system
- Profiling metadata and statistics are captured in the metadata repository to drive your data rules, ongoing data quality auditing, and automated data cleansing processes; you can also define data rules specific to your business or your problem domain, and test compliance with those rules during the data profiling process

The Oracle Data Quality and Profiling source and target data sources along with development languages and tools supported are:

Data source	Data target	Development languages and tools
Any data source	Oracle	GUI, CLI

The most likely instances or use cases when Oracle Data Quality and Profiling would be the Oracle product or tool selected are:

- Physical federation where source data requires significant data cleansing
- To avoid DIY data quality and data profiling solutions

> Physical federation provides a high performance environment where users can go to one place at any time to find the 'single data source of truth'. However, keeping all data sources in sync can prove to be a complicated problem to solve. Fortunately, Oracle provides many choices (Oracle GoldenGate, Oracle Data Integrator, and Oracle CDC) to keep the federated database and source data sources in sync.

Virtual federation products

Virtual federation is about leaving the data where it is and providing the user community with a view to the data through the tool of their choice, including a web browser. Instead of moving data around like physical federation, an Oracle product is used to provide users with a single view of their data. Virtual federation using Oracle products can be done at the developer level using SQL, using Java development tools to service-enable any data source, drag and drop development using Oracle JDeveloper, and by end users using Oracle Business Intelligence tools.

Oracle Gateways and Heterogeneous Services

The core of Oracle's database virtual federation strategy is **Heterogeneous Services (HS)**. Heterogeneous Services provides transparent and generic gateway technology to connect to non-Oracle systems. Heterogeneous Services is an integrated component of the database. Therefore, it can exploit all the capabilities of the Oracle database including PL/SQL and Oracle SQL extensions.

The two methods of connecting to non-Oracle databases through Oracle HS are:

- Oracle Transparent Gateways are tailored specifically for the non-Oracle systems and provide an end-to-end (Oracle-to-non-Oracle) certified solution.

- Oracle Generic Connectivity is based on ODBC and OLEDB standards so it allows connectivity to any non-Oracle system that is ODBC or OLEDB compliant. This solution is free and available with the database. It is recommended for non-Oracle systems for which Oracle does not provide a gateway solution.

Both Generic Connectivity and Transparent Gateways are based on Oracle Heterogeneous Services. These solutions are SQL-based federated integration solutions and have existed since Oracle version 8.0. They are some of the best kept secrets that Oracle has to offer. The Oracle Gateway source and target data sources along with development languages and tools supported are:

Data source	Data target	Development languages and tools
DB2 LUW, mainframe, iSeries, SQL Server, Sybase, or any ODBC data source	Oracle (HS runs in the Oracle database)	SQL, PL/SQL

The most likely instances or use cases when the Oracle Gateways would be the Oracle product or tool selected are:

- Your IT department has strong SQL skills or the database organization will be running the virtual federation project

- You would like to support any reporting, BI, reporting or portal tool, web mashup, or custom application to access the data

Oracle Business Intelligence Suite

Oracle has had many business intelligence solutions over the years including: Essbase, Oracle Reports, Business Intelligence Beans, Oracle Personalization, Oracle Clickstream, Oracle XML Publisher (now Oracle BI Publisher), and Oracle Discover. The database has built-in features such as OLAP/cube support, partitioning, data mining, star schema support, bitmap indexes, materialized views, and more. Oracle's solution had been lacking an end-to-end (database-to-end-user) solution set that provided a dashboard approach to business intelligence.

The acquisition of Siebel provided Oracle with new products to offer an end-to-end solution called the Oracle BI Enterprise Edition (OBIEE). OBIEE includes a full set products from Siebel (Oracle Answers), Oracle BI Publisher, and ETL provided by OWB or ODI. The solution includes the ability to easily build BI dashboards without the need for a portal product. The suite includes Structure Query Reporter (SQR) which was a product offering from Hyperion. SQR has been around since the mid-1980s. Ironically, SQR was first developed by Sybase which is now owned by SAP. The Oracle BI Suite source and target data sources along with development languages and tools supported are:

Data source	Data target	Development languages and tools
ODBC, JDBC, XML, web services, URLs, COTS Applications: PeopleSoft Enterprise, JD Edwards EnterpriseOne, Oracle E-Business Suite, SAP R/3, and mySAP. OLAP sources including: Oracle Database OLAP Services, Microsoft Analysis Services Cubes, Hyperion Essbase, and SAP BW Infocubes	n/a	SOA/web services, Java, MS Office, SQR development language, eXtensible Business Reporting Language (XBR)

The most likely instances or use cases when Oracle BI Suite would be the Oracle product or tool selected are:

- The focus is BI read-only data access
- One dashboard is needed for all business intelligence information

Oracle SOA adapters

The Oracle SOA adapters provide both application and data level integration using standards based JCA adapters. When combined with the Oracle SOA Suite BPEL and Service Bus products, the SOA adapters form the foundation of an Enterprise Information System (EIS). Oracle SOA adapters support enterprise application solutions like Oracle E-Business Suite, Oracle PeopleSoft, Oracle Siebel, Oracle JD Edwards, as well as SAP, Microsoft CRM, Lawson, and other commonly deployed COTS solutions. These adapters are written by Oracle or third-party partners (Attunity and IWay) and are sold and supported by Oracle. Because they are JCA compliant, it is possible to use the adapters to perform two-phase commit across mainframe and Linux, Unix, and Windows (LUW)-based databases.

The adapters are grouped into application, technology, database, and legacy. Technology adapters support common EII technologies such as JMS, FTP, SMTP, SOAP, and REST. The database adapters include support for DB2, Sybase, SQL Server, and less mainstream databases such as MUMPS and Informix. The legacy adapters support both transactional (CICS and IMS-TM) and database (flat F\files, VSAM, IMS) sources.

Oracle SOA adapters are integrated into Oracle BPEL and the Oracle Server Bus (OSB). This allows you to do both process and messaging-based application integration. Using JDeveloper Oracle BPEL and Oracle Service Bus (OSB) modeling tools, you can easily integrate SOA adapters into your BPEL and OSB-based enterprise integration solutions. OSB source and target data sources along with the development languages and tools supported are:

Data source	Data target	Development languages and tools
Specific drivers for almost all databases, message brokers, SAP applications, Oracle Applications, and more	n/a	Java, web services

The most likely instances or use cases when the Oracle SOA adapters would be the Oracle product or tool selected are:

- Virtual federation at the Application Server/middle tier
- Web services-based information integration strategy

Oracle Web Center and Portal

The first portal product Oracle offered in 1999 was database and PL/SQL-based, and was named Oracle WebDB. You are probably seeing a common theme in this chapter. This common theme is that all Oracle EII and data migration offerings introduced prior to 2000 were database-based. This is because Oracle was a database company. Oracle even first attempted to offer a Java application server in the Oracle database in 1999 as part of the Oracle Internet Computing Platform.

Oracle Portal provides an environment for creating a portal Web interface, publishing and managing information, accessing dynamic data, and customizing the portal experience, as well as an extensible framework for J2EE-based application access. The Oracle Portal solution is based upon BEA AquaLogic User Interaction (Plumtree) and the original Oracle Portal product. BEA had another portal-based offering called BEA WebLogic Portal. Features of this product are being merged into a combined Oracle Portal and BEA AquaLogic User Interaction.

Oracle WebCenter is both a Portal solution and a Java-based UI framework that can be used to develop a complete Web 2.0, social networking, and information (including content management) management experience. Oracle WebCenter is developed using Java from the ground up (unlike Oracle Portal which was developed using PL/SQL) and is the strategic Portal product from Oracle. The best of Oracle Portal will be merged with Oracle WebCenter to provide one Oracle Portal offering. The Oracle WebCenter source and target data sources along with development languages and tools supported are:

Data source	Data target	Development languages and tools
Specific drivers for almost all databases, message brokers, SAP applications, Oracle Applications, and more	n/a	Java, PL/SQL, GUI

The most likely instances or use cases when Oracle WebCenter would be the Oracle product or tool selected are:

- Presentation tier, browser-based integration
- Mash-ups, centralization of all applications on one website

Oracle Business Activity Monitoring

Oracle Business Activity Monitoring (BAM) provides the ability to monitor business services and processes throughout the enterprise. Oracle BAM can be easily incorporated into any application or receive information automatically from other SOA components such as Oracle BPEL Process Manager. Oracle BAM empowers end users to react quickly to changing needs, based on application and system feedback, and to take corrective action as required. It allows business users real-time monitoring of business processes, web service interactions, data flows, and database activity.

Oracle BAM is a product that Oracle acquired along with a number of other products and technologies from PeopleSoft in 2005. PeopleSoft acquired the product right before the acquisition of PeopleSoft by Oracle. The product was a complete Microsoft solution, utilizing Microsoft .NET and SQL Server. Of course, one of the first major changes to the product was to port it to Java EE and an Oracle database. The Oracle BAM source and target data sources along with development languages and tools supported are:

Data source	Data target	Development languages and tools
Any data source, web services	Oracle (repository)	Java, web services, GUI

The most likely instances, or use cases when Oracle BAM would be the Oracle product or tool selected are:

- Real-time dashboards for business users and executive decision makers
- Gathering real-time data from databases, BPEL processes, and any web service-based source

> Virtual federation can be achieved by many means using Oracle products. The great thing is that you have choices, but this can also lead to IT department and end user confusion. You need to know what your business goal is before deciding on what solution is best for you.

Data services

Data services are at the leading edge of data integration. Traditional data integration involves moving data to a central repository or accessing data virtually through SQL-based interfaces. Data services are a means of making data a 'first class' citizen in your SOA.

Recently, the idea of SOA-enabled data services has taken off in the IT industry. This is not any different than accessing data using SQL, JDBC, or ODBC. What is new is that your service-based architecture can now view any database access service as a web service. Service Component Architecture (SCA) plays a big role in data services as now data services created and deployed using Oracle BPEL, Oracle ESB, and other Oracle SOA products can be part of an end-to-end data services platform. No longer do data services deployed in one of the SOA products have to be deployed in another Oracle SOA product. SCA makes it possible to call a BPEL component from Oracle Service Bus and vice versa.

Oracle Data Integration Suite

Oracle Data Integration (ODI) Suite includes the Oracle Service Bus to publish and subscribe messaging capabilities. Process orchestration capabilities are provided by Oracle BPEL Process Manager, and can be configured to support rule-based, event-based, and data-based delivery services. The Oracle Data Quality for Data Integrator, Oracle Data Profiling products, and Oracle Hyperion Data Relationship Manager provide best-in-class capabilities for data governance, change management, hierarchical data management, and provides the foundation for reference data management of any kind.

ODI Suite allows you to create data services that can be used in your SCA environment. These data services can be created in ODI, Oracle BPEL or the Oracle Service Bus. You can surround your SCA data services with Oracle Data Quality and Hyperion Data Relationship to cleanse your data and provide master data management. ODI Suite effectively serves two purposes:

- Bundle Oracle data integration solutions as most customers will need ODI, Oracle BPEL, Oracle Service Bus, and data quality and profiling in order to build a complete data services solution

- Compete with similar offerings from IBM (InfoSphere Information Server) and Microsoft (BizTalk 2010) that offer complete EII solutions in one offering

The ODI Suite data service source and target data sources along with development languages and tools supported are:

Data source	Data target	Development languages and tools
ERPs, CRMs, B2B systems, flat files, XML data, LDAP, JDBC, ODBC	Any data source	SQL, Java, GUI

The most likely instances or use cases when ODI Suite would be the Oracle product or tool selected are:

- SCA-based data services
- An end-to-end EII and data migration solution

> Data services can be used to expose any data source as a service. Once a data service is created, it is accessible and consumable by any web service-enabled product. In the case of Oracle, this is the entire set of products in the Oracle Fusion Middleware Suite.

Data consolidation

The mainframe was the ultimate solution when it came to data consolidation. All data in an enterprise resided in one or several mainframes that were physically located in a data center. The rise of the hardware and software appliance has created a 'what is old is new again' situation; a hardware and software solution that is sold as one product. Oracle has released the Oracle Exadata appliance and IBM acquired the pure database warehouse appliance company Netezza, HP, and Microsoft announced work on an SQL Server database appliance, and even companies like SAP, EMC, and CICSO are talking about the benefits of database appliances.

The difference is (and it is a big difference) that the present architecture is based upon open standards hardware platforms, operating systems, client devices, network protocols, interfaces, and databases. So, you now have a database appliance that is not based upon proprietary operating systems, hardware, network components, software, and data disks. Another very important difference is that enterprise software COTS packages, management tools, and other software infrastructure tools will work across any of these appliance solutions. One of the challenges for customers that run their business on the mainframe is that they are 'locked into' vendor- specific sorting, reporting, job scheduling, system management, and other products usually only offered from IBM, CA, BMC, or Compuware. Mainframe customers also suffer from a lack of choice when it comes to COTS applications. Since appliances are based upon open systems, there is an incredibly large software ecosystem.

Oracle Exadata

Oracle Exadata is the only database appliance that runs both data warehouse and OLTP applications. Oracle Exadata is an appliance that includes every component an IT organization needs to process information — from a grid database down to the power supply. It is a hardware and software solution that can be up and running in an enterprise in weeks instead of months for typical IT database solutions.

Exadata provides high speed data access using a combination of hardware and a database engine that runs at the storage tier. Typical database solutions have to use indexes to retrieve data from storage and then pull large volumes of data into the core database engine, which churns through millions of rows of data to send a handful of row results to the client. Exadata eliminates the need for indexes and data engine processing by placing a lightweight database engine at the storage tier. Therefore, the database engine is only provided with the end result and does not have to utilize complicated indexing schemes, large amounts of CPU, and memory to produce the end results set. Exadata's capabilities to run large OLTP and data warehouse applications, or a large number of smaller OLTP and data warehouse applications on one machine make it a great platform for data consolidation.

The first release of Oracle Exadata was based upon HP hardware and was for data warehouses only. The second release came out shortly before Oracle acquired Sun. This release was based upon Sun hardware, but ironically not on Sun Sparc or Solaris (Solaris is now an OS option). The Exadata source and target data sources along with development languages and tools supported are:

Data source	Data target	Development languages and tools
Any (depending upon the data source this may involve an intensive migration effort)	Oracle Exadata	SQL, PL/SQL, Java

The most likely instances or use cases when Exadata would be the Oracle product or tool selected are:

- A move from hundreds of standalone database hardware and software nodes to one database machine
- A reduction in hardware and software vendors, and one vendor for hardware and software support

Keepin It Real

The database appliance has become the latest trend in the IT industry. Data warehouse appliances like Netezza have been around for a number of years. Oracle has been the first vendor to offer an open systems database appliance for both DW and OLTP environments.

Data grid

Instead of consolidating databases physically or accessing the data where it resides, a data grid places the data into an in-memory middle tier. Like physical federation, the data is being placed into a centralized data repository. Unlike physical federation, the data is not placed into a traditional RDBMS system (Oracle database), but into a high-speed memory-based data grid. Oracle offers both a Java and SQL-based data grid solution. The decision of what product to implement often depends on where the corporations system, database, and application developer skills are strongest. If your organization has strong Java or .Net skills and is more comfortable with application servers than databases, then Oracle Coherence is typically the product of choice. If you have strong database administration and SQL skills, then Oracle TimesTen is probably a better solution.

The Oracle Exalogic solution takes the data grid to another level by placing Oracle Coherence, along with other Oracle hardware and software solutions, into an appliance. This appliance provides an 'end-to-end' solution or data grid 'in a box'. It reduces management, increases performance, reduces TCO, and eliminates the need for the customer having to build their own hardware and software solution using multiple vendor solutions that may not be certified to work together.

Oracle Coherence

Oracle Coherence is an in-memory data grid solution that offers next generation **Extreme Transaction Processing (XTP)**. Organizations can predictably scale mission critical applications by using Oracle Coherence to provide fast and reliable access to frequently used data. Oracle Coherence enables customers to push data closer to the application for faster access and greater resource utilization. By automatically and dynamically partitioning data in memory across multiple servers, Oracle Coherence enables continuous data availability and transactional integrity, even in the event of a server failure.

Oracle Coherence was purchased from Tangosol Software in 2007. Coherence was an industry-leading middle tier caching solution. The product only offered a Java solution at the time of acquisition, but a .NET offering was already scheduled before the acquisition took place. The Oracle Coherence source and target data sources along with development languages and tools supported are:

Data source	Data target	Development languages and tools
JDBC, any data source accessible through Oracle SOA adapters	Coherence	Java, .Net

The most likely instances or use cases when Oracle Coherence would be the Oracle product or tool selected are:

- When it is necessary to replace custom, hand-coded solutions that cache data in middle tier Java or .NET application servers
- Your company's strengths are in application servers Java or .NET

Oracle TimesTen

Oracle TimesTen is a data grid/cache offering that has similar characteristics to Oracle Coherence. Both of the solutions offer a product that caches data in the middle tier for high throughput and high transaction volumes. The technology implementations are much different. TimesTen is an in-memory database solution that is accessed through SQL and the data storage mechanism is a relational database. The TimesTen solution data grid can be implemented across a wide area network (WAN) and the nodes that make up the data grid are kept in sync with your back end Oracle database using Oracle Cache Connect. Cache Connect is also used to automatically refresh the TimesTen database on a push or pull basis from your Oracle backend database. Cache Connect can also be used to keep TimesTen databases spread across the global in sync.

Oracle TimesTen offers both read and update support, unlike other database in-memory solutions. This means that Oracle TimesTen can be used to run your business even if your backend database is down. The transactions that occur during the downtime are queued and applied to your backend database once it is restored.

The other similarity between Oracle Coherence and TimesTen is that they both were acquired technologies. Oracle TimesTen was acquired from the company TimesTen in 2005. The Oracle TimesTen source and target data sources along with development languages and tools supported are:

Data source	Data target	Development languages and tools
Oracle	TimesTen	SQL, CLI

The most likely instances or use cases when Oracle TimesTen would be the Oracle product or tool selected are:

- For web-based read-only applications that require a millisecond response and data close to where request is made
- For applications where updates need not be reflected back to the user in real-time

Oracle Exalogic

A simplified explanation of Oracle Exalogic is that it is Exadata for the middle tier application infrastructure. While Exalogic is optimized for enterprise Java, it is also a suitable environment for the thousands of third-party and custom Linux and Solaris applications widely deployed on Java, .NET, Visual Basic, PHP, or any other programming language. The core software components of Exalogic are WebLogic, Coherence, JRocket or Java Hotspot, and Oracle Linux or Solaris. Oracle Exalogic has an optimized version of WebLogic to run Java applications more efficiently and faster than a typical WebLogic implementation.

Oracle Exalogic is branded with the Oracle Elastic cloud as an enterprise application consolidation platform. This means that applications can be added on demand and in real-time. Data can be cached in Oracle Coherence for a high speed, centralized, data grid sharable on the cloud. The Exalogic source and target data sources along with development languages and tools supported are:

Data source	Data target	Development languages and tools
Any data source	Coherence	Any language

The most likely instances or use cases when Exalogic would be the Oracle product or tool selected are:

- Enterprise consolidated application server platform
- Cloud hosted solution
- Upgrade and Consolidation of hardware or software

> Oracle Coherence is the product of choice for Java and .NET versed development shops. Oracle TimesTen is more applicable to database-centric and shops more comfortable with SQL.

Information Lifecycle Management

Information Lifecycle Management (ILM) is a supporting solution for physical federation, data consolidation, and business intelligence. What all these data integration solutions have in common is that the database where the information is being stored continues to grow as daily activity is added to the centralized database. This is not only an issue of data storage costs, but also performance of the applications that access these databases and the cost of managing growing volumes of data. ILM provides a mechanism to automatically move data from primary high speed storage to lower cost storage.

Oracle Information Lifecycle Management

Oracle ILM is a combination of features that are part of the Oracle database and a lightweight GUI that can be used to build an ILM solution. These Oracle database features include Oracle table partitioning, Oracle advanced table compression, and **Virtual Private Database (VPD)**. Oracle VPD is used in an ILM solution by eliminating the number of rows returned to end users based upon what data the user has the authority to access, therefore maintaining the performance as data volumes grow. Oracle ILM Assistant uses some of these features and is a GUI tool to help implement Oracle ILM. The Oracle ILM Assistant allows you to define lifecycle definitions, a calendar of events, simulates the impact of partitioning on a table, advises how to partition a table, and generates and schedules scripts to move data when required. The Oracle ILM Suite source and target data sources along with development languages and tools supported are:

Data source	Data target	Development languages and tools
Oracle	Oracle	GUI, CLI, SQL, PL/SQL

The most likely instances or use cases when Oracle ILM would be the Oracle product or tool selected are:

- Growing database volumes where data has become difficult to manage and maintain

- Increased hardware, software, and support costs because of exponential data growth

> Oracle ILM is a package of Oracle products (partitioning) that have existed for quite some time. Oracle does put a GUI on top of these products to make managing Oracle data archiving in less expensive storage easier.

Oracle-to-Oracle

Oracle-to-Oracle data integration is treated separately as Oracle offers products that have been optimized for moving data between Oracle database instances. These products can only be used when both the source and target databases are Oracle databases. Oracle has had a long history of Oracle-to-Oracle-based solutions, including Oracle Replication Server and Oracle imp/exp. These key legacy Oracle-to-Oracle integration solutions have been replaced by Oracle Streams and Oracle Data Pump, respectively.

Oracle Streams

Oracle Streams is a log-based solution that enables the propagation and management of data, transactions, and events in a data stream either within an Oracle database, or from one Oracle database to another. The stream routes published information to subscribed destinations. Streams supports capture and apply from Oracle to non-Oracle systems. However, the apply or capture from non-Oracle systems must be custom-coded, or through an Oracle Transparent or Generic Gateway. In addition, messages can be sent to and received from other message queuing systems such as MQ Series and Tibco through the Oracle Message Gateway.

Oracle Streams replaced the Oracle Replication Server in 2006 as the Oracle replication product of choice. Oracle Replication was originally a trigger-based solution and this was perceived negatively by the customers. Oracle Streams offered a log-based solution which was more to the liking of enterprise customers. The Oracle Streams source and target data sources along with development languages and tools supported are:

Data source	Data target	Development languages and tools
Oracle	Oracle	SQL, PL/SQL, CLI

The most likely instances or use cases when Oracle Streams would be the Oracle product or tool selected are:

- High speed near real-time Oracle-to-Oracle replication
- Oracle disaster recovery solution

Oracle Data Pump

Oracle Data Pump is a replacement for the original EXP and IMP utilities. Available from Oracle 10*g*, Data Pump is the new export and import mechanism that provides increased performance and more features then EXP/IMP. As from Oracle 11*g*, original IMP/EXP is no longer supported for general use, but is still available for use with Oracle 10*g* or earlier databases. Oracle Data Pump can be used for logical backup of schema/table, to refresh the test system from production, database upgrades (either cross-platform, or with storage reorganization), and moving data from production to offline usage (such as a data warehouse, ad hoc query). Data Pump complements other Oracle database features such as RMAN physical backups and Oracle Warehouse Builder for Load operations. The Oracle Data Pump source and target data sources along with development languages and tools supported are:

Data source	Data target	Development languages and tools
Oracle	Oracle	CLI

The most likely instances or use cases when Oracle Data Pump would be the Oracle product or tool selected are:

- Creation of test and QA databases
- Cloning of Oracle databases
- Database upgrades

> Oracle Data Pump is the choice when it comes to moving between databases when real-time streaming is not possible because of network bandwidth constraints, or network connectivity is not even possible. When a high speed network is available, Oracle Streams will probably be the best option.

Oracle XStream

Oracle XStream is a new product released with Oracle 11*g*. The underlying technology is based upon Oracle Streams. XStream consists of Oracle database components and application programming interfaces (APIs) that enable client applications to receive data changes from an Oracle database and send data changes to an Oracle database.

Oracle XStream provided several capabilities which are above and beyond Oracle Streams:

- In-memory exchange of messages to the target database, application, or queue
- Sending Oracle database changes through a message to a Java or C application

Data source	Data target	Development languages and tools
Oracle	Oracle (in theory could be any database, a flat file, or another application)	SQL, PL/SQL, CLI

The most likely instances or use cases when Oracle XStream would be the Oracle product or tool selected are:

- High speed in-memory messaging
- Capturing and sending Oracle database changes to applications, queues, other Oracle databases or non-Oracle databases

Application integration

Application integration takes many of the products and technologies we discussed in this chapter to provide a complete integration solution for orchestrating agile, user-centric business processes across your enterprise applications. The products that are bundled with the Oracle SOA Suite are the foundation of Oracle Application Integration Architecture (AIA), so this Oracle SOA product suite will be discussed first.

Oracle's **Application Integration Architecture (AIA)** offers pre-built solutions at the data, process, and user interface level, delivering a complete process solution to business end users. All Oracle AIA components are designed to work together in a mix-and-match fashion and are built for easy configuration, ultimately lowering the cost and IT burden of building, extending, and maintaining integrations.

Oracle SOA Suite

The products included in this suite are: Oracle BPEL Process Manager, Oracle Human Workflow, Oracle Integration Adapters (Oracle SOA Adapters), Oracle Business Rules, Oracle Business Activity Monitoring, Oracle Complex Event Processing, Oracle Service Bus, Oracle B2B, Oracle Business Process Management (BPM), and Oracle Web Services Manager. These products can all be purchased together or separately. *Chapter 9, Information Lifecycle Management for transactional applications* will discuss the Oracle SOA Suite and each product in the suite in detail.

Oracle Advanced Queuing

Message-based application and data integration is one of the oldest forms of integration used by companies. **Message Orientated Middleware** (also known as **MOM**) uses message queues and formatted messages to exchange information between applications or databases. MOM solutions such as those from Tibco, IBM, and Microsoft are well known in the market. Oracle **Advanced Queuing (AQ)** has been a component of the database since Oracle Database version 8.0.3, but is not as well known as other IT vendor solutions, since it is Oracle database-based and the main interface to AQ is PL/SQL. Oracle Advanced Queuing (AQ) provides database-integrated message queuing functionality. Oracle AQ leverages the Oracle database so that messages can be stored persistently, propagated between queues on different machines and databases, and transmitted using Oracle Net Services, HTTP(S), and SMTP.

Oracle AQ supports both point-to-point and publish-subscribe (topics) forms of messaging. A point-to-point message is aimed at a specific target. Senders and receivers decide on a common queue in which to exchange messages. Each message is consumed by only one receiver. A publish-subscribe message can be consumed by multiple receivers. Publish-subscribe messaging has a wide dissemination mode—broadcast, and a more narrowly aimed mode—multicast, also called **point-to-multipoint**.

Oracle Application Information Architecture

Just as the name implies, Application Integration Architecture, this solution from Oracle is not a product but an architecture. Due to it's architecture, the solution is a combination and integration of Oracle products to provide you with the holy grail of EII in a common architecture. The architecture consists of Oracle BPM and BPA, Oracle Service Bus, Oracle BPEL, Oracle B2B, and all of the Oracle technology and application SOA adapters.

The first step in building an AIA solution is to model your business processing environment using business process management and business process automation tools. Oracle provides products for Business Process Management (BPM) and Business Process Automation (BPA) through a pre-integrated portfolio of products that span modeling tools for business analysts, developer tools for system integration, business activity monitoring for dashboards, and user interaction for process participants.

The next step is to define and create all of your integration points. Oracle Integration B2B has built-in adapters for RosettaNet, EDI, ebXML, and low-level protocols like TCP/IP, HTTP, FTP, SOAP, MIME, SMTP, and more. This means trading partner IT infrastructure can be installed and configured in weeks, not months. Oracle SOA application and technology adapters, explained in the *Oracle SOA adapter* section of this chapter, are used to integrate your own technologies and applications.

The last step is to 'wire' everything together within your AIA environment. Oracle Service Bus integrates with Oracle BPEL, Oracle BAM, and Oracle Fusion Middleware, while Oracle JDeveloper provides development capabilities for applications that use Oracle SCA facilities. Using Oracle JDeveloper, integrating applications becomes a drag-and-drop exercise using pre-packaged adapters for file, database, message queues, and COTS access. The AIA source and target data sources along with development languages and tools supported are:

Data source	Data target	Development languages and tools
Any data source	Any data source	GUI, SQL, Java, .NET

The most likely instances or use cases when AIA would be the Oracle product or tool selected are:

- SOA application and data integration based upon a pre-built architecture blueprint and set of Oracle products
- Future proofing your EII, EIS and EAI infrastructure

Oracle AIA is exactly that—an architecture. This means that it includes products that you use to build an application integration solution. The particular products you use depends on you. Oracle AIA is where Oracle is headed for its entire database, Fusion Middleware, and application products, so it is probably in your best interest to align yourself with this architecture.

Products matrix summary

We have discussed each product in detail and provided use cases to help guide you as you move towards a more current information integration architecture. Before we end this chapter, we believe that providing you with a matrix will help in your decision making.

Product	Data or App-centric	SQL, CLI or Java-based API	Data replication	Trans formations	DB or Fusion family	Initial data load capable	When to use
SQL Loader	Data	SQL, CLI	No	Yes	DB	Yes	Data migration
OWB	Data	SQL, PL/SQL	Yes	Yes	DB	Yes	Data migration
Migration Workbench	Data	SQL, CLI	No	Yes	DB	Yes	Data migration
ODI	Data	SQL	Yes	Yes	Fusion	Yes	Data migration, Data integration
Performance and Tuning Packs	Data	SQL	n/a	n/a	DB	n/a	Data migration
GoldenGate	Data	CLI	Yes	Yes	Fusion	Yes	Data integration
CDC Adapters	Data	Java	Yes	No	Fusion	No	Data integration
MDM	Data	Java	Yes	Yes	DB	Yes	Information federation
Data Quality & Profiling	Data	Java	n/a	n/a	Fusion	n/a	Data migration, data integration, information federation
Gateways and HS	Data	SQL	No	Yes	DB	Yes	SQL based Information federation
OBI EE	Data	Java	No	No	Fusion	No	Presentation based information integration

Product	Data or App-centric	SQL, CLI or Java-based API	Data replication	Trans formations	DB or Fusion family	Initial data load capable	When to use
SOA Adapters	Data and App	Java	No	Yes	Fusion	No	SOA integration, information integration
WebCenter Portals	Data and App	Java	No	No	Fusion	n/a	Presentation-focused information integration
BAM	Data and App	Java	No	No	Fusion	n/a	Presentation-focused information integration
ODI Suite	Data	SQL, Java	Yes	Yes	Fusion	Yes	Information integration, data migration, SOA integration, application integration
Exadata	Data	SQL, CLI	n/a	n/a	DB	n/a	Data consolidation
Coherence	App	Java	No	No	Fusion	n/a	In memory data grid
TimesTen	Data	SQL	No (Oracle-to-Oracle)	Yes	DB	Yes	In memory data grid
Exalogic	App	Java	n/a	n/a	Fusion	n/a	In memory data grid
ILM	Data	SQL, CLI	No	n/a	DB	n/a	Information integration, data archiving
Streams	Data	SQL, PL/SQL	Yes	Yes	DB	No	Oracle-to-Oracle data migration and integration
Data Pump	Data	CLI	No	No	DB	Yes	Oracle-to-Oracle data migration and integration
External Tables	Data	SQL, PL/SQL	No	Yes	DB	Yes	SQL-based data integration

Product	Data or App-centric	SQL, CLI or Java-based API	Data replication	Trans formations	DB or Fusion family	Initial data load capable	When to use
XStream	Data	SQL, CLI	Yes	Yes	DB	No	Oracle-to-Oracle data migration and integration
SOA Suite	App and Data	Java	No	Yes	Fusion	No	Web services-based data and application integration
Oracle AQ	Data	SQL, PL/SQL	No	No	DB	No	Message-based application integration, message-based data movement
AIA	App and Data	Java	No	Yes	Fusion	n/a	SOA and web services information integration

As this matrix shows, certain Oracle products are focused on a specific use case or task. You have options with products depending upon your developer's strengths: Java, PL/SQL, SQL, scripting using CLI, or even .NET. There is some overlap in the Oracle EII and data migration product offerings. However, even when there is overlap, one product has a strength that the other product does not have that makes it more appropriate for the problem you are solving. For example, there is overlap in OWB and ODI. OWB may be a great solution for building an Operational Data Store when your developers are PL/SQL gurus and your target database is Oracle. If your developers are Java and SQL proficient and your target ODS is Teradata, DB2, or some other RDBMS, then the solution for your ODS would be ODI, or perhaps ODI Suite.

Most companies are building a service-orientated information integration architecture. This is why using the components that are part of the Oracle Application Information Architecture (AIA) are important to start implementing an **Enterprise Application Integration (EAI)** solution. AIA is the strategic technology for enterprise integration and the integration platform for all Oracle Fusion Application products.

> The real trick is in understanding business drivers, business requirements, and day-to-day information usage patterns. Once you have these, the previous matrix can make the decision much easier. Keep in mind that AIA is strategic to Oracle and Oracle business applications (Oracle PeopleSoft, Oracle E-Business Suite, Siebel, and more) that you probably use today in your company.

Products not covered

There are two sets of data-related content management—unstructured data products that were not covered in this chapter:

- Oracle XMLType data type (a database feature)
- Oracle Content Management

This database feature and Oracle product suite were not covered as this book focuses on relational database information integration and data migration. Certainly, the Oracle XMLType data type can be used to consolidate and manage XML formatted documents. Oracle's Enterprise Content Management (ECM) Suite, mostly acquired from Stellent, is a best-of-breed ECM solutions encompass Document and Records Management, Web Content Management, Digital Asset Management, Imaging and Business Process Management, Information Rights Management, and Risk and Compliance. However, the Oracle ECM product line also does not fall into traditional relational databases-based integration or migration.

Summary

This chapter provides a holistic picture of Oracle information integration, data migration, and data consolidation products, technologies, and tools from the Oracle Database to Fusion Middleware to Oracle Applications. We could not possibly cover each Oracle product in detail, but that was not the intention of this chapter. The Oracle products, tools, and solutions covered in this chapter serve as the foundation for the detailed discussion of the key Oracle EII and EAI, data migration, and consolidation products covered in the rest of this book.

Oracle has come a long way since it was a database-centric data integration company. Many of the newest solutions were acquired. Oracle has not only moved more towards a middle tier model, but also to a heterogeneous offering. The cause for this move may have been the heterogeneous technologies Oracle acquired (GoldenGate, Collaxa/Oracle BPEL), COTS acquisitions (JDEdwards legacy version only runs on DB2 iSeries) or recognition by Oracle that not everyone is on an Oracle database. Whatever the cause, Oracle has now embraced heterogeneous information integration.

After reading this chapter, you should now have a much better idea of what Oracle products to use for your EII, EAI, data migration, and consolidation initiatives. You should have the knowledge to know when to use which Oracle products for data integration and migration, presentation-based information integration, physical federation, virtual federation, application integration, and service-based integration. A major decision you and your organization must make is whether you will take an evolutionary or revolutionary approach to data consolidation and information integration:

- **Evolutionary approach**: Keep all custom-coded data migration, information integration, and data integration tools, products, and technologies in place. Develop all new data integration using Oracle Data Integrator. Develop all new application and process integration using Oracle SOA Suite. Implement all new Oracle Application Integration using Oracle AIA.

- **Revolutionary approach**: Move all custom-coded data migration, information integration, and data integration tools, products, and technologies to Oracle Data Integrator, Oracle GoldenGate, Oracle SOA Suite, and Oracle AIA. All new development will obviously be completed using these products and technologies. In addition, you will consolidate all data on Oracle Exadata and create a data grid using Oracle Exalogic.

- **Part evolutionary and revolutionary**: Create a physically or virtually federated common data store using Oracle Exadata, exposing this federated database using Oracle WebCenter. You could also monitor the current data flows using Oracle BAM. Then slowly move all custom tools, technologies, and products to Oracle Data Integrator, Oracle GoldenGate, Oracle SOA Suite and Oracle AIA. Of course, all new development would be done using the appropriate Oracle product.

In the next chapter, we will get our hands dirty with a real customer example, including code samples and details on using the products to achieve an 'end-to-end' data and application integration business problem.

3

Application and Data Integration Case Study

The company in this case study is a leading US-based insurance company and has been in business since the early 1900s. They have evolved from a life insurance company to a full service insurance and financial services provider. The company provides group dental, life, disability, accidental death, and dismemberment policies, as well as annuities and retirement plans. The focus of this case study is a 401K management system that is used by Fortune 1000 companies to provide retirement plans to their employees. This system performs most processing in nightly batch cycles.

Like most established, successful, and long-standing companies, this company has attempted to modernize portions of their IT application portfolio for over 20 years. The focus of many of these efforts has been to move the applications totally off the mainframe using both a re-host or re-architecture approach. The re-host and re-architecture approaches are described in detail in Packt Publishing's *Oracle Modernization Solutions* book (`https://www.packtpub.com/oracle-modernization-solutions/book`). Moving completely off the mainframe can be time-consuming, have a relatively lengthy Return on Investment (ROI), and in many cases its, abandoned because the projects become unmanageable unless a phased approach is used.

Many companies spend millions of dollars and have several failed modernization attempts before finding success. This particular company has spent millions of dollars on two modernization projects. They have attempted both a re-host and re-architecture with nothing to show for it. The result has made the organization very sceptical that either of these approaches can be made to work 'this time'. The company is probably correct as the application being modernized does not lend itself to either a re-host or re-architecture.

Why not re-host? Most of the processing involves copying, sorting, and reformatting the mainframe flat and VSAM files. The COBOL applications contain mostly infrastructure code instead of business logic. This would mean moving 'as is' processing and code that is inefficient, redundant or not even required onto open systems.

Why not re-architecture? The application supports seven transaction types. Each transaction type has a significant amount of common code but also has transactions-specific code. Replacing this mainframe custom code in the form of JCL and COBOL with a Java EE or .NET solution would be difficult, as separating common code from transaction-specific code from infrastructure code, would be a significant undertaking. In addition, there are no business or IT subject matter experts available (they are no longer with the company) that could help define the functional and technical specifications.

The approach being used this time is information and application integration using service-orientated enablement of mainframe legacy data and applications, along with exposing modern Oracle database tables and IBM MQSeries as web services. This will allow the company to achieve a quick win, phase in the additional transactions, and start the migration of data and processing off the mainframe in a controlled manner.

This chapter is a real-life example of a successful **Proof of Value** (**POV**), or pilot project, which utilizes data integration of the Oracle database, mainframe VSAM, and flat files data services, application integration of COBOL, data integration using transaction-based web services, process integration using Oracle BPEL, and information integration through IBM MQSeries. It is an end-to-end Oracle-based data, process, message, and application integration project using many of the products we learned about in *Chapter 2, Oracle Tools and Products*.

What is the POV?

The POV is more than just an exercise in what can be done using the Oracle information and application integration products. There was a specific technical reason behind each product choice. The Oracle products used were chosen because they provide the following technological benefits:

- Incremental migration of transaction processing off the legacy system — We are moving one transaction processing stream from the mainframe, that is adding a new member maintenance. The Oracle BPEL Designer and JDeveloper is used to model and design the new member maintenance process.

- A major re-engineering effort with minimal effort—The batch system is being replaced with new Oracle technology, but we are not incurring the risk and cost associated with rewriting the core business logic. The Oracle SOA Adapters will allow us to leverage mainframe applications and data.

- Complete new process and way of processing—Instead of running sequential batch jobs on the mainframe, the new process is orchestrated using Oracle JDeveloper and deployed to Oracle BPEL Process Manager.

- A target Oracle-based information and application integration architecture made possible using service-orientated architecture products—The customer now has the foundation in place for a new architecture based on SOA and a relational database. The Oracle Fusion Middleware, SOA Suite, and Database will make this new architecture possible.

- Migration of a batch, scheduled process to near real-time, event-based processing—The Oracle SOA platform is capable of supporting **Complex Event Processing** (**CEP**) in real-time as the business transactions occur instead of waiting to process transactions at night. Oracle CEP will not be implemented during this POV but can easily be added to the solution.

This project is very typical of mainframe batch processing migration to open systems and Oracle. Mainframe batch processing is an outdated mode of business automation processing that is technically based upon COBOL code, Job Control Language (JCL), job schedulers like CA-7 Autosys, VSAM files, and flat files. These old technologies are difficult to move in a 'big bang' (moving all technologies off the mainframe during one project) approach to the Oracle Database and Fusion Middleware. Open systems business automation processing is typically achieved through **Business Process Execution Language** (**BPEL**) process manager products. BPEL process managers let you orchestrate web service implementations, human interaction, and system workflow quickly and easily using graphical, drag-and-drop techniques. The tools are end user focused, allowing users to orchestrate their own systems. The execution language for orchestration is BPEL, and the run-time engine is Java EE. BPEL supports both human and automated orchestration. Enterprises typically use BPEL process managers to streamline and rethink existing business processes. This is what was achieved in this POV where the core mainframe technology (COBOL, VSAM files, and flat files) were kept on the mainframe. The business automation processing was moved from JCL and a job scheduler to Oracle BPEL Process Manager.

The Oracle BPEL and Database technical advantages over mainframe batch processing include:

- Customer online access—Online, real-time access to information when it is being processed and after it is processed.

- Internal access to information and processing status — Even within companies having online terminals, reliable, high-speed networks were too costly to make online systems common. The easiest and most often fastest way was to send all the day's work to the data processing department each night. Using Oracle, the information can be accessible immediately instead of waiting until the next day, after the nightly batch cycle.

- IT infrastructure limitations removed — The cost of high-speed networks, online disk storage, computer memory, and business applications prevented systems from being online and interactive. The least costly and most efficient way to do business was in batches. Using open systems infrastructure and Oracle software these limitations are removed.

- The way business was done — Because of IT infrastructure and online limitations, most business processes revolved around the idea of data entry (input), data processing (processing), and reporting/file extraction (output). That is the way business was done, so IT systems supported this way of doing business. Technologies like Oracle BPEL introduce a new way of processing.

- Information integration limitations lifted — Information integration with in-house and third-party systems needed to happen at night using a flat file exchange. The reason it had to be done at night is because batch processing handled a majority of daily transactions. A flat file was used because this was the easiest and quickest way to exchange the information. Oracle BPEL, Oracle SOA Suite, and Fusion Middleware provide a variety of methods, including web services, to perform information integration.

- Backup and archiving — Legacy data stores traditionally could not be backed up or archived while the data store was online. Some of these limitations have been lifted but processing has not been changed and the latest version of the data store is not being used. Therefore, batch systems have a lot of processing that backs up, does log archiving, data store compression, and data store corruption detection. Moving to the Oracle database removes these limitations so OLTP and batches can take place concurrently.

- Report formatting and creation — On the mainframe, the batch process must format files for reporting, execute customer programs to generate the reports and run print programs to handle high-speed printing and distribution. Once the system is on Oracle, the BPEL process can simply execute a SQL statement against the database to produce both reports and generate flat files.

Solving a business problem

Like most IT projects, this project was undertaken to solve a business problem. The three most tangible business benefits expected from this project are:

- Reduced business costs
- Reduced IT costs
- Increased customer **Service Levels Agreements (SLAs)**

This customer is typical of most major corporations as most of their daily transaction processing happens at night. Anytime you buy something with a credit card, make a phone call, pay for a visit to the doctor, or pay your mortgage there is a high probability the transaction is processed on a mainframe. There is also a high probability that the transaction was processed in a nightly batch cycle. Many corporations miss their nightly batch cycle window ten percent of the time. This means that when it is time to start capturing new transactions during the day, the transactions for the previous night have not been completed. When we first asked the company how often they missed their batch window, the response was on average two percent of the transactions, with other times being 10 to 20 percent of transactions every night. So this was not a case of missing batch windows once every ten days, they are missing nightly cycles (for example their batch window) every night! It simply varied from 2 percent to 20 percent of transactions every night. This has significant monetary impact to the company as these transactions are 401K buy, sell, and hold orders, where in today's volatile stock market could mean a 10 percent to 20 percent change in value between when the order was executed and when it was processed by the insurance company. The insurance company is responsible for the delta in value when the transaction was executed and when the insurance company actually processed it. So, if a 401K participant sells 2,000 shares of stock that was at $20 a share, and it takes three days for the insurance company to actually process the transaction, and the stock price is at $15, the insurance company needs to cover the $10,000. Now extrapolate this potential cost coverage to thousands of transactions a night. This amounts to a lot of money.

IT costs are lowered by implementing Oracle SOA technologies that provide stress relief for the nightly batch processes, and Plug and Play integration with Oracle database tables, IBM MQSeries and legacy CICS transactions, VSAM data, flat flats, and COBOL modules. These technologies are much easier to implement, manage, support, as well as to develop in. A five year Total Cost of Owner (TCO) study done by Oracle on Composite SOA for Telecoms in 2008 produced some interesting results regarding SOA cost savings. Most people may think that the development costs may be the biggest cost savings. However, the initial implementation (installation and development) saved 20 percent, while the upgrade costs provided a 55 percent saving, and maintenance produced a 50 percent saving.

As with most of the legacy modernization projects, the biggest benefits are intangible. These are benefits which may not have an immediate hard dollar business ROI or reduced TCO, but can provide significant business benefit and have extensive growth benefit:

- **Businesses expect 24/7 access**: The nightly batch window is continuing to shrink with business occurring all over the world and business expecting 24/7 access. Moving to Oracle SOA architecture with an Oracle relational database can provide this 24/7 access, while mainframe technology prevents VSAM and flat files from being accessible while nightly batch processing is being completed.

- **Near real-time processing**: Business owners expect to have almost immediate access to transactions. By reducing the processing time of transactions, business decision-makers can have web dashboards built to provide this feedback.

- **BPEL orchestration**: BPEL is the new way to perform batch processing and orchestrate business processes. There is still overlap and synergies between batch job scheduling and BPEL processing, as explained in the article entitled *Batch Processing in a Services World*: `http://bpelresource.com/113/batch-processing-services-world/`. However, orchestration of business processes using BPEL is the future of business processing.

- **Self-documenting applications**: We are using orchestration, Oracle BPEL Process Manager, and SOA technology to capture and preserve intellectual property. BPEL is a self-documented technology; a software developer can look at the BPEL processes and generated code, and understand the functionality of the system. This makes it easy for business users to understand the application processing. It also makes it significantly easier for IT personnel and business users to communicate their needs with each other. New IT staff can easily learn the way transactions are processed. You also avoid the 'one person knows this system' dilemma that causes many IT departments from making make any changes to the current way of processing.

- **Increased agility**: Adding a new data file, application, transaction, message, or process integration will now take a number of days instead of weeks or months. Whole new business processes can be incorporated into the environment in weeks instead of months. Business rules can be added, changed or deleted in minutes instead of days.

- **Increased efficiency through reuse**: The same data, transaction, messaging, and application adapters can be used when new data sources, message queues or brokers, or new applications need to be integrated into the system. The integration processes used as part of the new member process (the process being migrated off the mainframe for this case study) can be used in other business processes with little or no changes.

Estimated level of effort

The initial estimate for the elapsed time of the project was a four week plan with an allowance for seven weeks. The timeline broke down as follows:

- Week of July 19
    ◦ Complete functional specifications
    ◦ Complete technical specifications

- Week of July 26
    ◦ Test hardware and networking
    ◦ Install Oracle SOA Suite, Oracle SOA Adapters, Oracle Connect, Oracle Database, and Attunity software
    ◦ Expose VSAM and flat files as web services
    ◦ Expose COBOL program as a web service
    ◦ Expose CICS transactions as web services
    ◦ Create Oracle database table adapter web service
    ◦ Create IBM MQSeries adapter web service
    ◦ Unit test the application, message, and data integration web services

- Week of August 2
    ◦ Orchestrate end-to-end business process in Oracle BPEL using Oracle JDeveloper
    ◦ Test queues to Microsoft BizTalk
    ◦ Test queues to IBM MQSeries
    ◦ Test orchestration flow in Oracle BPEL Process Manager

- Weeks of August 9 and 16
    ◦ Lag time to complete any remaining activities

- September 7
  - ° Demo to Oracle team and insurance company middle level managers

- September 16
  - ° Presentation and demo to IT leadership at insurance company

The elapsed time is one way of representing the level of effort. As part of the pilot, the resource type and time effort for each resource type was estimated along with specific activities:

Resource type	Time effort	Activities
Oracle Fusion Middleware, SOA and BPEL	80 hours	Installation and configuration of Oracle SOA Suite, Oracle JDeveloper and Oracle Database.
		Orchestration of end-to-end integration process using Oracle JDeveloper BPEL Designer.
		Unit testing of Oracle database, VSAM file, flat file, COBOL application, CICS transaction, MQSeries data and application integration.
		Deployment to Oracle SOA Suite BPEL Process Manager.
		Testing of end-to-end process using BPEL Process Manager.
		Functional and technical specification lead.
Oracle Legacy Studio and Oracle Connect	80 hours	Installation and configuration of Oracle Connect on mainframe.
		Create copybooks (schema definitions) for all mainframe VSAM and flat files.
		Define VSAM, flat file, COBOL and CICS adapters.
		Expose all data and application adapters as web services.
		Unit testing of all adapters/web services.
		Assist with functional and technical specifications.
Attunity Expert	20 hours	Assistance with Oracle Connect installation and configuration.
		Assistance with mainframe file, COBOL and CICS adapter creation.
		Mainframe expertise.

Resource type	Time effort	Activities
Company Subject Matter Expert (SME) and architect	80 hours	Define current architecture.
		Define functional and technical specifications.
		COBOL, copybook, VSAM, flat file and CICS analysis, discovery, and fact-finding.
		Liaison between Oracle and insurance company mainframe and technical staff.
		Answer questions from Oracle and Attunity resources during pilot development.

An Oracle database administrator, mainframe system administrator, mainframe application developer, and mainframe data administrator would all have been useful additions to the team. These resources were called upon, but the lack of assigned resources held up the speed of delivery for this project.

Software and hardware requirements

The choice was made to implement the target software solution using an all-Oracle stack. The use of one stack makes maintenance, support, upgrading, and the employee learning curve much easier. The hardware chosen for the POV may or may not be the production hardware stack. In typical fashion for a POV/pilot, a Lintel (Linux and Intel) stack was used to make it faster and cheaper, and easier to find skilled personnel. The configuration was kept to a minimum, so hardware capacity planning will need to be done to determine the production configuration.

Software

The software required is often referred to as the **bill of materials**. The bill of materials for this information and application project is listed here. As URLs change, and the software is constantly updated and re-packaged, you may want to check the Oracle website to make sure you have the correct software to complete this use case on your own company. The following section consists of the complete bill of materials and how the products were used:

- Oracle Database 11*g* (`http://www.oracle.com/technetwork/database/enterprise-edition/downloads/index.html`) — Used to store the new member transactions and SOA Suite metadata repository.

- Oracle Application Server 11*g* R1 (10.3.3) (`http://www.oracle.com/technetwork/middleware/fusion-middleware/downloads/index.html`) — Used for database, application, mainframe file, MQSeries web service, Java Server Page (JSP) presentation tier, Java EE Connector, and SOA Suite container run times.

- Oracle SOA Suite 11*g* R1 (`http://www.oracle.com/technetwork/middleware/soasuite/downloads/index.html`) — Used for BPEL Process Manager runtime, and Oracle Database and MQSeries adapters.

- Oracle Fusion Middleware Adapters (`http://www.oracle.com/technetwork/middleware/downloads/fmw-11-download-092893.html`) — This software is found under the Adapters and Connectors (11.1.1.2.0) subtab. Used for mainframe data, transaction, and application integration.

- Oracle JDeveloper, Version 11.1.3.3 with SOA extensions (`http://www.oracle.com/technetwork/developer-tools/jdev/downloads/soft11-098086.html`) — Used to develop end-to-end integration and a business process flow using Oracle BPEL Designer and JSP development for the presentation tier.

- Oracle Enterprise Manager (`http://www.oracle.com/technetwork/oem/grid-control/downloads/index.html?ssSourceSiteId=ocomen`) — Used to manage the Oracle Database, Fusion Middleware, and SOA Suite.

- Oracle Enterprise Linux Version (`http://edelivery.oracle.com/linux`) — Used as the operating system.

- Oracle Virtual Box 3.2 (`http://www.virtualbox.org/`) — Used to easily share the POV deployment with the customer and Oracle employees. Oracle has many pre-packaged tutorials to download and use. The authors don't want to create material that is already available; the Oracle Technology Network has many tutorials here: `http://www.oracle.com/us/technologies/virtualization/oraclevm/061976.html`.

Hardware and network

The hardware and network deployment were chosen for ease of procurement, installation, configuration, and maintenance. Since performance or scalability were not part of the POV success criteria, the configuration was not enterprise ready:

- Server configuration:
    - 4-core Intel and Windows server
    - 8 GB RAM
    - 500 GB hard drive
    - Monitor for Oracle Enterprise Manager, BPEL process testing

- Internet connectivity: In case any software needed to be downloaded, to share project documents on an Oracle-based collaboration suite, e-mail access, and for researching issues

- Intranet connectivity: The orchestration server needs to be able to connect to the mainframe, a message queue, and internal databases like Oracle

- Two development work stations — Windows-based Intel machines: one machine for SOA development using Oracle JDeveloper, the other machine for Oracle Legacy Studio to create, configure, test, and expose legacy artifacts as services

> The Oracle software stack, for the most part, was all Oracle owned or Oracle branded Original Equipment Manufacturer (OEM) software from Attunity Software. The Attunity COBOL adapter software is not OEM'ed by Oracle so needed to be purchased directly from Attunity Software. The entire software stack is all pre-validated to work with the Oracle Application Server Weblogic, Oracle SOA Suite, and Oracle adapter framework.

Original architecture—nightly batch process

The current system is a typical legacy application that uses **time-delayed processing**. This means that all the work from the day is collected in a set of files and then processed at a specific time each day. The bulk of the processing is done by mainframe utilities like **IEBGENER** (Access Method Services), **Syncsort**, and **IDCAMS**. IEBGENER is an IBM utility used to write to the flat sequential files. IDCAMS is an IBM utility used to read and write to the Virtual Storage Access Method (VSAM) data store. Syncsort is a file sorting utility from the company of the same name. One COBOL program contains all the business logic and business rules to add new members to the application. Job Control Language (JCL) is used to control the flow of processing, writing to temporary data sets, and calling programs and utilities to format files for processing.

Batch cycle diagram—technical architecture

The online application consists of COBOL Customer Information Control System (CICS) programs accessing VSAM through 22 transaction codes. Although there is an online component to this application, all member master file updates, deletes, and inserts are completed in the nightly batch cycle. The entire nightly batch cycle consists of two JCL processes with a total of 20 steps in the two jobs. These 20 job steps mostly invoke IBM utilities (IEBGENER, IDCAMS). The 20 jobs invoke three COBOL programs to apply business rules and execute logic to process transactions that occurred during the day. At the end of the nightly batch cycle, the master database file (a VSAM file) is rebuilt so that the next day's online processing can start in the morning. The technical architecture of the current batch processing on the mainframe looks as follows:

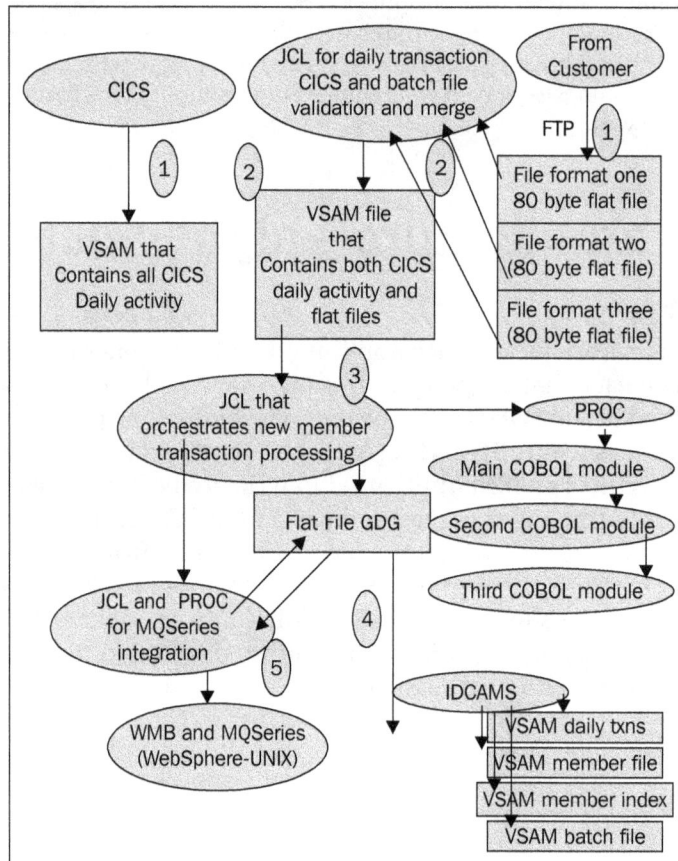

The overall business process flow shown in the previous diagram, from input transactions to MQSeries feeds and VSAM files prepared for the next day's activity, is as follows:

- **Input transactions**: The new member transactions come from two different sources during the day:

    ○ Customer files sent by FTP (File Transfer Protocol)–The company receives files from clients (major customer accounts) throughout the day through secure FTP. These files are held until the nightly batch processing cycle when they are processed.

    ○ CICS online transactions - The online transactions occur during the day through IBM mainframe 3270 'green screen' terminals. These transactions are not processed real-time but are aggregated and held for nightly batch processing using the same batch process as the customer files that are sent by FTP.

- **Batch and online transaction**: The customer files sent by FTP and CICS transaction files are merged during this processing. The merge process not only combines two different file formats, but also does data cleansing, removes duplicate transactions, and transaction validation.

- **Application processing of transactions**: The mainframe JCL and **Job Execution System (JES)** are the process orchestration 'engine' on the mainframe. Two sets of JCL call a PROC that in turn calls three COBOL modules. These three COBOL modules perform the processing to add new members, update members, and delete members. The COBOL modules process the transaction through JCL coding, using temporary flat files and VSAM files for intermediate processing. The COBOL module also writes all processed transactions to a **Generation Data Group (GDG)** flat file. GDG is a method on the mainframe to group a set of related files so they can be referenced individually or as a group. Mostly, GDGs are used to store and access files by the day they were created.

- **Prepare new VSAM files for next day**: The output GDG file is used along with the IBM IDCAMS utility to populate the four main VSAM files that will be used for processing the next day's transactions.

- **MQSeries feed to company portal**: IBM WebSphere Message Broker (WMB) and IBM MQSeries are used to feed other open system portal-based systems and Microsoft BizTalk.

Functional specifications

This application was chosen for a pilot/POV because it is a standalone application, and one transaction code, or type, can be processed alone (adding a member name) and be shown end-to-end. Demonstrating end-to-end processing was important to the customer as it would prove that Oracle could handle all the processing that takes place to the add the member transaction type on a nightly basis. Finding a standalone application in any IT environment, particularly legacy mainframe system, can be very difficult. Most applications rely on different databases located in different data centers, call application code that is part of other applications, and/or are dependent on integration with internal or external systems in order to complete an end-to-end process. Even though the application has 22 transaction types or codes, the processing is set up so that just one of the transaction codes (add new member) can be completely processed for the pilot.

The functional specifications define the transaction type and the flow the transaction type will take through the proposed solution. The functional specifications identify, from a business perspective, what the solution needs to accomplish. The endstate processing model includes the following:

- **Process AN** (**Add Name**, also referred to as **add member**): The transactions from an input from an Oracle Database table and output to VSAM files and MQSeries. The output files continue to be written to the same output targets (VSAM and MQSeries) as the current mainframe system does.

- **Straight through processing**: Straight through processing is not the same as real-time processing. Straight through processing is a financial services term that is used to refer to processing a transaction from beginning to end without manual intervention. Straight through processing was not possible on the mainframe as manual steps were required. Of course, real-time processing is to process transactions as they are received instead of in batches at a predefined (scheduled) time.

- **Reporting, monitoring, concurrency, and process restart**: This POV begins to show the reporting and monitoring capabilities using Oracle BPEL Designer to orchestrate processes. Oracle BPEL Process Manager, the BPEL runtime engine, produces reports for each activity in the processes and reports any errors, warnings, and results produced. A developer, DBA or system administrator can use a web console to monitor the processing as it takes place. More intensive reporting and monitoring can be done by placing Oracle BAM sensors on the BPEL process and monitoring the BPEL process using the Oracle BAM console. Due to the lack of time and to limit the scope of the POV, concurrency and process restart were not including in the POV, but this functionality can easy be added to the BPEL process.

- **Flashy demonstration**: The demonstration should have a lot of visual effects from processing through monitoring.

- **Demonstrate the benefits of orchestration**: The foundation of the pilot is BPEL processing and the benefits it has over JCL and JES mainframe processing. The benefits BPEL (and the Oracle Database) have over mainframe JCL and JES processing have been discussed in earlier sections of this chapter.

- **Self-documentation**: BPEL orchestration is self-documenting by nature and this needs to be highlighted in the pilot. Documentation in the current system is lacking and JCL/JES are impossible for a business user to understand. The customer is experiencing high resource expenses and time due to maintaining and enhancing an application that is not documented and impossible to understand.

- **Access any process, data or application as a service**: It can take weeks or even months to add new processing, data inputs or outputs, and applications to the current architecture. The pilot needs to show how new services can be added in minutes. This point goes to the heart of this book—how SOA technologies enable quick, easy, and less costly process, application, and data integration.

- **Easily replacing components without impacting other components in the orchestrated processing**: Legacy systems are costly to maintain and upgrade, because updating even a small piece of code can cause the entire application to break. The pilot needs to show how existing components can be replaced or updated with no impact to the overall processing or current code base.

Functional design diagram

The functional design is a business-focused high-level view of the new business process. It obviously does not have any technical details, implementation specifications, or specifics on what vendor technologies will be used.

The diagram depicts that new member transactions will be input into an orchestration business process through a batch or online. The transactions will be processed using BPEL orchestration through the same process that happens on the mainframe every night. The end of the orchestration business process outputs the transactions to VSAM files and MQSeries just as it does currently.

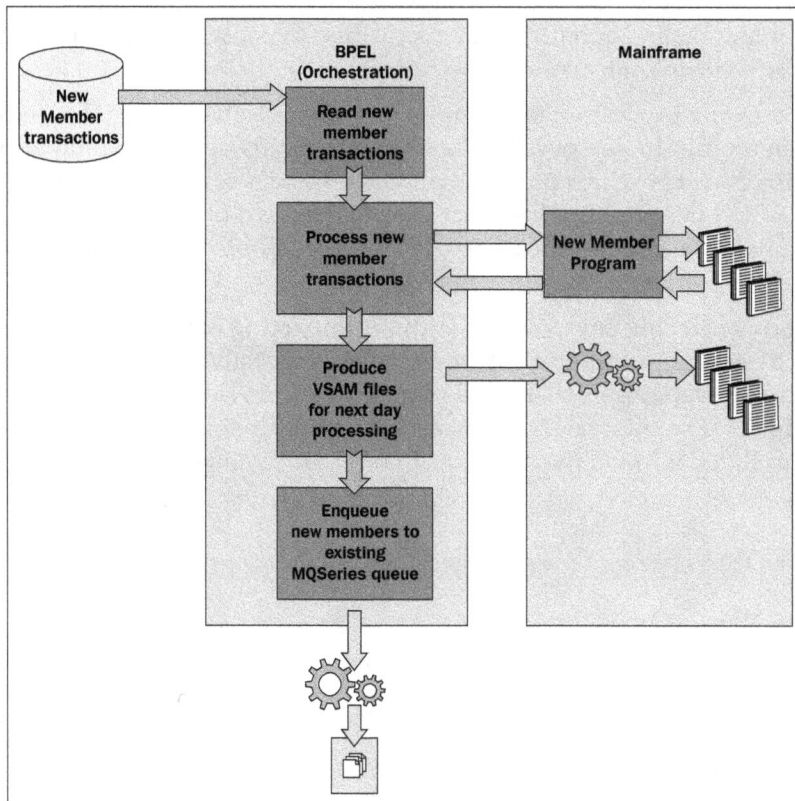

Functionally, we had a great handle on what we were setting out to accomplish and what the end state would look like. As you will see, knowing functionally what you are doing does not necessarily mean you have a concise and clear technical idea.

Technical specifications

Oracle's BPEL orchestration, legacy and technology adapters, and web services-based information integration solution (Oracle Fusion Middleware) replaces the existing time-delayed batch process with a straight through process. The architecture decided on, leaves the core business rules processing on the mainframe in a COBOL program. However, the core business processing now occurs inside of Oracle BPEL Process Manager instead of JCL and JES. In addition, integration with other applications takes place using Oracle BPEL Process Manager using Oracle SOA Adapters.

The target technical architecture demonstrates the ability to replace the current add member batch process by using Oracle, process, data integration, and application integration technologies to achieve the same result as the legacy system. The technology mapping from the legacy to the Oracle SOA integration-based solutions is as follows:

- **Read new member transactions**:
    - Legacy technology – JCL, PROCS, JES, and COBOL programs using flat files on the mainframe.
    - Oracle open systems technology – Oracle BPEL Process Manager using Oracle Database technology adapter exposed as a web service to read an Oracle database table.

- **Process new member transactions**:
    - Legacy technology – JCL, JES, and PROCS executing COBOL modules that read and write VSAM files and create flat file outputs.
    - Oracle open system technology – Oracle and Oracle partner product solutions with Oracle Fusion Middleware Legacy VSAM adapter, Oracle Fusion Middleware Legacy CICS adapter, Attunity Flat File adapter, Attunity COBOL adapter. The COBOL program is exposed as a web service. Just like in the legacy solution, the mainframe program will operate 'as is' and produce all the necessary VSAM and flat file output transactions.

- **Produce VSAM files for next day processing**:
  - ° Legacy technology—JCL calling IBM IDCAMS utility to copy flat files from flat files to VSAM.
  - ° Oracle open systems technology—Oracle BPEL Process Manager with Flat File adapter exposed as web services (for flat file reading) and VSAM adapter exposed as a web service to write to VSAM files.

- **Enqueue the member maintenance add transaction for the existing MQSeries queue for WCC** (WebSphere Customer Center now known as InfoSphere):
  - ° Legacy technology: IBM MQSeries—Oracle Open Systems technology with Oracle BPEL Process Manager, Oracle Fusion Middleware MQSeries Technology adapter exposed as web service.
  - ° Transaction monitoring—This was not possible in the legacy system. The combination of Oracle BPEL Process Manager and Oracle Business Activity Monitor (BAM) make this possible on open systems.

Technical specifications diagram

The overall business process flow is now controlled by the Oracle BPEL Process Manager; the integration work is done by Oracle legacy and technology adapters that are part of the Oracle SOA Suite:

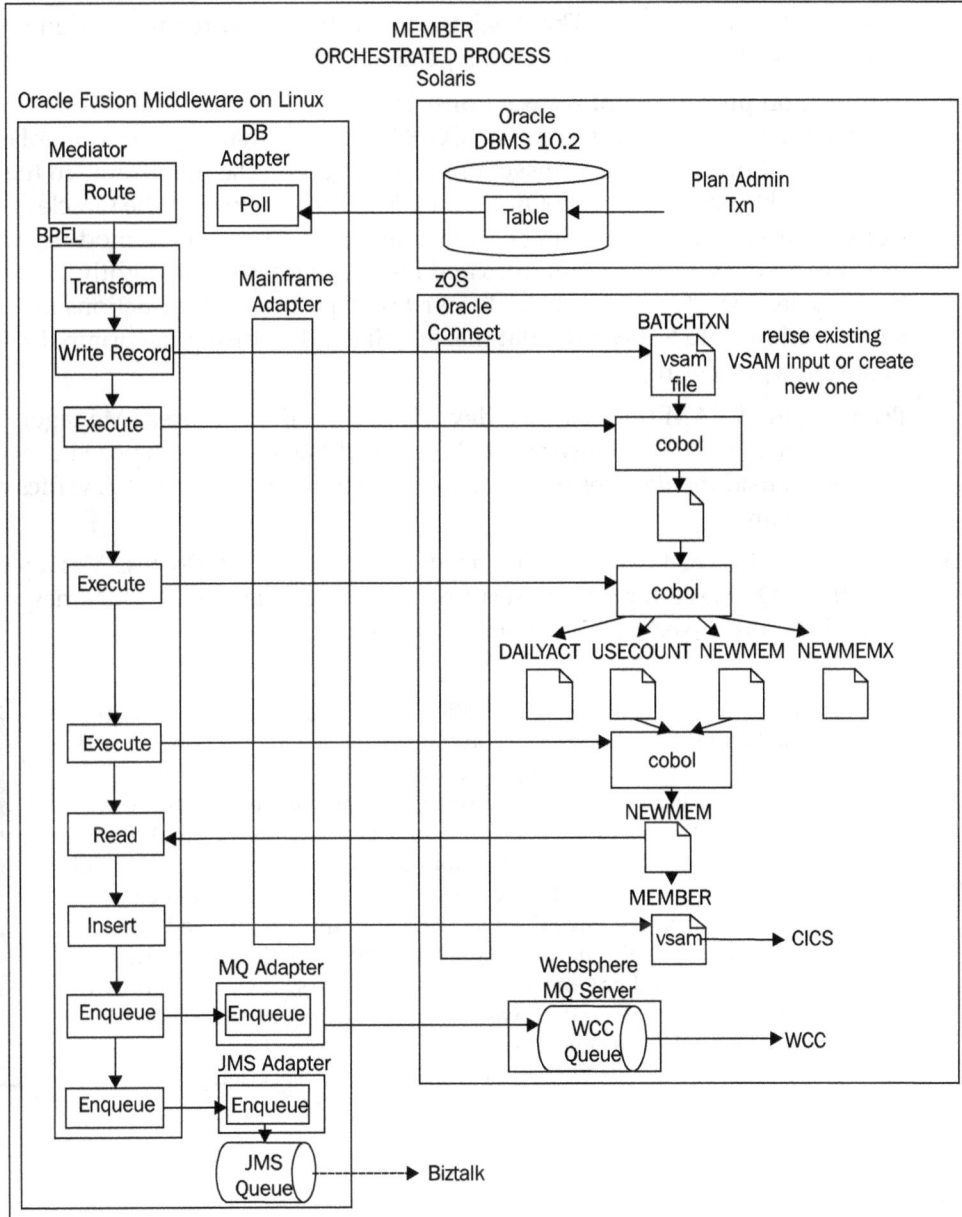

Interestingly, the business flow that took place on the mainframe is the same using Oracle BPEL. Obviously, the technology behind it has changed significantly. The overall business process flow from input transactions to MQSeries feeds, and next day VSAM files is now achieved in this manner:

- **Input transactions**: Read from the current Oracle database to retrieve all the new member transactions. The database connectivity and reading is done through the Oracle Database technology adapter.

- **Application processing of transactions**: The mainframe JCL and JES are replaced with BPEL processing. The COBOL module that adds new members is called and processes the transactions as it would on the mainframe in the legacy batch system. The COBOL module is accessed through the Oracle Connect product that is running on the mainframe. The COBOL module executes all the same business rules and logic as it does in the nightly batch cycle. The COBOL module also writes all processed transactions to a **Generation Data Set (GDG)** flat file, just like it did during the original mainframe processing.

- **Prepare new VSAM files for next day**: The Oracle BPEL Process Manager uses Oracle Fusion Middleware VSAM and Flat File adapters exposed as web services to read the flat files on the mainframe and write to the VSAM files on the mainframe.

- **IBM MQSeries feed to company portal**: The Oracle BPEL Process Manager calls the MQSeries adapter web service to write records to IBM MQSeries that will be processed by Microsoft BizTalk and feed to other systems.

In hindsight, the technical specification should have been much more detailed and robust. However, you cannot document that which you do not know. This project was highly experimental when it first started. So, we intentionally left the technical specifications non-specific and were very fluid in determining the actual end technical architecture. We knew all the Oracle products that were required and at what time in the BPEL business flow they would be executed. Going into the pilot development phase we still did not have the exact names of the mainframe VSAM and flat files. In addition, we did not have the file definitions (schemas) for the files. We did not know the format that the system (the company portal) on the other side that was receiving the MQSeries records was expecting. All these unknowns led to scope creep and scrambling to discover technical details, both of which led to project delays.

Assumptions, out of scope, and success criteria

A POV cannot be successful unless the customer and IT vendor define upfront what the definition of success is. The customer needs to know the end game, or the POV will never be considered complete, and both parties will blame each other for the lack of success. The assumptions are important to make sure the customer and Oracle both understand how the project will be implemented and what the end architecture will be. Assumptions also clear up any areas that are not well-defined at the start of the project so there is no misunderstanding of what the unknowns are going into the project. Items that were discussed and perhaps considered to be part of the solution but have been excluded are in the Out of scope section. Out of scope also defines very clearly any items that seem like they should be part of the project but both parties have decided they are not because of time or resource constraints.

Assumptions

The assumptions regarding POV were put in place to avoid **scope creep** (which are new functionality, features or Oracle products that keep getting introduced into the project success criteria) because some of the technical implementations details were not known at the beginning of the project. The assumptions also ensure that the POV would prove Oracle SOA Suite products can be used to replace a fragile and complicated legacy workflow application.

The five assumptions for this POV are:

1. A very simple solution would be to call the mainframe batch jobs from Oracle BPEL. This would prove that Oracle can be used to orchestrate workflow on the mainframe. This would be accomplished using Oracle BPEL to call wrapper functions on the mainframe that simply execute the appropriate job steps on the mainframe. However, it would not prove that the Oracle SOA Suite can be used to replace batch processing on the mainframe. Therefore, the first assumption is that the POV cannot be done by simply executing mainframe batch jobs. The real value behind using the SOA Suite is reducing the processing cost of the mainframe, as well as all the benefits of BPEL orchestration listed earlier in the chapter. Calling batch jobs on the mainframe using Oracle BPEL Process Manager would not demonstrate these benefits.

2. There are 22 transaction codes. However, this POV will only implement one of them, which is the add new member (AN) transaction code.

3. The POV only implements `add new member`. There are no updates or deletions of members, only inserts. The POV focus needed to be limited to one slice of the entire member maintenance process, which is add new member.

4. The POV will only need to web service-enable one application module. This is the `ADDMCOBL` COBOL module on the mainframe. The program does all of the `add new member` processing. Therefore, the other two COBOL modules that are part of the add member batch job stream will not be web service-enabled.

5. The existing Oracle Database has all new member transactions in it already. Instead of reading flat files on the mainframe to start processing transactions, it is much easier to read the transactions that are stored in the Oracle Operational Data Store (ODS). As part of moving to open systems, the company has already moved some of the data to an Oracle database. Therefore, this POV can leverage the fact that new member data is already stored both in flat files on the mainframe and in an Oracle-based ODS.

Out of scope

The list of out of scope items can be endless in most projects as you can never do all the items that are desired. In a POV, the list of out of scope items is much smaller, because the scope is very limited. For this POV, the following items are out of scope:

- **Performance**: The hardware and OS had to be acquired on a tight budget so they are not sized to do performance benchmarking. In addition, the intent of POV is to show the benefits of BPEL orchestration and integration using Oracle Fusion Middleware **Java Connector Architecture (JCA)** web service adapters. The POV is not intended to demonstrate how fast the processing can run compared to the mainframe batch cycle.

- **Error handling**: The POV environment is very controlled, so none of the input records used will have any errors in them to cause issues with processing. The failure or error messages from the COBOL modules or MQSeries will not be handled. If errors, warnings or issues arise, they will not be handled and the data used in the POV will have to be changed so no issues arise.

- **Restart ability at the point of failure**: The POV assumes that no hardware or software failures will occur when running the demonstrations. In other words, the entire set of add member transactions will fail or succeed as one unit of work. If there is a failure, the transactions that were added need to be backed out and the BPEL process restarted from the beginning. Oracle BPEL Process Manager supports both **Java Transaction Services (JTA)** and dehydration, so transaction processing can be restarted at the point of failure. Therefore, this capability can easily be added later.

Success criteria

Demonstrate an Oracle-based orchestration and integration software solution with straight through processing for the add member transaction. The system created during the POV needs to read from an Oracle database, read and write to VSAM and flat files on the mainframe, execute COBOL programs and CICS transactions on the mainframe, and publish messages to IBM MQSeries. Success is achieved by processing the add member transactions using the COBOL programs, VSAM files, and flat files just as it would happen on the mainframe every night. However, the core orchestration, process scheduling, process reporting, and monitoring now executes off the mainframe using Oracle BPEL Process Manager. The IBM MQSeries integration is now run off the mainframe.

The assumptions, risks, and challenges were well documented. However, because of the fluid nature of what technically was possible and how it is going to be done made it difficult to document some of the risks and challenges.

Technical implementation details

We will now cover the specific integration web services and explain how the Oracle BPEL Process Manager is used both as an orchestration engine and integration service bus. We will not go into great detail on the Oracle database technology, legacy data adapters, COBOL application adapters, and MQSeries adapters as there are more than enough white papers, documentation, and viewlets (step by step interactive product demonstrations) on the **Oracle Technology Network (OTN)** web site. We will go into detail on the BPEL process flow used in this POV as the functionality is obviously unique to this project. Each of the following sections will discuss the processes in the BPEL process flow implemented in the POV.

Reading from the Oracle Database

The transactions are stored in an existing Oracle Database 10*g* instance. The Oracle Database adapter is created in Oracle JDeveloper and automatically exposed as a web service to be consumed by Oracle BPEL Process Manager. The job of the database web service adapter is to read a new member transaction that will be added to the production VSAM data file and be accessible through the mainframe terminal applications the following day. A complete viewlet for the Oracle Database adapter can be downloaded from here: `http://download.oracle.com/otndocs/tech/products/integration/service-bus/OSBDBDEMO.zip`

This adapter is straight forward for obvious reasons. Oracle is a database company and Oracle owns both the group that writes the database and the JCA adapters that connect and process transactions to the Oracle database.

Writing to flat files

The COBOL module that will process the new member transactions in the next step reads from a flat file (MEMBER and NEWMEM2 GDG members) that contains all the new member transactions to be added. Therefore, a legacy Flat File adapter will be used to write the transactions read from the Oracle table to a mainframe flat file. The adapters and corresponding web services, one for each file, were created using the Oracle Studio for Legacy Adapters. The Flat File adapter is not a solution offered directly from Oracle, but offered by Attunity. However, since Oracle Connect and the Oracle Studio for Legacy Adapters are both products are OEM from Attunity, it was simple to add the license to support flat file processing to the Oracle Connect product.

The COBOL file copybooks had to be created for the two flat files since the COBOL module did not have a standard file description section with a file copybook. COBOL file copybooks are analogous to XML schema and relational database table **Database Definition Language (DDL)** files. COBOL file copybooks contain the definitions of the records in the file. The file copybooks are included in the COBOL module in the working storage section. The working storage section is part of the program memory where all data is stored. The COBOL file copybook contains many different record layouts, depending upon the record type. This is a common coding practice used with COBOL on the mainframe. This is not at all like your standard relational table in an Oracle database where a schema is predefined and contains only one record layout (in the relational world called a **table definition**) per table (analogous to a file on the mainframe). In case of a mainframe COBOL flat file, the program reads in a record and then determines what file copybook record type to use to read the data.

> The most difficult aspect of getting this adapter to work was creating the copybook (flat file record definition) that matched the physical file. Once this was done, integrating the file adapter web services into the Oracle BPEL process using the JDeveloper BPEL Designer was easy.

Executing the z/OS COBOL module

Executing COBOL modules on the mainframe z/OS system is application integration with a twist. The twist is that the COBOL module needs to read from a flat file populated by Oracle BPEL and write to a VSAM file that will be read by Oracle BPEL. In typical application integration scenarios, the application modules are executed and the results sent back in a SOAP message. The COBOL module ADDMCOBL does all the real work of processing the new member transaction. This COBOL module was exposed as a web service using the Oracle Studio for Legacy Adapters. The only change made to the program was to replace the COBOL command STOP RUN with a COBOL GOBACK statement so that the Oracle Connect process running on the mainframe did not think there was a fatal error in the COBOL module execution. The COBOL module writes the completed transactions to two VSAM files: MEMBER and NEWMEM2. Like the Flat File adapter, the COBOL module adapter is not a solution offered directly from Oracle, but offered by Attunity. However, since Oracle Connect and the Oracle Studio for Legacy Adapters are products OEM from Attunity, it was simple to add the license to support the COBOL program adapter.

The COBOL adapter and interaction (essentially the web service for a COBOL module) proved a challenge as it was a batch program that had no input and output parameters. COBOL programs typically have a communication area known as a **COMMAREA**, which is used to pass input and output parameters from the calling COBOL module. As this program was typically initiated through JCL in a batch under JES, all the DD NAMES (symbolic names for the actual data files) were mapped to physical file names in the JCL. Since the Oracle BPEL Process Manager is now driving the business process flow, there is no JCL in the process flow. Therefore, DD NAMES had to be mapped to physical files in the Oracle Connect product. Also, debugging a COBOL batch program exposed as a web service proved much more difficult than debugging a COBOL programming running under IMS-TM or CICS transaction managers on the mainframe. There is no way to turn on logging for a COBOL module run on the mainframe that is not under the control of a transaction manager (IMS-TM or CICS). The POV development team had to resort to the age-old method of program debugging—print statements ('I read the first record', 'I just wrote to a file', and so on.).

As done with the Flat File adapter, the COBOL adapter was created using the Oracle Studio for Legacy Adapters. The COBOL adapter was then exposed in the BPEL process using the Third-Party adapter in JDeveloper. Had this not been a COBOL program, but a more modern language such as Java or .NET, the application integration would have been easier as a couple things would have changed:

- **No need to create a COBOL adapter**: Modern languages that run on open systems don't need an adapter created using the Oracle Studio for Legacy Adapters.

- **BPEL third-party adapter not required**: For Java, there is no need to access the Java application using the Third-Party adapter in JDeveloper as was done with the COBOL module. There are a number of methods to access a Java module from an Oracle BPEL process:

    ° Java web service–Using the JDeveloper BPEL Java Web Service wizard you can expose your existing Java program as a web service.

    ° SOAP service–The Java code can be wrapped as a SOAP service.

    ° Directly embedding Java code–The Java code can be embedded directly in the BPEL process using the Java BPEL exec extension.

Reading from VSAM files

The VSAM files MEMBER and NEWMEM2 are now accessed in order to retrieve the processed new member transactions. The VSAM files were just populated in the previous step using the COBOL adapter on the mainframe and exposed in the BPEL process using the Third-Party adapter in JDeveloper. This BPEL web service uses a CICS adapter that reads from the VSAM file on the mainframe. It was first thought that the BPEL process could use a VSAM adapter web service as this is a VSAM file. This was not the case as the VSAM file was under the control of the mainframe CICS transaction manager. Therefore, the CICS adapter needed to be used to access the VSAM files.

The transactions that come back are mapped to local variables that can be passed into the next process to write to IBM MQSeries. This mapping is done using the JDeveloper BPEL designer XSLT (XSL Transformations) Mapper wizard. The wizard allows for drag-and-drop mapping of XML transaction file fields to local variables.

Reading from VSAM files was more time-consuming than first thought. We kept getting errors on the read of VSAM and could not understand why. As these VSAM files are under the control of CICS, it was determined that going through CICS was the only way to read these files.

Writing to IBM MQSeries

The Oracle MQSeries adapter was used to enqueue the transactions processed on the mainframe into IBM MQSeries. The version of MQSeries is no longer supported by IBM and therefore not certified with the Oracle MQSeries adapter. However, the adapter worked properly and it was not an issue for the POV. For the production deployment the IBM MQSeries product will need to be upgraded. As no documentation existed for the MQ Message payload format, the format was reverse-engineered by looking at code on the mainframe. This was a painful way to determine the message format, but it was the only method available.

BPEL process

The completed process in BPEL Process Manager looks as follows:

Instance	Type	Usage	State		Time
Trace					
Click a component instance to see its detailed audit trail.					
Show Instance IDs ☐					
🔲 CTAEnrollmentService	JCA Adapter	Service	✔	Completed	Oct 26, 2010 7:29:11 PM
📊 EnrollmentProcess	BPEL Component		✔	Completed	Oct 26, 2010 7:29:23 PM
🔲 UPDTRANS	JCA Adapter	Reference	✔	Completed	Oct 26, 2010 7:29:11 PM
🔲 GSXNMCB0	JCA Adapter	Reference	✔	Completed	Oct 26, 2010 7:29:14 PM
🔲 NEWMEMX	JCA Adapter	Reference	✔	Completed	Oct 26, 2010 7:29:15 PM
🔲 MEMBERXVSAM	JCA Adapter	Reference	✔	Completed	Oct 26, 2010 7:29:16 PM
🔲 NEWMEM	JCA Adapter	Reference	✔	Completed	Oct 26, 2010 7:29:16 PM
🔲 MEMBERVSAM	JCA Adapter	Reference	✔	Completed	Oct 26, 2010 7:29:17 PM
🔲 NEWMEMMB	JCA Adapter	Reference	✔	Completed	Oct 26, 2010 7:29:17 PM
🔲 MEMBERMBVSAM	JCA Adapter	Reference	✔	Completed	Oct 26, 2010 7:29:18 PM
🔲 NEWMEMML	JCA Adapter	Reference	✔	Completed	Oct 26, 2010 7:29:18 PM
🔲 MEMBERMLVSAM	JCA Adapter	Reference	✔	Completed	Oct 26, 2010 7:29:19 PM
🔲 NEWMEMMF	JCA Adapter	Reference	✔	Completed	Oct 26, 2010 7:29:19 PM
🔲 MEMBERMFVSAM	JCA Adapter	Reference	✔	Completed	Oct 26, 2010 7:29:23 PM

This view allows you to see all the adapter interactions that are done using the
Oracle BPEL JCA adapters exposed as web services. As each adapter is executed,
details of the input and output payloads are recorded. The exact processing that
occurred is viewed in the BPEL web console.

Security

Security was not a high priority item for the POV. Therefore, for Oracle Database
and Fusion Middleware, basic authentication using a username and password
was used. There was one user for the Oracle Database and one for Oracle Fusion
Middleware. The mainframe legacy web services all used **Resource Access Control
Facility (RACF)** to secure COBOL, VSAM, CICS, and flat file access. The mainframe
administrator created one RACF user for all of the mainframe web services access.

Actual level of effort and outcome

The four to seven week plan turned into an actual elapsed time for the project of 20 weeks. The timeline broke down as follows:

- Weeks of July 19 and July 26—Completed functional and technical specifications
- Weeks of July 26 through October 4—Created all the adapters and exposed them as web services
- Weeks of October 4 through November 19—BPEL orchestration, testing of end-to-end BPEL processing and fixing issues
- November 19—Demo to Oracle team and insurance company middle level managers
- November 23—Presentation and demo to IT leadership at the insurance company

The resources required and the actual hours required from each resource were as follows:

Resource type	Time effort	Explanation for additional effort
Oracle SOA Suite and BPEL Process Manager	160 hours	Interacting legacy web services and MQSeries much more time-consuming then originally thought.
Oracle Legacy Studio and Oracle Connect	120 hours	Three installations of Oracle Connect were required. Both installations took longer because of privilege issues on mainframe. It also took longer to expose VSAM, flat files, CICS transactions, and COBOL program as web services.
Attunity Expert	80 hours	Extra helped need with Oracle Connect installation and configuration, VSAM adapter configuration and COBOL adapter configuration required extra effort.
Insurance Company SME	160 hours	It took more time to find the VSAM and flat files and create test files. Also, more time to create copybooks manually, performed the second Oracle Connect installation. A lot of interaction with mainframe team and MQSeries technical lead.

The outcome was the successful processing of 1,000 new member transactions. An unexpected outcome was performance. It takes 12 seconds between the time when a transaction is picked up from the Oracle staging tables until it makes it to the VSAM files (which are written to the mainframe using the COBOL web service). This performance was achieved with no performance tuning, parallel processing, or special hardware. The original nightly batch process is a series of steps which, depending on when the transaction arrives, can take between one to three days to complete a transaction.

Challenges and lessons learned

Challenges and lessons learned can be summarized with the statement *'the devil is in the details'*. The project team had a clear idea of the Oracle architecture, new processing design, integration interface points, and transactions flowed. What was lacking were details regarding the file names, the file definitions, message formats, application integration specifics, the exact number of data integration points, and many other small but important details such as the copybooks for the VSAM files. The project consisted of many small tasks which made it easy to manage completion of tasks. If a couple of tasks slipped a few days this would be fine; the problem was that when you have many small tasks, all slipping, this adds up to a significant increase in project effort. Details on these challenges and lessons learned from this project are:

- **Installation and configuration of Oracle Connect on the mainframe**: The installation and configuration of this software can take anywhere from two days to three weeks. *Why the wide variation?* Most of this has to do with security and privileges on the mainframe. In this case, the privileges to write to mainframe libraries needed a number of iterations to solve, and the user privileges to run the process on the mainframe involved customer support tickets to be raised, which took days to be resolved. The installation on the mainframe was repeated three times before everything was in place to run the Oracle Connect process. This obviously delayed the ability to create the COBOL, flat file, and CICS adapters using the Oracle Studio for Legacy Adapters.

- **Extensive mainframe artifact and processing 'archaeology' after the start of the POV**: Archaeology was the term given to the process used to understand the technical details of the current application, and extract and use the artifacts of the current system in the new environment. Lots of time was spent performing archaeology on the COBOL program, VSAM and flat file data sets, COBOL copybooks, MQSeries messages, and JCL to understand the current process flow.

- **Lack of direct contact with mainframe specialist**: The mainframe experts were busy keeping the day-to-day operations running. They were also not assigned to the POV team, and there was some scepticism from this team that the POV team could actually get the POV to work. However, the mainframe specialists were very helpful during the process. During interactions with the mainframe team, lack of terminology understanding and the technologies between both groups caused small tasks to take days instead of minutes or hours.

- **Lack of COBOL copybooks for VSAM and flat files**: The COBOL copybooks (DDL) for the VSAM and flat files were actually in the working storage section of the COBOL program and were difficult to find. Typically, these copybooks are in separate files in a source code management system. Because the VSAM files are overloaded (different record layouts contained in the same data set), the typical method of having a file copybook in the COBOL program file description section was not in place. Instead, the file description was simply a string of bytes with no field definitions.

- **Creating DDL file manually**: The mainframe DDL files were created manually using sections of file definitions in the COBOL program. This DDL also had to be scrubbed to remove numerous redefines, occurs clauses, and '88 levels' that were not necessary. The Oracle Connect product does not behave nicely if the COBOL file copybook defining the VSAM or flat file has a lot of redefines and OCCURS clauses.

- **Batch COBOL program is not as easy to web service-enable as CICS COBOL program**: Batch COBOL programs, unlike CICS/online programs, do not have an input/output section (such as COMMAREA). This is not a requirement for the Attunity COBOL adapter, but you must have a dummy input parameter in order to be able to create the adapter. This requirement was not known until after the POV started.

- **Not your typical Oracle integration POV**: Most Oracle POVs use Oracle BPEL or the **Oracle Service Bus (OSB)** to process a simple message and call very well defined .NET and Java web services. The payloads are typically small and there are no data type mapping issues. These POVs don't include legacy integration even though, according to industry analysts, 50 percent of SOA implementations involve interaction with mainframes or mid-range systems. In a number of ways, this project was not your typical application integration POV.

- **Mapping data in Oracle BPEL**: The VSAM and flat files return hundreds of data fields, and these data items need to be mapped into the BPEL process so they can be written out to files for the next step, or sent on to IBM MQSeries. Any change to the VSAM copybook caused all the fields to have to be remapped, which was a tedious process, even when using the BPEL Designer XSLT mapper wizard.

- **Oracle 11g BPEL and legacy adapter incompatibilities**: These were issues associated with dealing with cutting edge releases of Oracle Fusion Middleware, Oracle SOA Suite, and Oracle legacy adapters. Workarounds were found for the bugs but it took time to debug and implement the bug fixes or workarounds.

> The next time Oracle engages with such a complex integration project, that involves the mainframe as well as open systems integration, the Oracle team will have a more well defined project plan, have detailed technical specifications, and not have the attitude that 'we can figure that out later'.

Cultural change in technology organizations

Making cultural changes in the technology organization is a prerequisite to the technology progress. IT has to renovate while maintaining a business-as-usual posture—the current operations need to be supported and run uninterrupted. The renovation is to move from technology silos, to layers, then to move from application thinking to shared services thinking. Shared services are another name for cloud computing in a consolidated data center.

Hard things are hard to do, and implementing integration activities in a silo environment is one of the hardest. At this large company, as well as most major organizations, the solutions in place are designed, developed, and implemented in silos. These silos are organized by business units (such as employees benefit insurance order entry, employee benefit insurance billing). Each business unit is its own silo. Then within each silo (within each business unit) is a collection of technology silos (such as IBM MQSeries, mainframe OLTP, mainframe FTP, Unix OS, and Unix FTP). This causes a duplication of hardware, software, business logic, data, processes, and other IT resources. This duplication causes companies to implement complex integration architectures to connect these standalone business units. These integration architectures drive up the overall cost of hardware, software, people, and support costs. This causes the shift from silos to shared services to not only be a challenge in terms of technology, but also in terms of people (company culture).

> Replacing legacy business processes and the supporting legacy
> technology is never a technological challenge. Oracle and Java-based
> solutions can solve any business problem and in most cases increase
> performance, provide better management and reporting, reduce the time
> to deliver the information, and provide a more reliable, adaptable, and
> available solution. The difficulty in implementing a modern information
> integration solution is company, cultural, and people-related. Proving
> the ROI and reduced TCO can typically be done. However, getting
> independent minded business units and people to change their way
> of thinking, and IT departments that are split between the 'mainframe
> camp' and the 'distributed system newbie' is sometimes insurmountable.

Next steps

This project covered just one batch transaction, one COBOL program out of three
that are executed every night, and one of the JCL streams. This was the initiation
of the project, however, and not the final solution. The full project is to move all
member 401K processing off the mainframe. In order to achieve this, the following
activities are planned as either one or many smaller projects:

- **Complete new member transaction type to make production-ready**:
  Reliability, Availability, Scalability and Performance (RASP) were not
  part of the POV. In order for the new member processing to be moved off
  the mainframe, RASP must be built into the architecture. This includes
  adding parallel processing, processing restart at point of failure, notifications,
  monitoring, tuning of the process, dynamically adding hardware and
  software resources, and automatic failure.

- **Move other transaction types off the mainframe**: This involves orchestration
  of other batch COBOL programs as web services using Oracle BPEL Designer
  and deploying to the Oracle BPEL Process Manager. This first involves
  migrating two to three more transaction types out of the 22 remaining off the
  mainframe; then continuing this process until all transaction types are off the
  mainframe.

- **Trigger transactions on the mainframe through IBM MQSeries**: Instead
  of polling the Oracle database for transactions, the idea is to make the
  transaction processing real-time by trigger transactions through IBM
  MQSeries on the mainframe.

- **In-band transformations**: Translation activities add time to the transport, and therefore time to all transaction processing activities. If the translation happens on a node that is attached to the middleware, it is out-of-band. If the translation happens inside the middleware, then it is in-band. Moving translations to the middleware not only increases the speed of translation but also consolidates all transformations into one location for reuse and ease of maintenance.

- **Move other new member maintenance processing off the mainframe**: Begin to move some of the business logic and rules that are now in COBOL into a business rules engine (Oracle Business Rules engine).

- **Move data off the mainframe**: The last step would be to move data and data access off the mainframe. This would involve migrating the VSAM and flat files to an Oracle Database.

> The approach is to complete the new member processing using Oracle BPEL and adapters while adding RASP capabilities, then move other transactions into the BPEL process. Once this is completed, the approach is to complete the move off the mainframe by moving business rules, business logic, data, and data processing off the legacy mainframe system.

Summary

This chapter is a classic, real-life example of information and application integration challenges that face major corporations. The insurance company has a 25-year-old mainframe system that still runs core 401K investment programs for Fortune 500 companies. This legacy system needed to integrate with a modern Oracle database and messaging-based systems. The combination of the Oracle Database 11*g*, Oracle legacy adapters for application integration through COBOL programs, Oracle legacy adapters for data integration with VSAM and flat files, and Oracle MQSeries adapters were deployed to solve this complex application and information integration business problem. Oracle BPEL Process Manager was used to orchestrate and manage the information and application flow.

The most overlooked aspect in complex integration projects are the technology, legacy, and application adapters. Companies spend a lot of time evaluating and testing the BPEL orchestration engine, message bus, **Service Component Architecture (SCA)**, **Business Process Management (BPM)**, and governance products. What is almost an afterthought are the adapters, connectors or gateways needed to bring the variety of data sources, application languages, and messaging systems together. Adapters in any integration scenario are the key; without adapters that are performant, scalable, reliable, and that integrate easily into your BPEL engine or messaging infrastructure, you have nothing. It is also important to be able to have a vendor like Oracle, that supports every data source, technology or application you have, and provides transactional support across all adapters using technology such as JCA.

Now that we have covered an end-to-end solution, we will start to take a very detailed technical deep dive into specific Oracle information and application integration solutions. Before we do this, we will start with data migration. In the next chapters, we choose to focus of one of the many Oracle data migration technologies—Oracle SQL Developer. The robust activity which the authors have seen in the last couple of years for companies choosing to migrate from Sybase, DB2, SQL Server, and Informix to Oracle makes this a logical selection as the next Oracle product discussed.

4
Oracle Database Migrations

Organizations go through migration processes to bring about changes in their IT departments involving hardware, operating systems, and databases. The business drivers for such changes in IT departments can be attributed to:

- Consolidation of database platforms, change in hardware and operating systems, and to decommission certain de-supported/obsolete products/technologies
- To incorporate the latest hardware, software, and computing paradigms, for example. Blade servers, virtualization, adoption of Oracle Grid Architecture, cloud computing, and so on
- To reduce operational costs as a result of consolidation and improved efficiency, bring agility, and provide more business value to the company

Many of these changes result in migrating databases from multiple vendors to Oracle, as well as migrating Oracle databases from one platform to another. Even though we call the process database migration, in reality it may include changes to the frontend applications as well.

Migration from a non-Oracle to Oracle database typically involves:

- Assessment of the current environment and requirements analysis
- Migration of database schema objects (tables, indexes, triggers, views, procedures)
- Migration of data to Oracle
- Application porting, involving changes to embedded SQL, and API changes in applications based on the database access drivers being used
- Functional/integration testing
- Production system setup
- Delta incorporation (application code and delta of data changes)
- Production rollout

Some of the previously mentioned tasks, for example application porting/testing can be resource-intensive based on how the application is implemented, that is the languages used (3GLs, 4GLs), APIs used for database access, SQL compliance with ANSI standards, availability of test cases/suites, and so on.

Before embarking on a migration project it is advisable to perform impact analysis on applications of the planned database migration. The assessment exercise will not only help in estimating the migration effort accurately, but also assess the business risk. Some customers may need to operate both old and new platforms in parallel for a short period as a fall back strategy, which may require additional tools/technologies such as bidirectional replication solutions based on changed data capture (CDC) principles.

Database migration scenarios

Most common database migrations involve migrating from:

- Sybase, SQL Server, DB2, and so on, to Oracle due to a combination of the previously discussed drivers for such migrations.

- Migration of an Oracle database from one platform to another. This effort is typically undertaken due to changes in the underlying platform, for example operating systems change (Unix to Linux, Windows to Linux), periodic hardware refresh cycles, a platform change (HP to IBM, IBM to Oracle SUN, and so on), and moving from 32 bit platforms to 64 bit platforms.

Complexities of the database migrations depend on factors such as:

- A large number of database(s)/schema objects
- The complexity of the business logic: embedded within stored procedures/ triggers involving temporary tables, multiple result sets, database-specific functionality involving system tables/functions
- The size of the stored procedure/triggers/views in terms of lines of code (LOC)
- Very large databases (multi-terabytes+)
- The downtime availability for mission critical databases
- A lack of well-documented test cases and automated testing suites

Using tools for tasks like schema, data migration, conversion of stored procedures, trigger, and views can cut down the time required to complete the project. They are especially helpful for migrating very large databases.

Without porting the online and batch applications, the migration is incomplete. So porting applications is also an important task in database migrations. Not many tools are available for code remediation in applications to make it work against Oracle. Application programs implemented in different languages/4GLs, for example Power Builder, Visual Basic, C/C++, and Java/J2EE, and so on, complicate the migration process due to the effort involved in migrating embedded SQL statements and other database access routines to Oracle.

Regardless of the level of automation provided by migration tools/technologies, comprehensive testing of the migrated application/database remains an important aspect of the migration process.

Migrating an Oracle database from one platform to another

As mentioned earlier, IT departments change hardware platforms (including OS) to upgrade to the latest versions as part of periodic refresh cycles, or their desire to embrace a different hardware/operating system platform. As the source and target database remains the same (Oracle) in such a scenario, little or no change is required to database schema/objects or the application.

This project can also become a database upgrade project where upgrading to a newer version of the database is also added to the project plan. In such cases, the database upgrade can be performed either on the source before the platform migration or on the target after the platform migration, based on the complexity of the database/application.

Typical activities that comprise these types of migrations are:

- Install Oracle Software on new platform
- Configure storage/network for the new database server
- Perform data migration from the source platform to the target platform
- Functional/performance/regression testing
- Re-direct client requests to the new database server and test
- Delta incorporation (data/application updates) after the initial migration
- Go live

These activities certainly do not cover all the other activities that customers go through in order to migrate an Oracle database from one platform to another. Careful planning for strategies around data migration, delta incorporation, testing, and so on is very important for a successful completion of the project.

One of the important tasks in this type of project is data migration from the source to the target platform. Very large databases (several terabytes +) and large online user populations with 24/7 uptime requirements need careful planning, efficient data migration tools, data replication software, and so on. Databases that are small or medium-sized with a regular maintenance window can have the data migrated within the maintenance window before going live on the new platform.

Most common approaches for migrating data from one Oracle database to another are:

- **Using Oracle Data Pump**: It is an Oracle database utility that is part of the standard installation. Data Pump allows Oracle database/schema/tables to be exported into a proprietary format from the source database and to import the data into another Oracle database on another platform. Data Pump generates a platform independent file for data movement between Oracle databases only. It also allows for direct import/export over the network between two Oracle databases.

    ○ **Recommendations**: Ideal for small to medium-sized databases with a planned maintenance window for data migration.

    ○ **Benefits**: Works across different platforms seamlessly. It can also spawn multiple threads when desired. Oracle Enterprise Manager can be used for administering Data Pump.

- **Using Transportable Tablespaces**: The Transportable Tablespace feature in the Oracle database allows users to copy data files belonging to a tablespace directly from the source database to the target, along with an export copy of the tablespace metadata as a mechanism for data movement. On the target system, the data files are placed at the desired location and metadata for the tablespace can be imported into the target database, making the tablespace available for use just as it was at the source database. This feature requires that the objects in the tablespaces chosen for transportation to another system do not have dependencies on objects in other tablespaces at the source database, that is tables in one tablespace having referential integrity constraints on tables in another tablespace, and so on. Tablespaces need to be put in read-only mode when copying the data files from source system to target.

    ○ **Recommendations**: Very useful feature for periodic data publishing or migrating subsets of data at a time.

- **Using Oracle Data Guard**: Generally, Oracle Data Guard is used for disaster recovery purposes by maintaining a standby database at a remote location. Data Guard maintains the standby Oracle database by shipping the transaction logs from the source database to the target and applying them to the target database. It supports maintenance of the standby database in two modes—**physical** and **logical**. A physical standby database is an exact replica of the primary database (block-to-block). All changes taking place on the primary database are replicated to the standby database in this mode. Logical standby, also known as **SQL Apply mode**, can contain a subset of the primary database's data. Basically, it allows the filtering of data that is made available at the standby site. In Oracle database 11*g* R2, the Active Data Guard feature is also available and lets a standby database be used for reporting purposes, while it is being continuously update with changes from the primary database (recovery mode). No data changes are allowed on the standby database while in this mode. The Oracle database backup and recovery utility **Recovery Manager** (**RMAN**) complements Oracle Data Guard in creating a standby database from a primary database by easing the process of duplicating the database and transferring the data files to the remote site, even when the database files are in use at the primary site. This requires minimal downtime for the primary database and can assist in Oracle database migrations in heterogeneous migrations. This method of database migration of course requires that the primary database is configured with archive logging. It is the only zero data loss, high availability solution for Oracle databases.

  - **Recommendations**: This option is best suited for environments that have primary Oracle databases configured for high availability, and cannot afford a significant amount of downtime for the primary database to facilitate database migration.

- **Using Recovery Manager (RMAN)**: Recovery manager is Oracle's premier backup and recovery tool. RMAN offers many features such as incremental backups, backup compression, database duplication, automatic block repair, and so on. RMAN can assist in database migrations in a couple of ways. With the database duplication feature it can create a copy of the database on a remote server (standby) from either the backups of the primary database or from an online primary database. Secondly, with its ability to create transportable tablespace sets, it can facilitate database migration with ease. RMAN can play a big role in performing a cross-platform database migration by converting endianness of the data files to match with the endianness of the target platform — from little endian to big endian and vice-versa. Endianness typically refers to how multi-byte data is represented on different systems, based on their CPU architecture. RMAN can convert the data files endianness during the database migration process either at the source or the target database. It is important to find out the endianness of the source and target platforms first and determine the approach for the conversion of the format.

  ○ **Recommendation**: RMAN utility can be used for migrating databases leveraging existing backups easily in cases where source databases cannot afford a significant amount of downtime for data extraction. It can also assist in cross-platform migrations involving Oracle databases by converting the data file format to match endianness of the target platform. It can also assist in creating transportable tablespace sets for database migration.

- **Using Oracle SQL Developer**: Oracle SQL Developer is a free product from Oracle for developers and DBAs. It provides a GUI for performing day-to-day tasks such as database objects maintenance (tables/indexes/stored procedures, and so on), security, schema maintenance, export/import of data, and also migration of data from other relational databases like SQL Developer. SQL Developer offers an option to copy data from one Oracle schema to another. The source and target schemas can reside on two separate Oracle databases.

  ○ **Benefits**: Easier to perform the task. Just point and click. Ideal choice for small databases (few gigabytes) with a planned maintenance window. SQL Developer can also be used for copying data from one schema to another for Dev/QA purposes.

Very large databases require a hybrid approach to data migration, potentially involving any of the following methods:

- Restoring a database from a most recent backup of the production database and exporting data from it

- Using replication technologies, like Oracle Streams or Oracle GoldenGate, to apply the delta of the changes that occurred between the time periods from which the last backup was performed till the completion of the initial copying process

- Oracle GoldenGate can also create an initial copy of the database if desired, but may not be the most efficient method for very large databases

- Copying static/read-only data using Oracle Data Pump for smaller database objects and then using Oracle SQL*Loader/External Tables utilities for very large tables

- Exporting data to flat files/importing data from flat files through Named Pipes (a feature available on most Unix/Linux/Windows platforms)

- ETL tools like Oracle Data Integrator (ODI) or Oracle Warehouse Builder (OWB) can also help move data from source to target platform or tools from other vendors that are already used by the customer

- Data can also be migrated using Oracle database gateways for non-Oracle databases

Migrating relational databases to Oracle

Migration of relational databases to Oracle usually involves using a migration tool that migrates not just the schema (tables/indexes), but business logic implemented in stored programs in the database such as stored procedures, triggers, views, and so on.

Over the years, all migration tools have matured in terms of functionality coverage and quality of the conversion. Oracle has improved its offerings in this space significantly by:

- Having just one tool, Oracle SQL Developer for all development/DBA/ migration activities. This enables developers who are involved in the migration to get familiar with the development/DBA tasks execution in SQL Developer. The old migration workbench is still around to support Informix to Oracle migrations, because Informix migration support is not available in Oracle SQL Developer.

- Improving source database functionality coverage for migration such as adding support for conversion of temp tables, result sets handling, efficient data migration capabilities, multi-project versioning, and so on. The latest SQL Developer has more fine grain capabilities such as:

    ◦ Command line APIs for performing migrations in a batch mode

    ◦ Ability to convert one object at a time (such as table, stored procedure)

    ◦ Better handling of resolving database linkages in the source database business logic such as Sybase, SQL Server, and so on

    ◦ Improvement in code coverage in terms of handling multiple result sets, temporary tables, and other features

The migration process is consistent regardless of which database is being migrated to Oracle. A typical migration process involves the following steps:

- Processing the source database metadata for all schema objects
- Conversion of the source database schema using the metadata models to Oracle
- Creating Oracle schema
- Porting of client-side code to ensure that all the SQL Statements and database APIs work with Oracle
- Data migration
- Testing
- Optimization of the Oracle database
- Delta incorporation for both application and data changes
- Production rollout

The most important tasks in such migration projects are:

- Migration of business logic implemented in the source database to Oracle
- Data migration
- Porting of online and batch applications to Oracle
- Testing of the migrated applications/business logic

Together these tasks constitute the bulk of the effort required for a migration project. Using tools for automation or productivity enhancement for these tasks can help meet the project goals.

Using Oracle SQL Developer Version 3.0 for migrations to Oracle

Using Oracle SQL Developer for migrations has several advantages. One of the most important advantages being that it is FREE and can be downloaded from Oracle Technology Network (`otn.oracle.com`) for immediate use. Secondly, it can be used to assess the source database complexity factors in terms of object count, functionality usage such as temp tables, result sets, error handling, transaction management, and so on. SQL Developer also provides many reports tailored for migration effort estimation.

SQL Developer is being continuously enhanced to reduce the effort required for porting the applications to Oracle. SQL Developer 3.0 is capable of scanning applications written leveraging Sybase CT-Lib/DB-Lib, Java, and Perl for SQL statements are incompatible with Oracle and optionally convert them to Oracle. The best part of this feature is the ability to enhance this feature to include any other language/construct through a rule-based implementation where users need to modify the rules used in scanning the source code.

As mentioned earlier in this chapter and elsewhere, SQL Developer is also Oracle's key database development tool. Users do not need to install Oracle database client software to connect to an Oracle Database. SQL Developer can use JDBC Thin Driver (Type IV) or JDBC Thick Driver (Type II) to connect to an Oracle Database. So it is very easy to deploy on desktops/laptops and manage it.

Oracle SQL Developer facilitates migrations with a Wizard-driven approach. The metadata capture process is a very simple because SQL Developer only queries the system tables in the source databases for metadata about all the database objects. It does not retrieve the actual data from the database nor does it perform actual conversion of the database objects at the source database, so it does not cause heavy resource utilization.

Prerequisites for using SQL Developer

Prerequisites for using SQL Developer configuration varies from task to task; that is, migrations, unit testing of PL/SQL code, and so on. Prerequisites for each of these tasks are well documented and SQL Developer also allows users to perform these tasks as they are needed.

Prerequisites for performing migrations using SQL Developer are:

1. Create a migration repository.
2. Register JDBC Drivers for non-Oracle databases for direct access.
3. Set up target Oracle schema (optional).
4. Create directory for migration project.

Creating a migration repository

SQL Developer requires a metadata repository where it stores all the source and target schema models. The migration repository requires a schema in Oracle database. The Oracle database can be of any version starting with Oracle10*g*. Oracle Database10*g* XE can also be used for creating migration repositories. The database user for migration repository needs the following roles/privileges:

- `RESOURCE`
- `CREATE SESSION` and `CREATE VIEW`

For multi-schema migrations the `RESOURCE` role must be granted with the `ADMIN` option, and also `CREATE ROLE`, `CREATE USER`, `ALTER ANY TRIGGER` with the `ADMIN` option.

After creating the migration repository user in the Oracle database, create a connection for this user in SQL Developer.

To establish a connection to the database as the migration repository user, right-click on the connection in the Connections navigator on the left side in SQL Developer; choose the option **Migration Repository | Associate Migration Repository**. This will create the repository in the user schema created in the previous step.

JDBC Drivers setup

Obtain the appropriate JDBC Drivers for the source database if making a direct connection to it from SQL Developer.

- For Sybase/SQL Server databases, JDBC Driver can be obtained from `http://jtds.sourceforge.net`

- For DB2 databases, the appropriate JDBC Driver can be obtained from `http://jt400.sourceforge.net/`
- For MySQL databases the MYSQL Connector /J drivers can be obtained from `http://www.mysql.com/downloads/`

JDBC Drivers can be registered in SQL Developer by selecting the **Third Party JDBC Drivers** option (**Tools | Preferences | Database**)

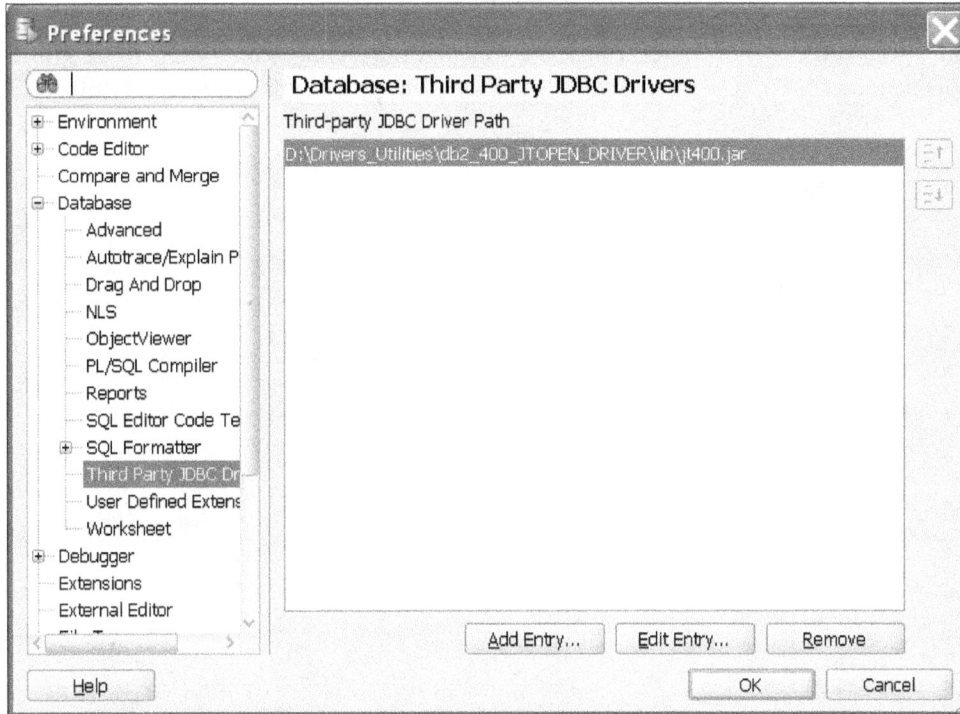

The JDBC Driver for source database is not required if there is no network connectivity between the desktop/server where SQL Developer is installed and the source database that needs to be migrated.

Creating a connection for a privileged database user in Oracle using SQL Developer

Only a privileged user in the Oracle database can create a new user/schema in Oracle. The privileged user in Oracle must have atleast the following roles:

- CONNECT WITH ADMIN option
- RESOURCE WITH ADMIN option

In addition to these mentioned roles, the following privileges also need to be granted to this user so that a new user/schema can be created using this user account:

- ALTER ANY ROLE
- ALTER ANY SEQUENCE
- ALTER ANY TABLE
- ALTER TABLESPACE
- COMMENT ANY TABLE
- CREATE ANY SEQUENCE
- CREATE ANY TABLE
- CREATE ANY TRIGGER
- CREATE PUBLIC SYNONYM WITH ADMIN OPTION
- CREATE ROLE
- CREATE USER
- CREATE VIEW WITH ADMIN OPTION
- DROP ANY ROLE
- DROP ANY SEQUENCE
- DROP ANY TABLE
- DROP ANY TRIGGER
- DROP USER
- GRANT ANY ROLE
- INSERT ANY TABLE
- SELECT ANY TABLE
- UPDATE ANY TABLE

Once a privileged user is created in Oracle with the previously mentioned roles and privileges granted to it, a database connection can be set up for this user in SQL Developer, which can be used later to create the target schema after the schema conversion process.

Existing DBA users can be used to create the Oracle schema as it is a one-time effort only and creating a separate user exclusively for this task may not be productive.

The following command can be used for creating a privileged database user to generate the target schema in Oracle:

```
Create user ora_user identified by ora_user default tablespace users
temporary tablespace temp;

Grant dba to ora_user;
```

> **Note:** In the previous example, the 'DBA' role was granted to the user but this can be customized to a particular environment based on security requirements.

After creating the database user, using SQL Developer or any other tools like SQL*Plus, create a database connection in SQL Developer for this database schema. To create a new connection to the source database, click on the green + icon in the Connections navigator on the left-hand side in SQL Developer.

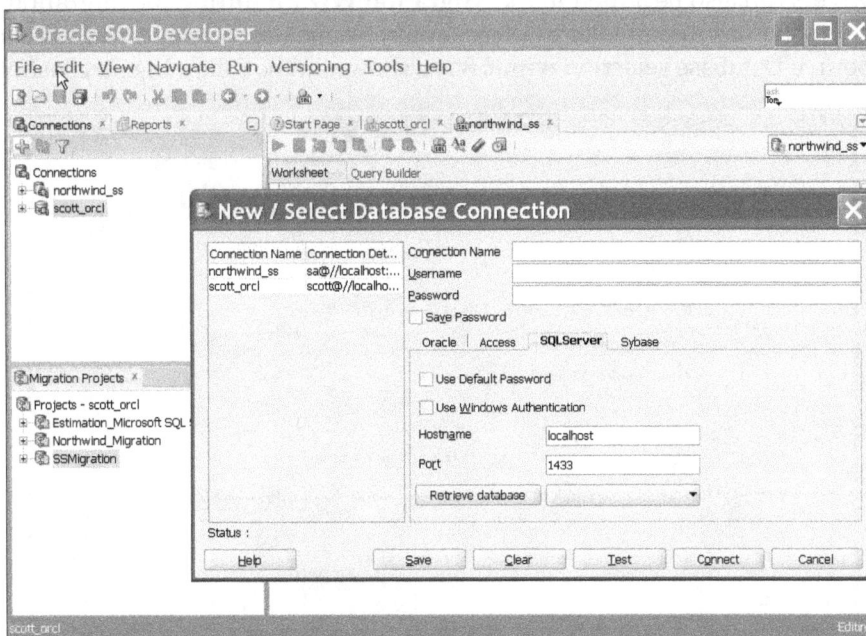

Register the source database JDBC Driver in SQL Developer. Select the **Third Party JDBC Drivers** option (**Tools | Preferences | Database**)

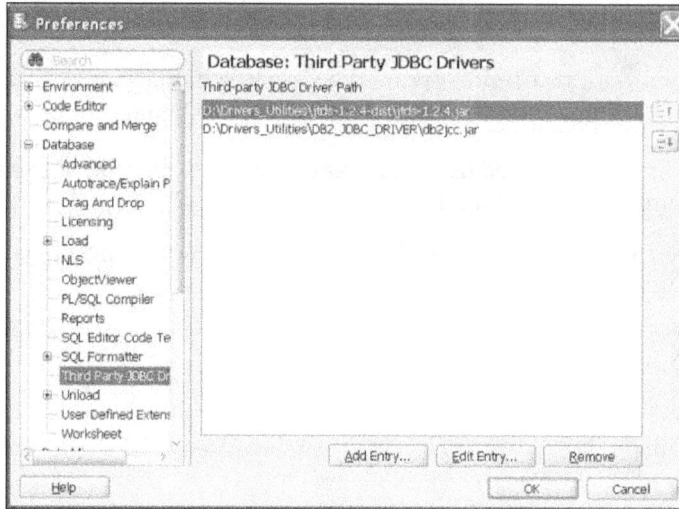

After registering the JDBC Driver for the source database as illustrated in the earlier section, the option for creating new connections to the source database is made available in the Connection Creation screen as illustrated in the previous figure.

JDBC Drivers can also be added in the **Migration Wizard** during the migration process, which is discussed later in this chapter, by clicking on the **Add Platform** link on the Source Database selection window, as shown in the following screenshot:

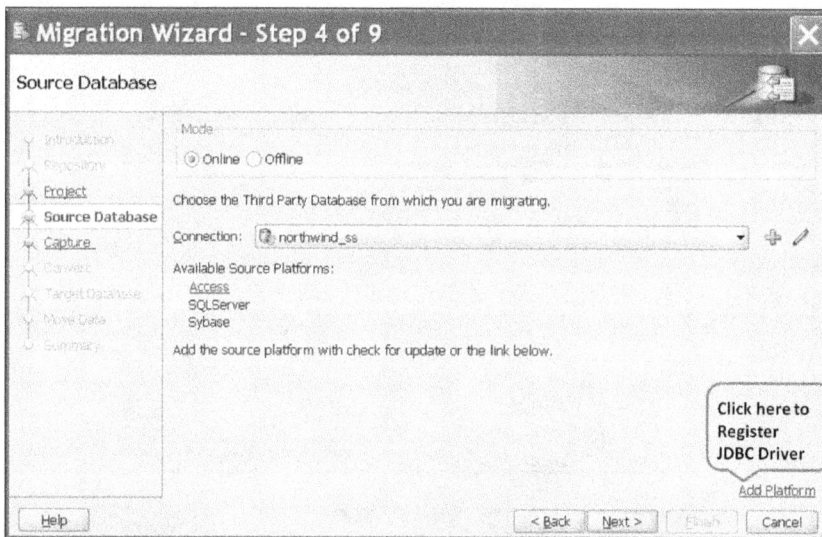

Clicking on the **Add Platform** link will bring up the **Third Party JDBC Drivers** addition screen which we discussed earlier in the prerequisites section to add JDBC Drivers.

Creating a directory for a migration project

A directory on the local file system is required by SQL Developer as a placeholder for all scripts and logs generated by SQL Developer during the migration project. A single directory can be used as a placeholder for multiple projects in SQL Developer.

Migration process using SQL Developer

Oracle SQL Developer facilitates migrations in seven steps. Each of these steps allows users to select source and target database connections created earlier in this chapter and online/offline mode for capture, convert, generate, and data move operations.

Users can launch the Migration Wizard from two locations in SQL Developer. They can right-click on the source database connection and choose the **Migrate to Oracle** option or they can access **Migrate** in the main toolbar (**Tools | Migration | Migrate**). To perform migrations in a step-by-step manner, where each step is performed individually so that the rest of the steps can be executed later, select the check box at the bottom of the respective screen (GUI). For an illustration on this option refer to the following screenshot:

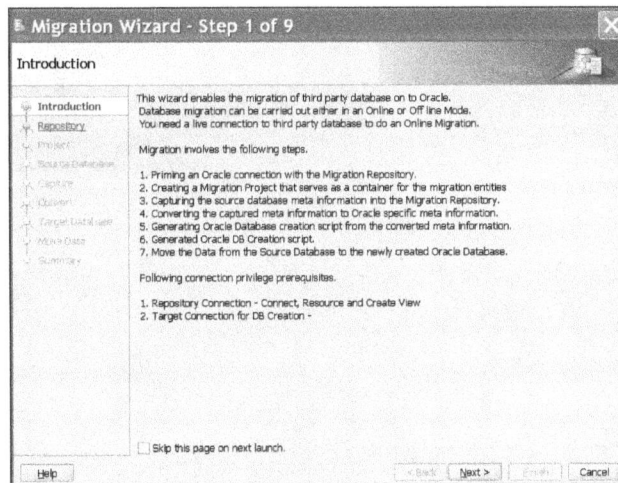

Insert image_2206_04_04.png

Migration steps in SQL Developer

As mentioned earlier, the seven steps outlined in the Migration Wizard allows a user to execute a full database migration process, from capturing the source database metadata to migrating data from the source database to Oracle in multiple ways, that is in online and offline modes.

Selection of the database connection for the repository

Since SQL Developer allows users to create multiple migration repositories for supporting migrations from many databases to Oracle concurrently, users have to pick the desired migration repository connection which will be used for their migration exercise.

SQL Developer also allows users to specify a particular migration repository connection as a default connection, so the selection becomes easier, particularly if there are several of them.

> It is better to create multiple repositories, if there are several databases to migrate (from different vendors or from the same vendor such as Sybase). This allows the migration effort to be divided into multiple groups, so that they can carry on their tasks without interfering with each other. It may also provide a security layer as to who can access the source schema/business logic.

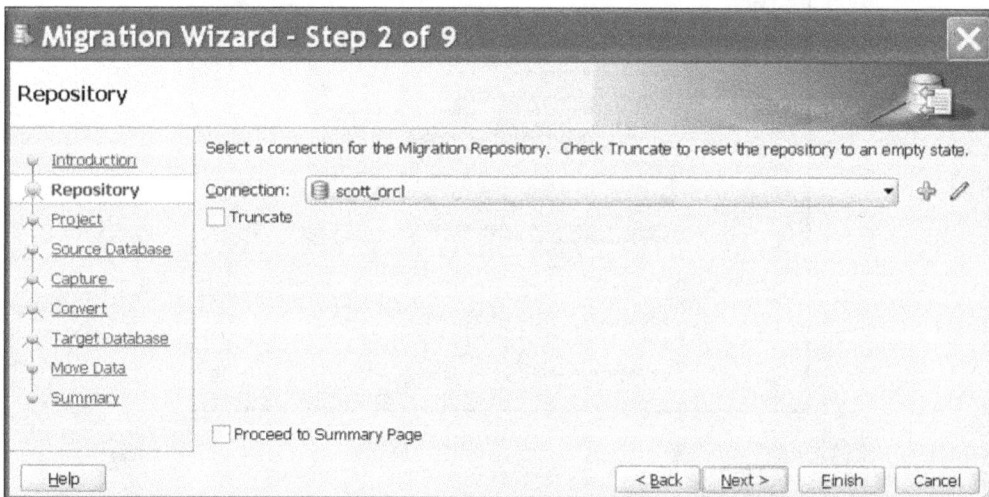

Project creation

A project in SQL Developer Migration Process acts as a placeholder for a migration project. Within each project, all the relevant information for a specific migration project, such as captured/converted models, and the different scripts that are generated during the migration process, are stored in the project context. So if a client is performing multi-vendor database migrations or several large database migrations, then they can choose to isolate each of these migration processes as separate projects so that they can be assessed, managed, and executed effectively.

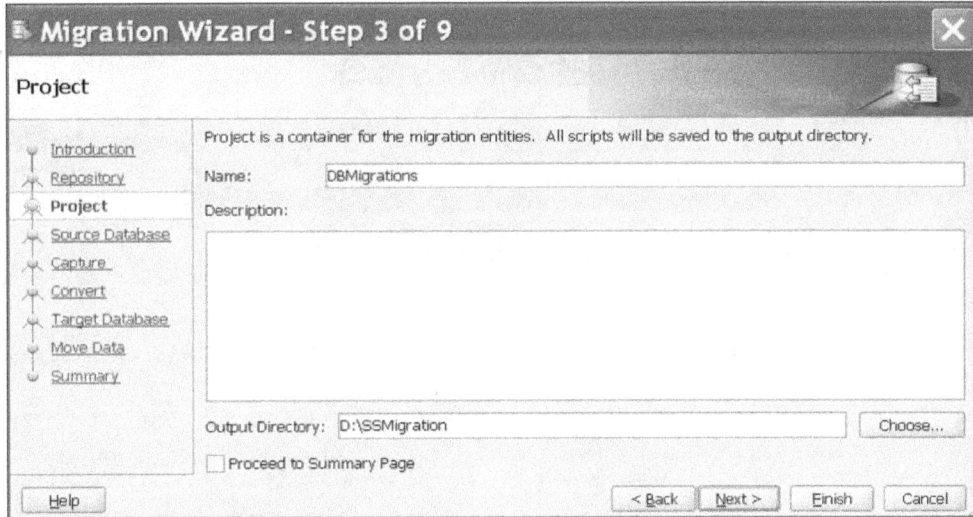

Gathering source database metadata

For a database/schema migration, SQL Developer needs to gather the metadata for the intended database/schema for conversion, as well as source database analysis which helps in migration project estimation.

SQL Developer allows the collection of the source database metadata in two modes — online and offline. For very large databases containing thousands of objects, it is better to use the offline capture process, because it does not require a live connection to the source database to avoid the risk of dropped network connection or the desktop/laptop going into sleep mode, and so on.

Online capture

As the name suggests, online capture involves SQL Developer connecting to the source database using a JDBC connection. To gather source database metadata, SQL Developer needs administrator level (SA) privileges for the databases to be processed. In both cases, SQL Developer will present the option of selecting a source database connection for capturing metadata from source database. After selecting the source database connection, the Migration Wizard will present a Summary screen listing all the available source databases to capture, letting the user pick the database(s) to migrate.

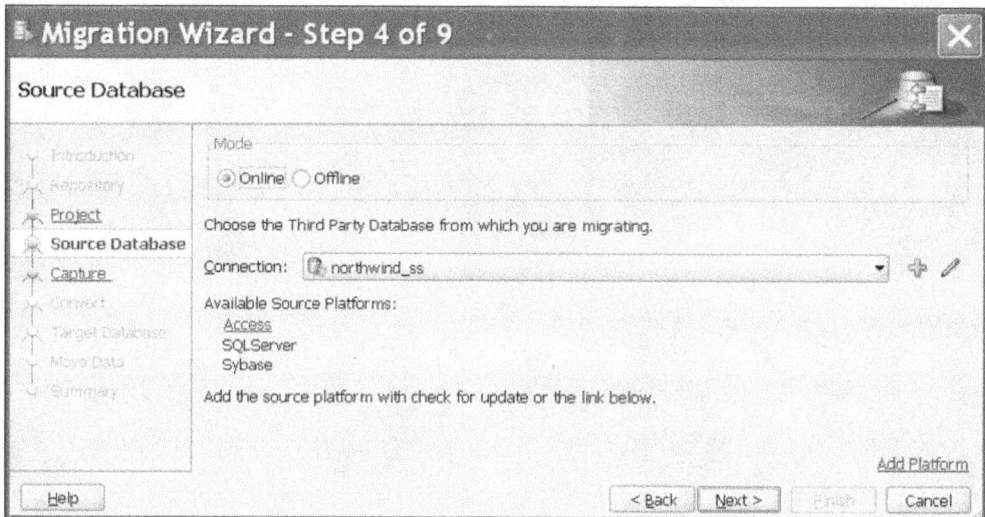

Offline mode

As the name suggests, the offline mode capture process involves executing a series of steps manually to gather the metadata from the source database and loading it into the SQL Developer migration repository for further action. The steps involved in performing the capture process are as follows:

1. Generate the database vendor-specific metadata collection scripts. This option can generate scripts for Windows OS (BAT files) or for Linux/Unix platforms (Shell scripts). This step requires setting up a directory where the scripts are generated by SQL Developer. The project directory created as part of the prerequisites can also be used for storing these script, albeit in a separate sub-directory so as not to confuse with any other scripts that get generated during the migration process.

2. To generate the scripts, navigate to **Tools | Migration | Create Database Capture Scripts** in SQL Developer as shown in the following screenshot:

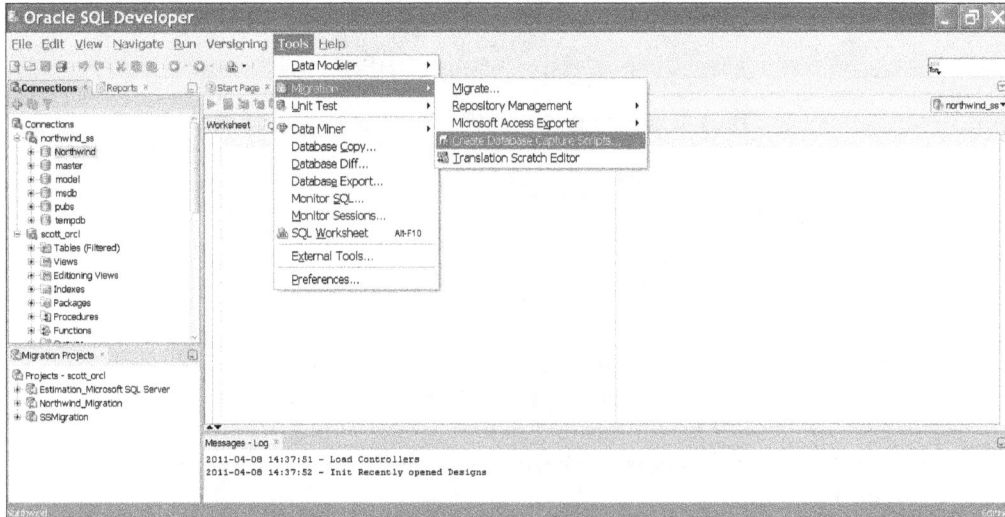

3. Select the directory where the scripts will be generated by SQL Developer and also choose the database vendor/version that will be migrated (as shown in the next screenshot):

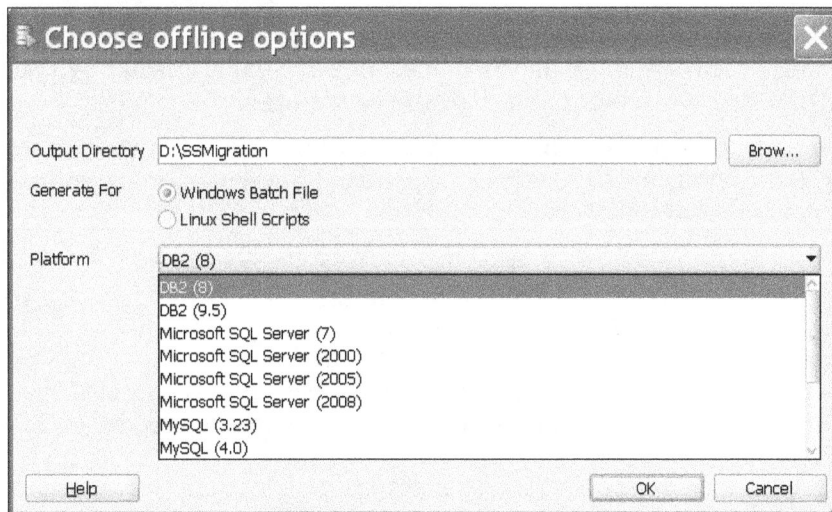

4. Offline capture scripts (refer to next screenshot) will be generated for the database vendor/version that is chosen and placed in the output directory specified.

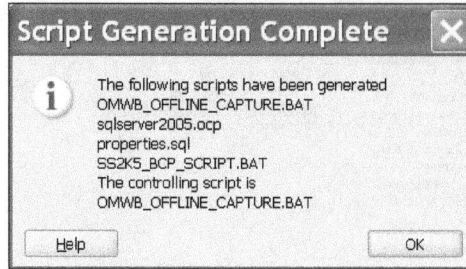

5. After the scripts are generated, they need to be transferred to the source database server and executed with appropriate parameters, depending on the database. It is recommended that all the files associated with the metadata capture process are kept in a separate directory from which they can be executed.

6. The driver script's name varies from database to database. However the naming conventions of these scripts are self-explanatory, making it easier to spot them. The parameters for running these scripts are documented within the scripts so it is advisable to open the scripts in a editor and understand the parameters required.

7. The parameters required for running this script are the administrator user name, password, and database name. For some databases like Sybase and SQL Server, the server name may also be required.

8. The driver script for gathering metadata from the SQL Server 2005 database is `OMWB_OFFLINE_CAPTURE.bat`, which can be executed on the source database server as follows:

```
OMWB_OFFLINE_CAPTURE login_id password database_name server_name
```

```
Where login_id is a login id which has been granted db_datareader
and view definition on database_name
password is the password for the login id
database_name is the name of the database to be captured
server_name is the name of the server on which the database
resides
```

```
An sample command using the offline capture utility can be:
```

```
D:\SSMigration\capture>omwb_offline_capture sa oracle northwind
localhost
```

9. As is evident, this command will work with one database at a time. So this script needs to be executed for each database.

10. After the offline capture scripts are run, all the files under the directory where the scripts were placed originally, including the newly-created sub-directories, need to be transferred back to the machine where SQL Developer is installed.

11. Once the offline capture files are made available locally to SQL Developer, the captured metadata can be loaded into the Migration Repository using the offline capture option in the **Source Database** capture step in **Migration Wizard**.

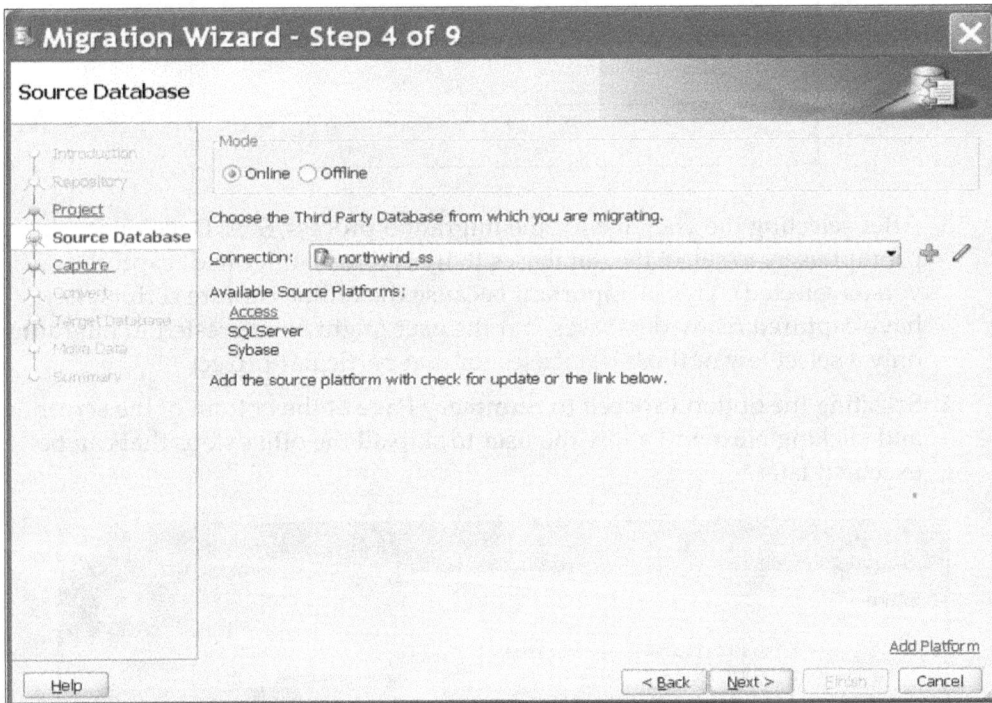

12. For the offline capture mode, users need to browse to the directory where all the files from the previous steps are placed on the server hosting SQL Developer. The main file to look for is named with the extension .ocp.

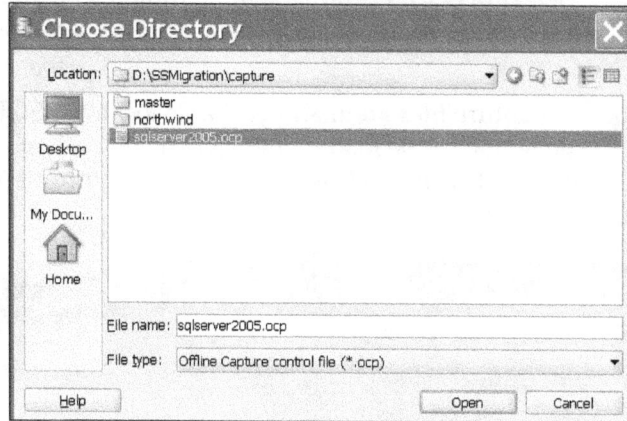

13. After selecting the .ocp file for the migration process, SQL Developer will prompt users to select the databases that need to be migrated (captured versus selected). This is important because the offline capture scripts may have captured many databases, but the user might be interested in migrating only a select few of those databases for that particular project.

14. Selecting the option **Proceed to Summary Page** at the bottom of the screen and clicking **Next** will allow the user to skip all the other steps that can be executed later.

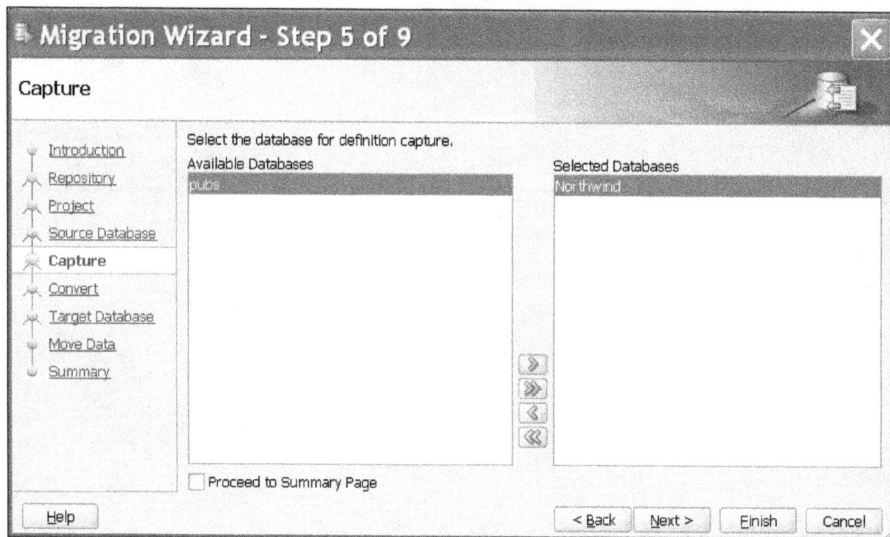

15. After completion of this step, the next option presented by the Migration Wizard is the **Convert** process. At this point, the **Capture** process for the selected database is not yet started. It will start when all the other steps in the Migration Wizard are completed and the **Finish** button is clicked on the **Summary** screen.

16. As discussed earlier, users can choose to skip the rest of the steps and go straight to the **Summary** screen by checking the **Proceed to Summary Page** option and clicking the **Next** button on this screen.

Convert the captured database model to an Oracle model

The conversion step, as the name suggests, converts the source database model into an equivalent Oracle model. The migration repository holds both the captured and converted models. During the conversion process, SQL Developer will generate the schema/objects suitable for Oracle, which can be viewed in the **Project Navigator** pane that appears below the Connections navigator on the left-hand side in SQL Developer. Again at this stage in the migration process, the physical schema is not generated, just the logical model for Oracle schema is generated and stored in the migration repository.

During the convert phase, users are presented with a screen listing various data types used in the source database and default Oracle data types that will be used by SQL Developer for mapping purposes. Users can choose to alter the default mapping rules and specify different data types in Oracle. The most common data types that need to be paid attention are: CHAR, VARCHAR2, TIMESTAMP, DATE, CLOB/BLOB columns. Usually all numeric data types are mapped to the NUMBER data type in Oracle.

Simple user defined types (UDTs) are converted to their base data types but complex UDTs are not converted. This is a limitation in SQL Developer for now.

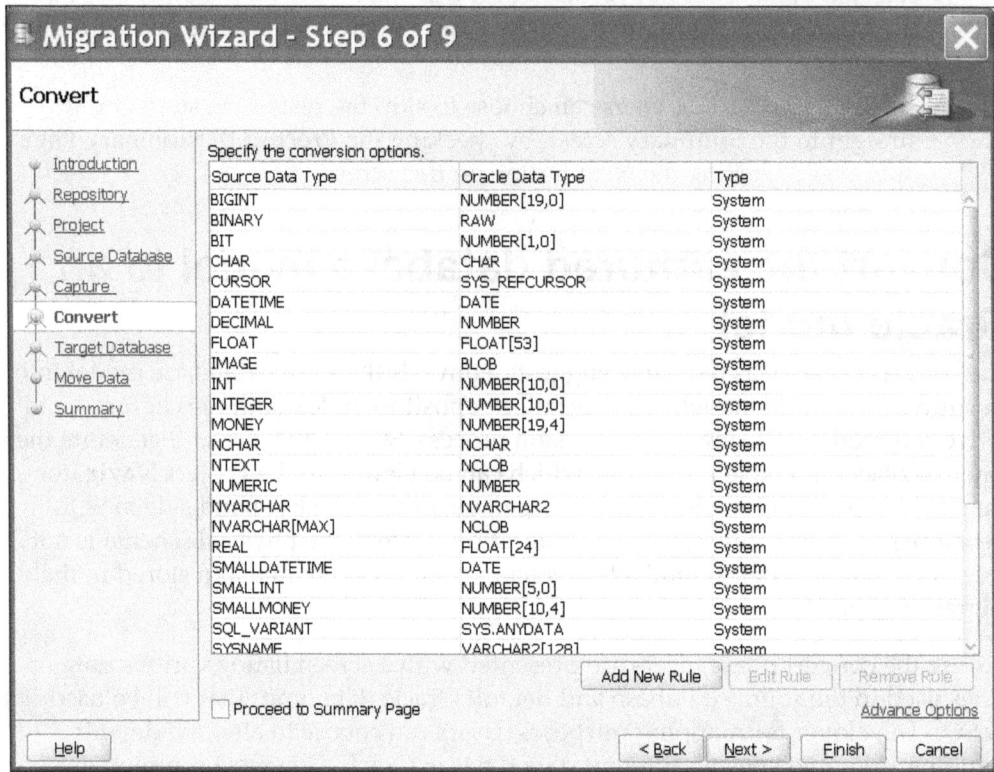

Target Oracle schema generation

The next step in the migration process is to define where/how the target Oracle schema will be generated. In online mode, SQL Developer can generate the Oracle schema by using a database user connection that has the privileges to create schemas (users).

If such a user connection is created as part of the prerequisites for using SQL Developer, then that connection should be used in this step to create the target schema as shown in the following screenshot:

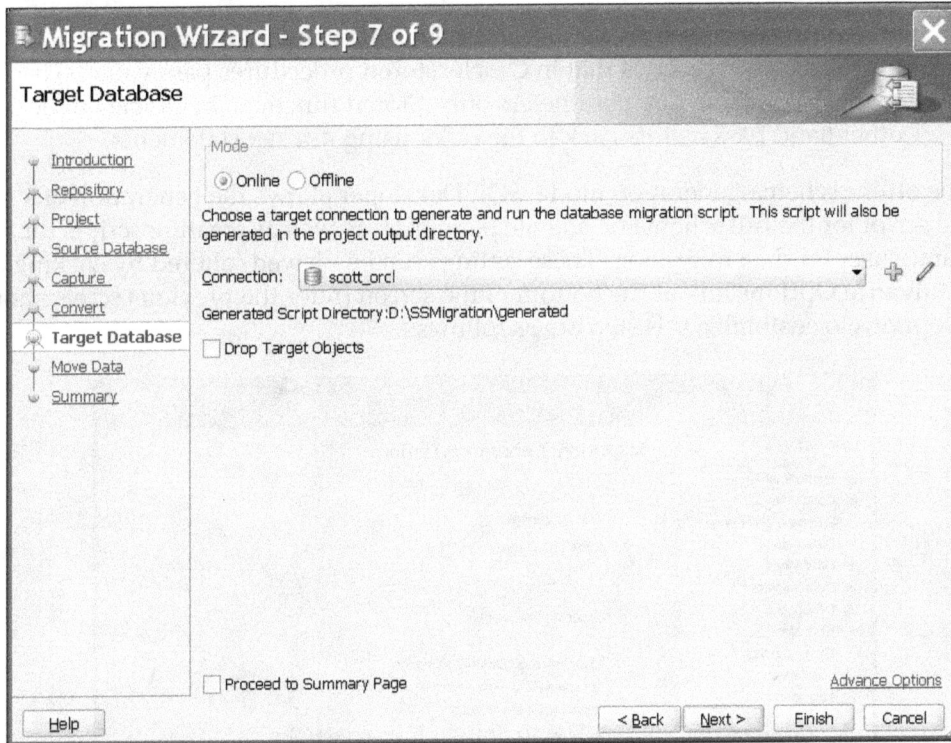

In case users have skipped the part creating a database user with administrative privileges in Oracle and a connection in SQL Developer, they are presented with that option again during the target schema generation step in the Migration Wizard. They simply need to create a connection for an Oracle database user that has all the privileges for creating the target schema (by clicking on the green + button next to the Connection name as shown in the previous screenshot). The schema to which the connection points to in this step is not the destination schema for the migrated objects. It is simply used to create the target schema (user) because schema creation activities require a database connection with administrative privileges.

The Oracle schema generated by SQL Developer may contain more or different objects than the source database because of the following reasons:

- Identity columns in the source database used for generating unique identifiers are converted to numeric columns in Oracle (NUMBER data type) with associated triggers and SEQUENCE to provide the same functionality in Oracle.

- Temporary tables used in source database stored programs such as Stored Procedures are converted into global temporary tables in Oracle. Global temporary tables need to be created just like regular tables in Oracle as part of the schema creation process.

- Stored procedures with RETURN statements are converted into Oracle functions. The reason is that in Oracle, stored procedures pass value(s) back to the caller using OUT parameters only. Stored functions in Oracle on the other hand pass results back to the caller using RETURN statements.

In the offline schema generation mode, SQL Developer allows the generation of a large script for the full schema or one file per object, as well as creating scripts for a separate user for data migration. These settings can be viewed/altered by clicking on the **Advance Options** link at the bottom of the screen (refer the previous screenshot). The options to customize this step are as follows:

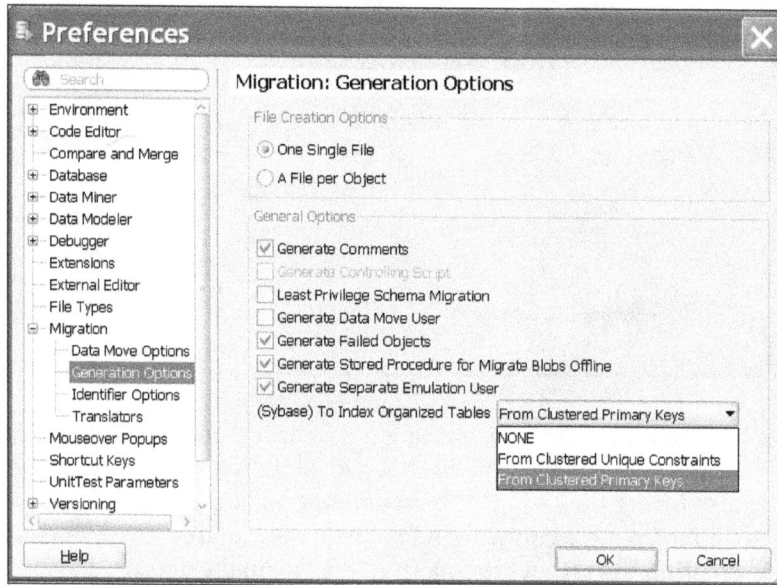

With the **Generate Failed Objects** option selected, SQL Developer will include the DDLs for objects that could not be converted by SQL Developer in the schema creation scripts, which will in turn allow users to identify failed objects on one hand and also investigate the reasons for the failure in conversion. In the offline schema generation mode, generated DDL script is placed in the Projects directory for later use.

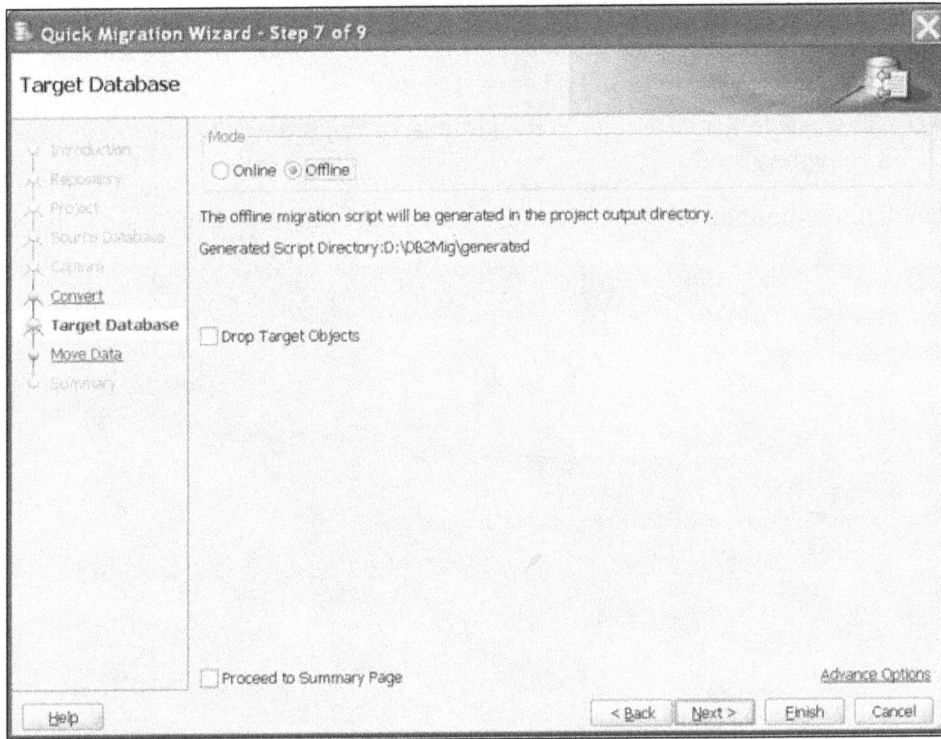

Data migration

SQL Developer facilitates data migration from source databases to Oracle in two modes. In the online mode, SQL Developer uses the JDBC connection for connecting and extracting data from the source database. In the offline mode, SQL Developer generates scripts to export data from the source database into flat files and Oracle SQL*Loader utility scripts for loading the data from flat files into Oracle. For the offline mode data migration, it generates the necessary scripts for the data unloading/loading as well as scripts for disabling/enabling constraints, driver scripts for launching the unload/load scripts to reduce the administrative tasks.

The online data migration mode in SQL Developer is a very useful feature for the following reasons:

- It allows us to customize the number of connections that can be used to transfer the data from the source database to Oracle. This option may help optimize the data migration process based on the network connectivity available between the source and target databases.

- Reuse of the JDBC connections created in the earlier steps for the capture process for both source and target databases.

- Users simply need to pick the source and target database connections to facilitate data migration from source to target, regardless of the number of tables in the source/target schema.
- Allows us to truncate data in the target schema, if the data migration process is being repeated.

For small to medium-sized databases, this is a viable option for data migration.

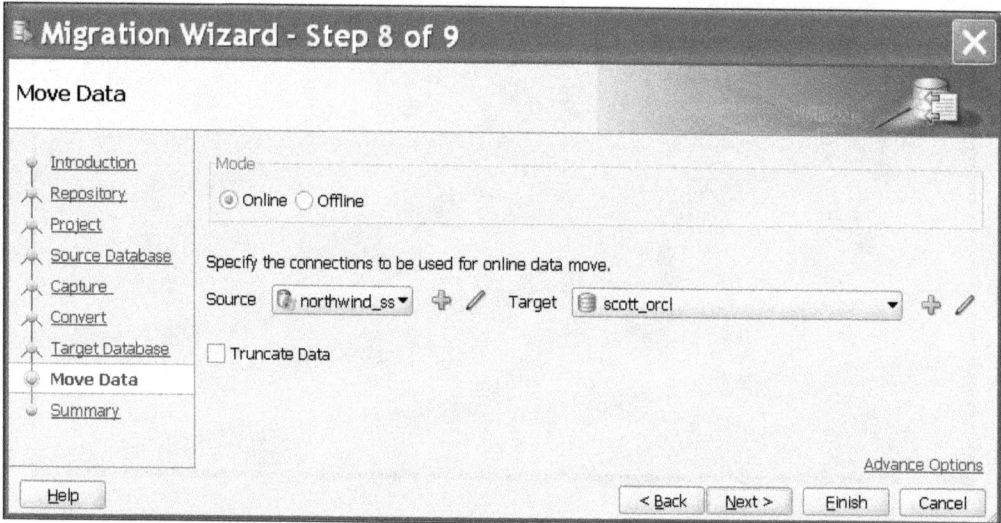

The data unloading scripts generated for the offline data migration mode leverage the source database utilities like BCP for Sybase/SQL Server and DB2 command line utility for DB2 databases.

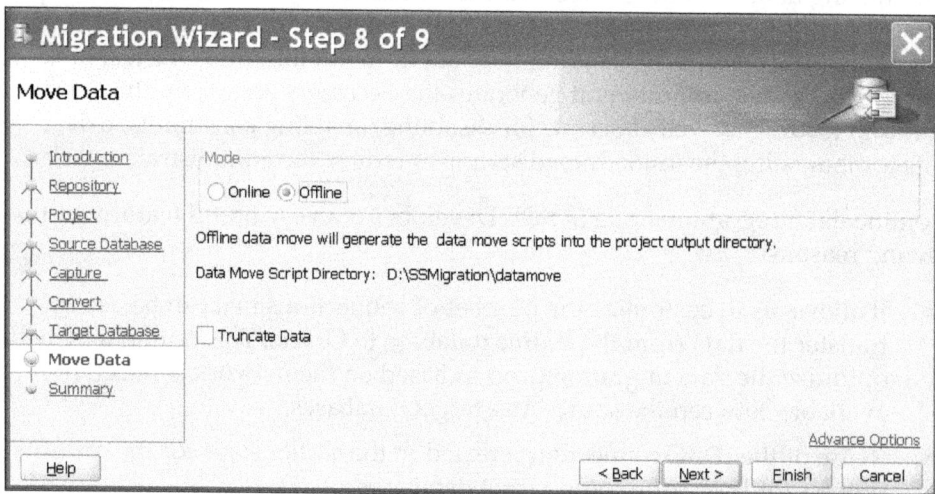

SQL Developer also allows users to customize the source database date/timestamp formats, end of line delimiters, column delimiters, and so on for seamless data migration (refer the next screenshot):

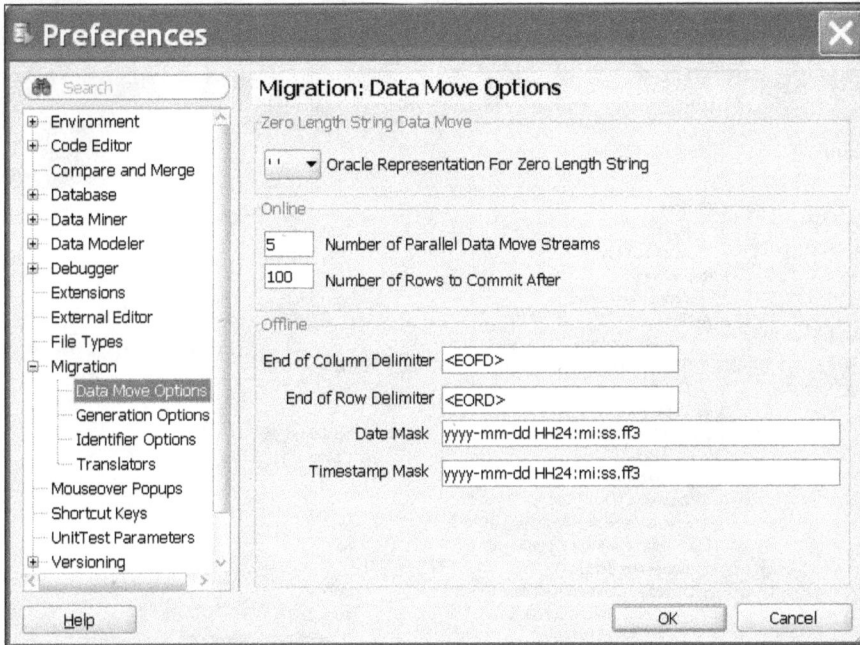

After the data migration options are chosen, users are presented with the **Summary** page, where all the options chosen for different migration steps/tasks such as **Capture**, **Convert**, **Data Migration**, and **Oracle Schema Generation** are displayed. Clicking on the **Finish** button starts the migration process and executes the steps according to the choices made during the process.

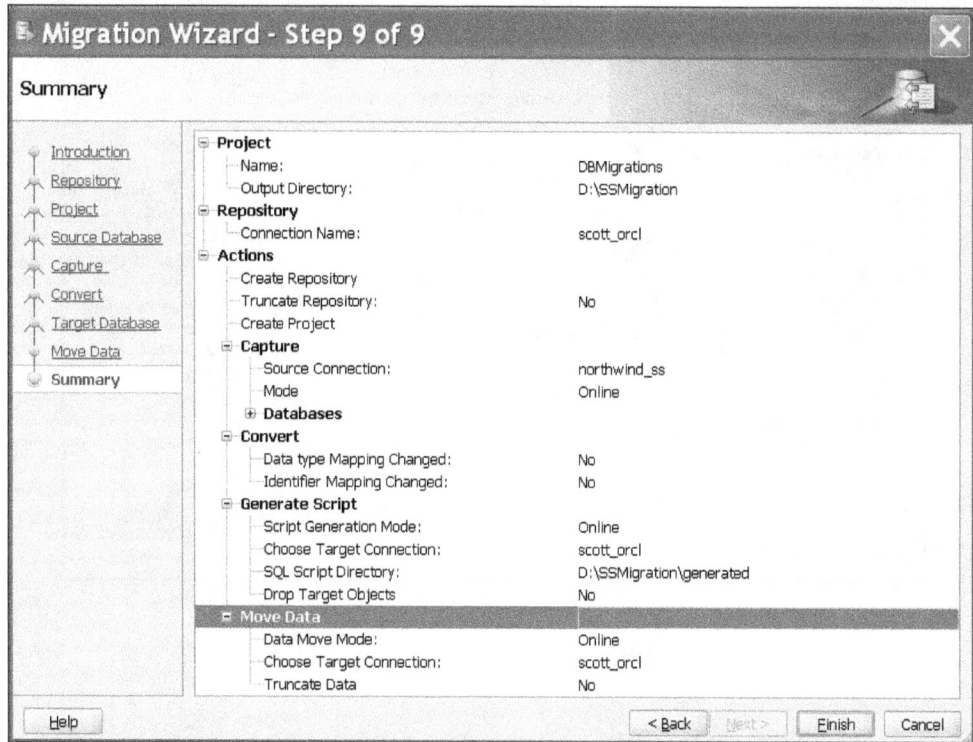

Migration Wizard - Step 9 of 9	✕

Summary

Introduction
Repository
Project
Source Database
Capture
Convert
Target Database
Move Data
Summary

- **Project**
  - Name: DBMigrations
  - Output Directory: D:\SSMigration
- **Repository**
  - Connection Name: scott_orcl
- **Actions**
  - Create Repository
  - Truncate Repository: No
  - Create Project
  - **Capture**
    - Source Connection: northwind_ss
    - Mode   Online
    - ⊕ **Databases**
  - **Convert**
    - Data type Mapping Changed: No
    - Identifier Mapping Changed: No
  - **Generate Script**
    - Script Generation Mode: Online
    - Choose Target Connection: scott_orcl
    - SQL Script Directory: D:\SSMigration\generated
    - Drop Target Objects   No
  - **Move Data**
    - Data Move Mode: Online
    - Choose Target Connection: scott_orcl
    - Truncate Data   No

Help   < Back   Next >   Finish   Cancel

After the migration has completed successfully, it is recommended that objects created in the Oracle database be verified with the source database objects in terms of object count, status of objects, for example: Valid/Invalid. It is also important to verify the migration logs/reports to find out which objects failed to migrate, as well as which objects have not been fully migrated, due to limitations in SQL Developer. In some cases, SQL Developer generates the stored procedures, triggers, views, functions, and so on, which compile in Oracle, but some statements may be commented out because it could not convert them. SQL Developer lists out objects that require manual intervention due to its limitations in conversion, such as the conversion of the @@ERROR and @@TRANS features of the Sybase database. These issues surface because of the architectural differences between databases rather than shortcomings of SQL Developer.

To assist with the manual conversion process as well as code enhancement and bug fixes, SQL Developer provides a feature called **Translation Scratch Editor**, which helps convert ad hoc T-SQL/Stored procedures into Oracle SQL, PL/SQL on demand. This is very useful for developers to convert embedded SQLs in other applications, as well as for optimizing the SQL Statements in Oracle.

The migration report generated by SQL Developer clearly lists those objects that have been renamed due to conflicts with the Oracle naming convention (reserved words in the Oracle database). Object naming conventions in Oracle does not allow the object name to begin with #, similarly Oracle database does not allow certain words to be used as a column name, for example: a table cannot have a column of name **DATE** which is of data type DATE. This is however possible in some other databases. A complete list of reserved words is published in the Oracle database documentation.

SQL Developer provides many reports detailing the entire migration process that includes objects captured, converted, generated, final status, and issues encountered. In addition, it also provides application code analysis reports, stored programs analysis reports that help customers in estimating the migration effort.

These reports can be accessed by clicking on the converted and captured projects under the **Project Navigator** pane on the left-hand side in SQL Developer.

Enabling a factory approach to database migrations using SQL Developer

SQL Developer enables database migrations in an interactive manner, that is, users need to set up connections, click through the migration wizard and choose desired options to perform the migrations. This method works well for migrating a very small number of databases. But many organizations have dozens and hundreds of databases, if not thousands, that they need to migrate. Using the SQL Developer GUI to migrate one database at a time is not an optimal method for 'en masse migrations'. This is where using a factory approach to migrations comes in handy. The factory approach to database migrations involves performing database migrations in a batch, non-interactive manner so that users do not have to sit and wait for the migration processes to be completed to click through the GUI.

To facilitate database migrations (schema and data) in a batch mode for many databases at a time, SQL Developer offers a command line interface which can be scripted to go after many source databases/systems and run the migration process from end-to-end, that is capture, convert, generate, and data move phases in a batch mode, reducing user interactions.

`Migration.bat` utility under the SQL Developer installation (`D:\` `sqldeveloper-3.0.04.34\sqldeveloper\sqldeveloper\bin`) can facilitate the factory approach to database migrations. This utility can be used for performing migration steps individually, that is, only the capture step or convert step as well as performing all the migration steps in sequence for each database. An example of invoking this utility is shown in the following code:

```
D:\sqldeveloper-3.0.04.34\sqldeveloper\sqldeveloper\bin>migration.bat
-help
HELP:
Syntax:
    Migration -help|-h=<actions> to get help on one or more actions.
where
    <actions> could be one or more (comma separated list) actions or
guide
    guide provides a walk through of a typical migration
Examples:
    Migration -help=capture
    Migration -h=capture,convert
    Migration -h=guide

Valid actions:
capture, convert, datamove, delcaptured, delconn, delconverted,
driver, generate, guide, idmap, info, init, lscaptured, lsconn,
lsconverted, mkconn, qm, runsql, scan and translate
```

As illustrated earlier, this utility can be used to create database connections for multiple databases, perform all database migration steps, maintain the migration repository, generate reports, and most importantly can be used to scan application code base for identifying and changing the SQL Statements that are not valid for the Oracle database. This utility can be invoked in a script to migrate many databases at a time, removing user interaction for each database.

Data migration using Oracle SQL*Loader/ External tables

Usually data loading into Oracle itself is a very quick process, but it takes some time to organize and assemble all the pieces together before the data gets loaded. On an Oracle Database Machine server 12 terabytes (TB) of data can be loaded in less than an hour as per the internal testing done by Oracle. Real data load rates on any system will depend on the server configuration, IO subsystem configuration as well as the database schema setup in terms of data types used, number of indexes on the tables, row/column sizes, and so on. With continuous improvements in technology, this rate will get even faster in the future. The Data Migration stage often becomes a multi-week process for large databases because of the need for an efficient process to migrate data from the source to Oracle. Having a very large number of tables to migrate complicates the process, because any method chosen needs to be as automated as possible so that administrators can avoid dealing with one table or script at a time. The most common activities that are part of the Data Migration process are:

- **Formulation of Data Migration strategy/plan**: Coming up with a plan to migrate several hundred or thousands of tables in an automated fashion is important for migrating data within a fixed time. Database Administrators need to consider many options for scripting the unloading, data transfer, and loading of data into Oracle. Typically, they need to consider options like utilizing native utilities provided by the database vendors, scripting, and ETL tools to perform these tasks.

- **Data unloading**: There are several options for data unloading from the source, including native utilities for unloading data into flat files, for example Sybase/SQL Server BCP, DB2 UNLOAD, using ETL tools like Oracle Data Integrator (ODI). Sometimes the main concern is where and how to stage the data files to load into Oracle later. For very large databases a very large staging area (disk space) may be required. Network transfer times through FTP may also pose a challenge for very large data sets. For very large datasets, compression can be used to reduce the file size to speed up the data transfer process. Time spent on compressing/uncompressing a data file after unloading and before loading in Oracle should be considered into the project timelines.

- **Data loading**: As mentioned earlier, the data loading process itself does not usually take much time. Loading of data in parallel for partitioned tables, multiple tables in an Oracle Real Applications Cluster environment should be considered to speed up the process. However, there are steps that need to be performed before data loading into Oracle like disabling constraints, dropping secondary indexes on tables (especially the very large tables). Then enabling the constraints, re-building indexes after the data loading process is complete. The most important step of all is to gather statistics on the tables/indexes after the data loading is complete.

- **Data verification**: Data verification is an important task in the whole data migration process. There are not many tools for performing side-by-side data comparison between the source and target. Custom scripts can be used for data verification after data loading. Data profiling/quality tools can also be used for this purpose. Some common elements to be verified post data migration are:

  - **Date/timestamp fields accuracy**: Incorrect usage of date/timestamp formats in Oracle might result in the truncation of time data

  - **Improper sizing of the columns**: Might result in truncation/ rounding of the numeric fields with decimal places such as amount fields

  - **Columns containing character data**: They might have junk characters in them due to incorrect translation because of differences in encoding between source and target databases (EBCDIC versus ASCII)

Using Oracle SQL*Loader

This is the most commonly used tool for data loading in Oracle. Many other ETL tools also utilize it for loading data in Oracle because it is free, very fast, and flexible. Oracle SQL*Loader is a free utility bundled with all editions of Oracle database. It can load data from flat files and support multiple data formats (fixed/variable length), different encodings (EBCDIC, ASCII). SQL*Loader has the ability to batch data loading so that it commits the records less often, improving performance.

SQL*Loader requires a control file which contains all the directives that are required for loading data from a flat file. It allows data manipulation while loading the data into Oracle. It also supports loading data into multiple tables from a single input file containing different varying length records. However, this typically is not required in migrations because data migration is done on a table-to-table basis. Only cases of data migrations from other non-relational databases may have a requirement to process data in such methods.

Using SQL*Loader features such as direct-path loading, skipping index maintenance, and parallel data loading, data loading processes can be optimized tremendously. The direct-path loading feature of SQL*Loader allows it to write the column arrays (data) directly to the data files bypassing the SQL Command processing in Oracle database. Hence, it is significantly faster than the conventional load option (default option) of SQL*Loader. The index maintenance on tables during data loading can slow down the whole process, because the database engine has to continuously update the indexes for every row that gets inserted into the table. Index maintenance can be avoided when loading data using SQL*Loader by using the SKIP_INDEX_MAINTENANCE command line option, or by explicitly disabling the indexes before the data load operation. After data is loaded into the table, indexes can be rebuilt efficiently using the parallelism feature of the database. Similarly, all constraints, triggers that effect the data in the table, should be disabled during the data migration process and re-enabled after data load when using SQL*Loader to improve performance overall. Using SQL*Loader data can also be loaded in parallel. For parallel data loading, the input data file needs to be split into multiple files, a separate copy of the control file is also required for each file. Then, using separate sessions, multiple data loading operations can be launched. This is a key approach for loading very large data sets in Oracle. Of course, it requires some manual effort for managing the whole process for example splitting files, managing control files, and managing/monitoring sessions to load the data. However this approach may not be required for all the tables in a database, only a select few.

The following is a sample control file for SQL*Loader which is part of Samples provided by Oracle:

```
LOAD DATA
INFILE 'ulcase7.dat'
DISCARDFILE 'ulcase7.dsc'
APPEND
INTO TABLE emp
  WHEN (57)='.'
  TRAILING NULLCOLS
  (hiredate SYSDATE,
   deptno    POSITION(1:2)   INTEGER EXTERNAL(3)
             NULLIF deptno=BLANKS,
   job       POSITION(7:14)   CHAR   TERMINATED BY WHITESPACE
             NULLIF job=BLANKS   "UPPER(:job)",
   mgr       POSITION(28:31)   INTEGER EXTERNAL TERMINATED BY WHITESPACE
             NULLIF mgr=BLANKS,
   ename     POSITION (34:41) CHAR   TERMINATED BY WHITESPACE
             "UPPER(:ename)",
   empno     INTEGER EXTERNAL   TERMINATED BY WHITESPACE,
   sal       POSITION(51)   CHAR   TERMINATED BY WHITESPACE
```

```
                   "TO_NUMBER(:sal,'$99,999.99')",
     comm          INTEGER EXTERNAL   ENCLOSED BY '(' AND '%'
                   ":comm * 100"
  )
```

Today's Newly Hired Employees

Dept Commission	Job	Manager	MgrNo	Emp Name	EmpNo	Salary/
----	--------	--------	-----	--------	-----	-----------------
20 $1,600.00 (3%)	Salesman	Blake	7698	Shepard	8061	
$1,250.00 (5%)				Falstaff	8066	
$1,250.00 (14%)				Major	8064	
30 $1,100.00	Clerk	Scott	7788	Conrad	8062	
8063 $800.00		Ford	7369	DeSilva		
$2,975.00	Manager	King	7839	Provo	8065	

Using Oracle External Table

The Oracle External Table feature allows data access from flat files just like the SQL*Loader utility. Unlike SQL*Loader which is a command line utility, External Tables is a core database feature so that it can be used in SQL Statements in the database. This feature allows users to read data from a file just like reading data from an Oracle table. Users can open cursors and process data row-by-row in PL/SQL Procedures/Functions. External tables are created like a regular table in Oracle and require information about the data file indicating location, format, line/column separators, and so on.

Oracle External Table eliminates the need for a separate staging table when loading data and processing the data in traditional ETL settings. One of the key advantages of Oracle's External Table feature in the data loading process is that it can parallelize the reading operation from flat files. So it can make use of all available system resources, for example: CPU, memory, multiple-nodes in a RAC environment with a single command. On the other hand, using the SQL*Loader utility to enable a parallel load of data, the data files need to be split into multiple files and then a separate thread for each flat file needs to be launched.

> If using parallelism across a RAC cluster in Oracle, make sure that data files are accessible to nodes that are being used for the data loading operation.

Here is a sample depicting creation, using External Tables to load data into Oracle:

```
CREATE TABLE emp_load
      (employee_number      CHAR(5),
       employee_dob         CHAR(20),
       employee_last_name   CHAR(20),
       employee_first_name  CHAR(15),
       employee_middle_name CHAR(15),
       employee_hire_date   DATE)
    ORGANIZATION EXTERNAL
     (TYPE ORACLE_LOADER
      DEFAULT DIRECTORY def_dir1
      ACCESS PARAMETERS
        (RECORDS DELIMITED BY NEWLINE
         FIELDS (employee_number      CHAR(2),
                 employee_dob         CHAR(20),
                 employee_last_name   CHAR(18),
                 employee_first_name  CHAR(11),
                 employee_middle_name CHAR(11),
                 employee_hire_date   CHAR(10) date_format DATE mask
"mm/dd/yyyy"
               )
        )
      LOCATION ('info.dat')
     );
```

The following lines consist of a sample command to load data from a file (info.dat) into an Oracle table named emp:

```
SQL> CREATE TABLE EMP tablespace USERS storage (initial 500m next 50m
maxextents unlimited) parallel (degree 4) AS SELECT * /*+ PARALLEL (emp_
load, 4) */ FROM emp_load;

Or

SQL> INSERT INTO /*+ PARALLEL (emp, 4) */ emp AS SELECT * /*+ PARALLEL
(emp_load, 4) */ FROM EMP_LOAD;

SQL>COMMIT;
```

Using Oracle Data Integrator (ODI) for data migration

Oracle Data Integrator can also assist with data migration tasks in a migration process. It does not require a separate server to run on as it has a very low footprint in terms of CPU/memory/disk space requirements. It also offers high performance data extraction/loading capabilities from source and target databases due to its abilities for leveraging native utilities.

Key benefits of using Oracle Data Integrator for data migration are:

- Both ETL and ELT methods for data loading can be used. Using the ELT method, the data staging step can be avoided, resulting in improved performance of the data loading process and reduced resource consumption.

- Supports many alternatives for data loading into Oracle, including utilities like SQL*Loader, External Tables, and JDBC connections between source and target databases. It can also generate the necessary scripts for running these utilities, run them on a schedule and alert end users about the status of the process.

- Can connect to many data sources out of the box, for example Server, Sybase, DB2, Informix, Ingres, flat files, JMS/MQ, and so on.

- Provides a flexible framework to create connectivity for new and less popular data sources through Knowledge Modules.

- Provides a GUI to map source tables, to target tables, and data manipulation formatting options.

- ODI can also reverse engineer source database tables for which currently there are no migration tools. This is possible by creating/modifying relevant Knowledge Modules for reverse engineering (RKM).

- Data from non-relational data sources can be appropriately transformed when loading into Oracle schema.

- Supports invocation of data loading processes through web services.

- End-to-end process design/development involving data unloading, transferring the files, data loading into Oracle tasks can be accomplished using GUI.

- ODI also offers a change data capture (CDC) mechanism for many data sources by using triggers to capture the changes in source databases. It also offers CDC capabilities for IBM DB2 database on Series I servers leveraging the log-mining method. This method requires journaling of source tables.

Production rollout using Oracle GoldenGate

Deploying a new database (after migration) for use by end users after testing, optimization requires careful planning. During the data migration process at the end of database migration projects, there is a need to capture the changes that occurred on the source database and applied to the new database before it is made available to the end users for live usage. Capturing changes in the source database after the initial data extraction may require special tools/technologies for the following reasons:

- The data volume is very high or the application performance cannot be impacted because of the capture process
- Applications cannot be taken offline for the duration of data migration process.

Oracle GoldenGate allows for capturing changes from a database with relatively low performance impact by accessing the transaction logs for capturing the data changes. GoldenGate also allows for transmission and applies the data changes to the target database in near real-time. GoldenGate maintains the order of the transactions on the source database when applying the same on the target database.

Oracle GoldenGate is the tool of choice for many customers for changed data capture because of its ability to capture changes and apply them to the target database with very low impact on performance on the source database.

In a database migration project, typical steps that users go through to set up GoldenGate, to capture the changes at the source database and apply them to the target database, are as follows:

1. Before starting the data extraction process on the source database, install and configure Oracle GoldenGate.

2. Configure and start the capture process to capture the changes as they take place in source database.

3. Make a note of the first system change number (SCN) that GoldenGate generates. This step is optional.

4. After ensuring that the capture process is successfully started, start the data extraction process to ensure that the data changes in the database are being captured as the data is being extracted.

5. If the application can be taken offline during the data extraction process, then the capture process can be started after the data extraction process completes. Once the capture process is started then the database can be made available to end users for transactional use.

6. Load the data into the target database that was extracted from the source database. Data loading can also be performed through many tools, as discussed earlier.

7. After completing the data loading process of the pump, an apply process can also be configured on the target database server for applying the changes captured from the source database.

Once all the changes from the source database are available and applied to the target database, then the target database can be made available for use by end users. The process of making the applications connect to the new database and allowing users to connect to it requires careful planning and consideration.

These steps represent a common scenario for data migration in the context of a large database migration project. These steps may need to be sequenced differently based on how the data extraction/migration processes are executed.

A few things to consider in a high transaction volume environment:

• Have the source and target systems sized properly and consider the performance impact of these additional processes

• GoldenGate processes such as capture, pump, and apply can also be optimized to meet performance/latency requirements

For most databases where application/database downtime is available during the planned maintenance window, which is usually few hours in a weekend, the data migration can be accomplished without requiring these additional products/ processes.

The most important aspect of this process is to make sure all data changes that occur on the source database after the data extraction process has begun, are subsequently captured and applied on the target database before it is made available for transactional use by the end users.

One other common use case for Oracle GoldenGate is to support the live operation of both environments in parallel. GoldenGate helps in such a situation by keeping both the databases in sync with each other. This is typically desired for mission critical systems as a way of maintaining a failback option.

Impact of database migrations on applications

Database migrations impact applications in many ways. Most common changes to applications include:

- Connection mechanisms including using vendor-specific drivers. Database drivers from different vendors have different connection string formats and parameters that they support.

- Applications have to be modified to issue vendor-specific (Oracle) SQL Statements. Such modifications may be minimal if the application uses ANSI standard SQL Statements. For example, SQL Statements with database-specific extensions such as date/timestamp arithmetic need modification.

- The database access APIs from different vendors differ on how they allow manipulation of cursors, LOBs, system-generated keys, and so on.

- Error handling may also require manual intervention as databases have different error codes for the same error condition. This task is easier to accomplish if the application uses a central library of error codes and messages so that the full application code base need not be scanned/modified.

Oracle ODBC and OLEDB drivers are very similar to other ODBC drivers in terms of functionality and support for various APIs. So applications leveraging ODBC or OLEDB drivers require minimal changes.

Oracle JDBC drivers currently distributed with Oracle Database11*g* R2 and earlier versions differ from other JDBC drivers on the market today in some respects, for example handling of result sets returned from the Oracle database, handling of autogenerated keys, and so on. In the future, hopefully these differences will be narrowed down considerably to allow for seamless migration.

DBA utilities/scripts that use command line utilities and proprietary commands from the database vendors also require changes to ensure smooth transition to the new environment.

Integration and reporting facilities may also require changes, depending on how they are developed or in what languages they are implemented.

User security may also require some effort as in most cases database passwords cannot be migrated to a new database. If the application stores the user passwords in the database instead of using an LDAP server then it may require additional effort in resetting the default passwords for database/application users and notifying users of the change in passwords.

Summary

Database migration projects are not just about data migration. They also involve changes to schema, applications, security, integration, reporting tools, backup, and recovery processes.

With the introduction of new technologies to reduce the application migration effort by way of emulating database functionalities, either at the database access layer or at the application tier, impact of database migrations on applications can be reduced to a certain extent. Aside from marketing claims on how easy it is to migrate databases in weeks, database migrations in general can be complex and time-consuming, especially when there is significant amount of business logic implemented in the database that needs to be migrated first. With judicious use of tools/technologies, a good portion of the migration tasks can be automated and the whole migration process can made manageable and economically viable. Using a factory approach for many of the tasks such as data migration, schema conversion, and so on, for the migration of a large number of databases can also help in reducing the overall effort required.

Oracle is making significant improvements in its migration capabilities to make the database/application migration process as automated and seamless as possible and reduce the overall effort involved.

5
Database Migration Challenges and Solutions

From a relational database perspective, the migration of one relational database to another is easier than migrating from a non-relational database to a relational database. However, this does not mean that this type of migration is a simple process, because of the impact on the ecosystem of which these databases are a critical part. In many respects, relational databases are quite similar, for example: data storage concepts, data management techniques, data access APIs and so on. However, they also differ significantly in the actual implementation of these common features, such as:

- Object naming conventions
- Null value handling
- Case sensitivity
- Default locking behavior
- Features/functionalities supported in stored programs

Data migrations between relational databases are easier when compared with migration from legacy databases. The reason being that relational databases are similar in many data management aspects, such as handling different types of data using similar data types, and their behavior, for example: fixed length character data (CHAR), varying length character data (VARCHAR or VARCHAR2 in Oracle), numeric data, large objects (LOB), and so on. They do differ in how they handle date and timestamp data, especially with the granularity of the data supported by these databases.

But data in non-relational databases, such as hierarchical/network databases, is organized in a completely different way; the data in these databases is not always stored like a relational database, that is, data organized in rows and columns in a tabular format. So direct mapping of data between relational and non-relational databases may not be possible in many cases.

As discussed earlier, there are vendors who claim that database migrations and application porting can be completed in a matter of weeks. In reality, database migrations and application porting can take much longer than a couple of weeks, based on the complexities in schema, business Logic, and application client implementations. Regardless of the methodology and tools for porting application/databases, testing the application, post migration remains a major challenge.

A combination of any of the following factors make an application/database complex to migrate:

- Large databases in terms of database size in terabytes
- Databases with business logic embedded in a large number of stored programs, for example: stored procedures, triggers, and views
- Large numbers of application client programs/interfaces with embedded SQLs
- Lack of documentation/use cases for post migration testing

Potential challenges in a database migration (to Oracle) project can be broadly divided into the following categories:

- Schema migration
- Database stored programs migration
- Application Migration

In this chapter, the focus will be on the challenges of database/schema migrations as it is related to the topic of data integration/migration. Application migration issues like database stored programs conversion are simply out of the scope of this book.

Database schema migration challenges

Relational databases differ in naming conventions for tables, columns, and other objects. They also differ in how the object names are stored in the database and how they can be referred to in SQL queries and transactions. All database migration tools currently in use by customers, including SQL Developer, do a pretty good job of converting non-Oracle database schemas to Oracle. The most common issues that show up during a database migration to Oracle are discussed in the following sections.

Database object naming/definition issues

The Oracle database has placed certain restrictions on what is allowed for naming/defining objects in the database and how these objects are subsequently accessed. Broadly, the object naming issues can be classified into four categories:

- Use of special characters in object names
- Use of reserved words in object names/definitions
- Case-sensitive object names
- Length of object names

SQL Developer assists in identifying, resolving these issues automatically by generating a report that lists objects affected by any of the previously mentioned issues. It also addresses the issue in its own way by renaming the objects, column names, and so on. Each of the previously mentioned categories are discussed in detail and SQL Developer addresses the specific issue, starting with the first category from the list.

Use of special characters in object names

In an Oracle database, object names cannot begin with special characters such as #, %, _(underscore), $, etc. However, a few of these special characters such as #, _ (underscore), and $ are allowed within the object names (not as first character). In a database migration scenario, such as SQL Server or Sybase to Oracle migration, one of the most common issues that crops up is object names that have the special character # (pound) as the first character (special temporary table names). There are two solutions to address this issue:

- **Rename the object**: In databases such as Sybase, SQL Server names of temporary tables in stored programs begin with #. When SQL Developer is migrating, the schema appends TT_ to the temporary table when generating the DDL for the temporary table and updates the dependent stored procedure accordingly.

- **Enclose the object name in double quotes** (""): This solution can also allow object names to be created with some of the special characters such as $, #, and so on. A code sample demonstrating this solution is presented in the section *Handling case-sensitive object names* mentioned in a later section.

With either of these solutions, this issue will have a system-wide impact. SQL Developer assists in this matter by reporting objects that have been renamed when migrating to a new database.

Use of reserved words in object names and their definitions

The Oracle database has a set of reserved words that cannot be used when naming a table, or a column in the table, because they have significance in the database's internal operations. For example, trying to create a table named DATE will fail with an error as shown in the following code:

```
SQL> CREATE TABLE DATE (FIRST_NAME VARCHAR2(30), LAST_NAME VARCHAR2(30),
DEPT VARCHAR2(10), DATE DATE);
```

ERROR at line 1:

ORA-00903: invalid table name

SQL>

Similarly, creating a table with a column named DATE of DATE data type will fail with an error message as shown below:

```
SQL> CREATE TABLE MY_TABLE (FIRST_NAME VARCHAR2(30), LAST_NAME
VARCHAR2(30), DEPT VARCHAR2(10), DATE DATE);
                *

    ERROR at line 1:
    ORA-00904: invalid identifier
    SQL>
```

The earlier example illustrates the fact that DATE is a reserved word which cannot be used as an object name or as a column name in an object definition. Oracle has published a complete list of reserved words that cannot be used as table or column names. This list of reserved words can be found in the Oracle SQL REFERENCE guide: http://download.oracle.com/docs/cd/E11882_01/server.112/e17118/ap_keywd001.htm#BABCJAEB.

There are two solutions for addressing this issue in a similar way to the issue of special characters in object names, renaming the column name that does not conflict with the reserved words in an Oracle database. The second option is to enclose the object name in double quotes ("").

During migration, SQL Developer converts the reserved words from the source database into acceptable object names in Oracle by appending an underscore _, for example: DATE in source database gets converted to DATE_ in Oracle. Basically, SQL Developer renames the column name to avoid the conflict. Changing the names of database objects can have an impact on the applications accessing these objects, as they need to be modified to reflect the new object names in Oracle. To address this and other scenarios where application modifications may be required, Oracle is working towards providing a comprehensive set of tools and technologies that will reduce this effort significantly.

Use of case-sensitive object names

Databases such as Sybase and SQL Server also allow users to create objects in mixed case letters. Users can set the collation parameter for these databases and then all objects that they create will be case-sensitive or case-insensitive depending on the collation parameter. Oracle on the other hand stores all object names in uppercase and allows access in a case-insensitive manner, that is, any query or SQL statement can contain the object names in any case and the database will execute the statement without any issues.

If case-sensitive object names are required in the Oracle database, then the object names have to be enclosed in double quotes (""). The following example demonstrates how to create a table with mixed case letters and enforce the rule that the table has to be represented in that manner in all SQL statements:

```
SQL> create table "MyCase" ("Case_id" number (10), "Case_description"
varchar2(50
));

Table created.

SQL> desc mycase
ERROR:
ORA-04043: object mycase does not exist


SQL> describe "MyCase"
 Name                                      Null?    Type
 ----------------------------------------- -------- ------------------
 -----------

 Case_id                                            NUMBER(10)
 Case_description                                   VARCHAR2(50)
```

```
SQL>
SQL> insert into "MyCase" values (1230,'New Case');

1 row created.

SQL> commit;

Commit complete.

SQL> select * from "MyCase" where "Case_id"=1230;

   Case_id Case_description
---------- --------------------------------------------------------
      1230 New Case

SQL> SQL> select * from mycase where "Case_id"=1230;
select * from mycase where "Case_id"=1230
              *
ERROR at line 1:
ORA-00942: table or view does not exist


SQL> select * from "MyCase" where Case_id=1230;
select * from "MyCase" where Case_id=1230
                             *
ERROR at line 1:
ORA-00904: "CASE_ID": invalid identifier
```

Length of object names

Many databases such as DB2 and SQL Server support object name length up to 128 characters. They also allow column names to be of 128 characters in length. Oracle on the other hand restricts the object name lengths to a maximum of 30 characters as of database version 11*g* R2 (11.2.0.2).

As a result of this restriction, in most migrations there is a possibility that some database objects will have to be renamed to conform to this limitation. This also impacts the applications that refer to these objects, because they need to be updated to reflect the new object names in Oracle.

Every migration tool has its own way of handling this limitation. SQL Developer truncates the object name to less than 30 characters and appends an underscore _ as a suffix. It then includes the affected object name (original and converted name) in its report titled Name changes.

Data type conversion issues

As discussed in *Chapter 4, Oracle Database Migrations*, data type support varies from database to database. Let us take a look at important data types that differ between Oracle and other databases.

Numeric data

NUMBER data type in the Oracle database supports all numeric data storage requirements in addition to FLOAT, BINARY_FLOAT, and BINARY_DOUBLE data types, whereas other databases have many data types such as BIT, INTEGER, SMALLINT, BIGINT, MONEY, and so on. The Oracle database allows columns with data types such as INTEGER, and INT when creating tables, which it converts to NUMBER data type internally. Oracle also supports the BINARY_FLOAT and BINARY_DOUBLE data types that are based on IEEE standards, and hence are not converted to NUMBER data type internally.

In PL/SQL Procedures, the Oracle database allows NUMBER subtype usage such as DECIMAL, NUMERIC, REAL, SMALLINT, and DEC also but it does not affect how the numeric data is treated when storing it or retrieving it from the database.

Using native data types such as FLOAT, BINARY_FLOAT, and BINARY_DOUBLE may result in improved performance when handling large volumes of such data, especially in data warehousing environments because the Oracle database does not have to perform any data type conversions—from internal to platform-specific as it does with the NUMBER data type which is a proprietary implementation character data.

Oracle and other databases differ mostly by the amount of data that is allowed to be stored in character data types like CHAR, and VARCHAR (VARCHAR2 in Oracle). SQL Server 2008 supports up to 8,000 bytes storage in CHAR or VARCHAR data types. Sybase supports up to 4,000 bytes in CHAR/VARCHAR data types. The following table shows the maximum length of the character data types that are allowed in most databases as a reference:

Data Type	Oracle	Sybase	SQL Server	DB2	Informix
CHAR	4,000	255	8,000	32,767	32,767
VARCHAR	4,000	32,767	8,000	32,767	256

Solution: For databases that support data lengths of more than 4,000 bytes, converting to Oracle entails using the CLOB (character large object) data type. SQL Developer allows users to map the source and Oracle data types appropriately during the migration process. Usage of large object data types instead of simple character data types may require application changes where appropriate. LOB (Large Objects) APIs may need to be used instead of direct manipulation of character data.

Identity columns

Many databases support the concept of identity or SERIAL columns in the tables. The main advantage of using this feature is that the database generates unique identifiers for these columns as new records are added to the table. This feature is beneficial for developers because they don't have to write any additional code to implement this functionality on their own. Up until release 11*g* R2 (11.2.0.1), Oracle does not support identity column feature.

Solution: Users migrating to the Oracle database version 11*g* R2 or earlier will have to implement an indirect mechanism to generate a unique identifier when a new record is added to a database table.

For example: the following command in Sybase will create a table with an identity column. Then the Sybase engine will update the column every time a new record is added to the table:

```
create table city_stores
    (store_id numeric(5,0) identity,
    store_description char(30) not null)
```

This feature can be implemented or emulated in Oracle in two ways. One approach is to use a combination of a trigger and sequence on the table to generate the unique identifier when a new record is added to the table. This approach is usually a three step process, as shown in the following steps:

1. Create a table with a numeric column to store the unique identifier. For example:
   ```
   CREATE TABLE dept (
   DEPT_ID          NUMBER(10)     NOT NULL PRIMARY KEY,
   DESCRIPTION   VARCHAR2(50)   NOT NULL);
   ```

2. Create a sequence in the database from which the unique identifiers will be generated every time a new row is added to the table.
   ```
   CREATE SEQUENCE DEPT_SQ START WITH 1 INCREMENT BY 1;
   ```

3. The command creates a sequence that starts with an identifier value of 1. The sequence can be reset to a different value as a starting point for a table that has data in it due to data migration from the source database. All that needs to be done is to determine the maximum value of the identifier and increment it by 1 as the starting value for the sequence.

4. Create a trigger on the table that will populate the unique identifier from the sequence and populate the identifier column in the table.

```
CREATE OR REPLACE TRIGGER dept_trg
BEFORE INSERT ON dept
FOR EACH ROW
WHEN (new.dept_id IS NULL)
BEGIN
   SELECT dept_sq.NEXTVAL
   INTO   :new.dept_id
   FROM   dual;
END;
/
```

This approach allows the generation of unique identifiers for a table without requiring code changes in Oracle. Implementing this approach can result in more database objects such as sequences and triggers in Oracle and potentially affects performance when loading large amounts of data into the table. Secondly, during data migration from the source database, as best practice it is common to disable triggers/constraints/indexes on the tables. So after the data is loaded into the table, the sequence object has to be reset to reflect the current maximum value in the unique column in the table and then the trigger needs to be re-enabled for future operations.

Oracle SQL Developer implements this approach for migration from other databases to Oracle. The schema generated by SQL Developer after the migration will have all the necessary database objects to enable this feature.

The second method is to access the sequence object directly in SQL INSERT statements to generate the unique identifier, when inserting a new record in a table. This approach requires the creation of a sequence for each table that needs to have a different set of unique identifiers generated. The sequence object can be created as shown in step 2 of the previous section. Instead of writing a trigger to generate the unique identifier from the sequence object, users can directly incorporate the sequence as shown in the following SQL Statements:

```
INSERT INTO DEPT (DEPTNO, DNAME, LOC) VALUES (DEPT_SQ.NEXTVAL, 'NEW
DEPT','USA');
```

This approach may involve a lot of code changes if identity columns are used heavily in the source database. If the identity column feature is used only in a couple of tables and the application components that insert data into this table are clearly identified and their number is very small then the second approach can be implemented easily (that is, directly using the sequence object in INSERT statements) as it has no performance overhead.

Date/timestamp data

All databases have different levels for support date/timestamp data. Some databases support a TIME data type to store the time of day. Some databases have separate data types for storing only the time of day, irrespective of the day of the week. Relational databases also differ in granularity of the time data supported by these data types.

The differences in date/timestamp data types supported by some of the most popular databases are depicted below:

Data type	Oracle	IBM DB2	Sybase	SQL Server	Informix
Date	Supports DATE and Time up to seconds	Supports only DATE data without time of the day	Supports only DATE data without time of the day	Supports only DATE data without time of the day	Supports only DATE data without time of the day
Time	Not supported	Supported	Supported	Supported	Not supported
DateTime	Supports using TIMESTAMP data type with time precision up to a microsecond	Supports using TIMESTAMP data type with time in milliseconds	Supported with time precision up to $1/300^{th}$ of a second	Supports with 3 variants of this data type: SMA LLDATETIME, DATETIME,DA TETIME2 data types for varying precisions for time of the day	Supported with time precision up to $1/100000^{th}$ of a second

Some databases also support special data types which are not a standard feature in all relational databases. For example, Sybase/SQL Server supports TIMESTAMP which basically contains binary data maintained by these databases, indicating the time when a particular row in a table was modified. Some applications depend on this information to determine if they need to lock that particular row to update it.

Solution: Oracle does not a have similar feature where it maintains the timestamp for every row in a table to indicate the last update timestamp, so if the application depends heavily on this feature then there are couple of alternatives for migrating to Oracle:

- Re-write the application to remove dependencies on the TIMESTAMP columns in the database
- Implement a pseudo-column to store the timestamp when the row was last updated and use a row level trigger to update the latest timestamp for all updates to the table

It is best not to implement any pseudo-lock optimization (optimistic locking) in client applications when accessing an Oracle database because Oracle supports true row-level locking, and rows in tables are not locked unless a user explicitly locks them. Other databases typically acquire locks when reading data from tables. Oracle on the other hand, acquires row-level locks only when updating the data, not when reading it.

User-defined data types

Migrating user-defined data types from other databases to Oracle can pose some challenges. SQL Developer attempts to convert the basic user defined types that are based on the built-in data types like CHAR, VARCHAR, etc. Usually migrating complex user-defined types from one database to another is difficult.

Solution: Complex user-defined data types from the source database cannot be converted to Oracle by SQL Developer. If an application uses user-defined types extensively then using a third-party tool to migrate such a database would be advisable. Alternatively design changes may be necessary to avoid using user-defined types.

Database feature mapping

Usually all relational databases support the concept of tables and indexes. However, many databases allow proprietary ways of data storage for better performance. In this section, migration of some of those special features to Oracle is discussed.

Clustered indexes

Clustered indexes are special tables supported in SQL Server, Sybase, and other databases. Although most databases have database objects that are called clustered tables and indexes, they differ in their goal and implementation.

In SQL Server, Sybase clustered indexes allow data storage/retrieval in a sorted order based on a set of columns. Usually, the clustered indexes are created on the basis of columns that are always used for data retrieval. They speed up the data retrieval in those databases significantly.

In DB2, clustered indexes actually involve specifying the clause when creating the index on the table. However, in this case the clustered index also dictates the order in which the data is stored in the table.

Solution: In Oracle the clustered index feature can be emulated by using either of the following features:

1. **Index organized tables (IOTs)**: IOTs differ from regular tables in the way data is organized. Regular tables in Oracle are 'heap' organized, that is, data is inserted in any block that has free space available and where they can fit in a random order, whereas in IOTs data is stored in an index defined on the primary key of a table. As a result, data is stored in the order defined by the primary keys, which eliminates the additional IOTs required to read the data blocks because data is now co-located with the primary key in the leaf blocks of the index. A separate primary key index is also not required when using an IOT.

```
CREATE TABLE countries_demo
    ( country_id      CHAR(2)
      CONSTRAINT country_id_nn_demo NOT NULL
    , country_name    VARCHAR2(40)
    , currency_name   VARCHAR2(25)
    , currency_symbol VARCHAR2(3)
    , region          VARCHAR2(15)
    , CONSTRAINT      country_c_id_pk_demo
                      PRIMARY KEY (country_id ) )
   ORGANIZATION INDEX
   INCLUDING    country_name
   PCTTHRESHOLD 2
   STORAGE
     ( INITIAL  4K )
  OVERFLOW
   STORAGE
      ( INITIAL  4K );
```

Notice the keyword, organization index, in the table creation statement. This clause dictates if the table will be heap organized or index organized. Omitting this clause will cause the table to be created as heap organized which is the default. Also, for regular tables the overflow clause of create command is not applicable.

2. **Table clusters**: A table cluster allows data blocks to be shared between tables that share columns between them so they can be grouped together. This feature certainly is not equivalent to the clustered index feature that other databases have, but this features another option to optimize querying of tables by storing the frequently joined table data in the same blocks. A cluster can also be created on a single table. However, table clusters should not be used with tables that are very active—data is added to them quite frequently. These clusters are suitable for static tables with a preferred access path. The following code snippet illustrates the creation of a table cluster:

```
CREATE CLUSTER emp_dept (deptno NUMBER(3))
    SIZE 600
    TABLESPACE users
    STORAGE (INITIAL 200K
        NEXT 300K
        MINEXTENTS 2
        PCTINCREASE 33);

CREATE TABLE emp (
    empno NUMBER(5) PRIMARY KEY,
    ename VARCHAR2(15) NOT NULL,
    . . .
    deptno NUMBER(3) REFERENCES dept)
    CLUSTER emp_dept (deptno);

CREATE TABLE dept (
    deptno NUMBER(3) PRIMARY KEY, . . . )
    CLUSTER emp_dept (deptno);
```

Database schema layout

Many databases such as SQL Server and Sybase support multiple databases in one instance. These databases also support the same schema to be created in more than one database. To allow access to these objects by users in a uniform manner, these databases also allow the database name to be referenced as part of the fully qualified object name. For example: a table named dept under a schema named MySchema which is created in a database named MyDatabase can be referred to as MyDatabase.MySchema.dept.

As Oracle does not support the concept of multiple databases under one instance, the fully qualified object name can only include the schema name such as Schema.ObjectName.

This presents a challenge where the source database allows multi-level object qualification that includes the database name and schema name, whereas in Oracle only a single level qualification is allowed.

Solution: There are couple of ways to address this issue in Oracle:

- Create each schema in each database (from source) as a separate schema in Oracle. Rationalize and consolidate schemas in order to avoid conflicts and duplication. The goal of this exercise is to preserve the schema names as much as possible in Oracle so that the application need not be changed much.

- Re-visit the schema layout design and create a fresh set of schemas in Oracle. This may require code changes if the database and schema names are hardcoded in the SQL Statements in the application.

Empty strings and NULL value handling

Most databases distinguish a character column having a NULL value versus having an empty string, so they support the comparative operators as shown below:

```
Column1 = '' or Column1 = NULL.
```

When a column in these databases is assigned a value of empty string (") then it is not the same as having a NULL value in that column.

In Oracle there is no concept of empty strings. They are all treated as NULL values. So if an application uses an equality predicate as follows: Column1 = " then the SQL Statement will not return any rows.

Solution: Since Oracle does not support the concept of empty strings, it is better to assign NULL values to columns that are expected to have empty strings. The application needs to be updated to reflect the equality predicate as follows: Column1 is NULL.

Data case-sensitivity

Applications need the ability to allow users to perform case-insensitive searches, the advantage being that users don't need to remember the specifics of data patterns (uppercase, lowercase, and mixed case) to search data in their databases. Some databases can be configured to behave in a case-insensitive manner by setting the collation sequence parameter as a database configuration parameter.

However, by default Oracle stores data in a case-sensitive manner. Oracle object names and usernames can be used in a case-insensitive manner, but data in the tables is stored in a case-sensitive manner.

Solution: Case-insensitivity can be implemented in Oracle at three different levels.

- **At the database instance level**: Add the following parameters to the database configuration file (`spfile.ora`) and restart the database instance.

  ```
  NLS_SORT=BINARY_CI (Default value is BINARY)
  NLS_COMP=LINGUISTIC (Default value is ANSI)
  ```

  These two parameters facilitate case-insensitive searches in the database, either by using wildcard searches, for example using the LIKE operator OR the output from sort operations.

- **At a user session level**: To enable case-insensitive searches at a session level, set the two parameters shown as follows:

```
alter session set NLS_SORT ='BINARY_CI';
alter session set NLS_COMP = 'LINGUISTIC';
```

The above commands can also be made part of a logon trigger so that when a user logs on, these parameters are automatically set for that user.

- **At a query level**: To enable case-insensitive searches for a query the following operators need to be used:

```
Select * from emp where NLSSORT ("ENAME",'nls_sort=''BINARY_CI''')
= (NLSSORT('Miller','nls_sort=''BINARY_CI'''))
```

> The NLSSORT (ENAME,nls_sort=''BINARY_CI'') clause on the left hand side of the predicate which is basically for ENAME column of table EMP. Similarly on the right hand side of the predicate the same clause needs to be used on the variable or the constant such as 'miller'. As a result, of using the NLSSORT clause the database performs a case-insensitive query and returns appropriate data.

Users can also use the UPPER() **or** NLS_UPPER() **functions on columns on both sides of the predicate.**

```
Select * from emp where NLS_UPPER(ENAME) = NLS_UPPER('Miller')
```

```
OR
```

```
Select * from emp where UPPER(ENAME) = UPPER('Miller')
```

The only difference between UPPER() and NLS_UPPER() is that NLS_UPPER() as the name suggests has National Language Support—it can be used to sort data in languages other than English.

Regardless of how the case-insensitivity is implemented, there may be a need to build indexes on the character columns on which these types of searches are performed. In the absence of indexes with the NLSSORT clause or NLS_UPPER() or UPPER(), Oracle query optimizer may choose to retrieve the data by performing full table scan instead of using an index. To avoid this scenario an appropriate functional index must be created on the column that is being used for searches as shown below:

```
CREATE INDEX ENAME_IDX ON EMP (NLSSORT
("ENAME",'nls_sort=''BINARY_CI'''));
```
OR

CREATE INDEX ENAME_IDX ON EMP (NLS_UPPER(ENAME));

Using query level implementation for case-insensitive searches will require code mofications whereas using session level or instance level implementation will not require code modifications, but certainly require that affected columns be identified and appropriate indexes are created on them as discussed earlier, so that query performance is not affected. Between session-level implementation and instance-level implementation, instance-level implementation has wider impact, because all queries, data elements will be affected as such extensive testing is required. For session-level implementation the only issue is that the NLS parameters need to be set every time a user establishes a connection either through a database logon trigger or specifying the parameters as part of connection properties or exclusively setting the parameters through ALTER SESSION commands in the application: Byte Order conversions.

Byte order essentially refers to how multi-byte data is represented on systems with different CPU architectures. There are two distinct byte orders that are in use today. One is the LITTLE ENDIAN which is most commonly used in systems based on Intel's x86 processors and the other is BIG ENDIAN which is typically used in systems based on SPARC, POWER/RISC processors. Legacy systems such as IBM mainframes (System Z) running zOS also use the BIG ENDIAN byte order. So it is important that conversion of byte order (or endianness) is considered when migrating data between BIG ENDIAN systems and LITTLE ENDIAN systems. Common operating systems/platforms and their byte ordering can be obtained from an unlikely source Oracle database. V$TRANSPORTABLE_PLATFORM view in Oracle database contains most commonly used platforms and their byte ordering. The following is a list of platforms as per Oracle database 11*g* R1 11.2.0.1.0:

```
SQL> select platform_name, endian_format from v$transportable_platform
order by platform_name asc;
Platform Name                              Byte Order
-------------------                        --------------
AIX-Based Systems (64-bit)                 Big
```

```
Apple Mac OS                                              Big
Apple Mac OS (x86-64)                             Little
HP IA Open VMS                                       Little
HP Open VMS                                            Little
HP Tru64 UNIX                                          Little
HP-UX (64-bit)                                          Big
HP-UX IA (64-bit)                                      Big
IBM Power Based Linux                    Big
IBM zSeries Based Linux                  Big
Linux IA (32-bit)                                                Little
Linux IA (64-bit)                                                Little
Linux x86 64-bit                                                 Little
Microsoft Windows IA (32-bit)     Little
Microsoft Windows IA (64-bit)     Little
Microsoft Windows x86 64-bit      Little
Solaris Operating System (x86)     Little
Solaris Operating System (x86-64) Little
Solaris[tm] OE (32-bit)                         Big
Solaris[tm] OE (64-bit)                         Big
20 rows selected.
SQL>
```

The byte ordering can be different for the same operating system running different chips (micro processors) such as Solaris /Intel x86 vs. Solaris/SPARC.

Conversion is required when transferring Oracle database data files (table space) between platforms with different byte orders. As discussed in *Chapter 4, Oracle Database Migrations*, Oracle utilities like Recovery Manager (RMAN) can convert the byte order for Oracle database data files either at the source system or on the target system. Data exported from Oracle database using DataPump utility and ASCII delimited files do not require byte order conversion. Oracle utilities like SQL*Loader can read data encoded in either byte orders without the need for any conversion.

EBCDIC/ASCII conversions

The EBCDIC and ASCII character set encoding system primarily differ in their usage of 8 bits for representing characters as well as support for certain characters, or lack thereof. EBCDIC encoding system was primarily used by legacy systems like IBM Mainframes. The ASCII encoding scheme was developed in the 1960's and used by most modern systems. Although legacy systems support ASCII encoding as well, many databases running on legacy systems like IBM Mainframe running System z (zOS) continue to store data in EBCDIC. On the other hand, most Unix/Linux systems support ASCII encoding scheme.

When migrating from a database on the legacy systems supporting EBCDIC encoding to a platform that is primarily using ASCII, the data needs to be converted to ASCII from EBCDIC. The data conversion can be done at three places.

- **At the source system**: Basically, at the source system the data can be converted to ASCII when extracting data into flat files for subsequent transfer to the target system. Before the data is converted to ASCII format however, any compressed data types that were used in the source system need to be converted to regular uncompressed data types like NUMERIC or DECIMAL data types first.

- **Conversion during data transfer**: Data can also be converted to ASCII from EBCDIC during the data transfer phase. When using utilities such as FTP, they can convert the data on the fly saving precious CPU cycles in the process.

- **Conversion on the target system**: Finally, conversion can also be done at the target system after it has been extracted from the source system and transferred to the target system. This is usually accomplished by special conversion tools or Oracle utilities, which can do the conversion while reading the data.

Almost all Oracle tools and utilities can read EBCDIC data and convert them into ASCII format while loading data into Oracle. So there is no need to convert data format from EBCDIC to ASCII manually before loading it into Oracle. Here is an example showing how Oracle SQL*Loader utility can be instructed to read EBCDIC data from a file into an Oracle database:

```
OPTIONS (
    SKIP=0,
    ERRORS=1000,
    DIRECT=FALSE
    )
LOAD DATA
CHARACTERSET WE8EBCDIC500
BYTEORDER BIG

INFILE  "C:\SAMPLE.txt"  "FIX 1000"
BADFILE "C:\SAMPLE.bad"
DISCARDFILE "C:\SAMPLE.dsc"
DISCARDMAX 1000
INTO TABLE SCOTT.SAMPLE
TRAILING NULLCOLS
(
    . . . . . . . .
)
```

In the previous code snippet the directive CHARACTERSET WE8EBCDIC500 tells the SQL*Loader utility that the source data is encoded using EBCDIC500 character set. There are many variations of EBCDIC formats in use on the legacy systems, so it is important to use the correct character set in use on the source system. EBCDIC500 appears to be the most common of all. The directive BYTEORDER BIG tells the utility that the byte order is BIG ENDIAN instead of SMALL ENDIAN. As discussed previously, legacy systems like IBM Mainframes running zOS are mostly based on BIG ENDIAN byte order. Another important issue that comes up with EBCDIC to ASCII data conversion is the difference in sort orders for EBCDIC and ASCII data formats. The sort orders differ significantly between EBCDIC and ASCII encoding schemes. For example, when sorting data in EBCDIC format in an ascending order the alphabets are ranked the lowest so they appear first in the list. Whereas when sorting data in ASCII format, the numeric data is ranked lowest and hence they appear first on the list followed by the alphabets.

Here is an example of the difference in the order in which data is returned for the same SQL query in Oracle on UNIX and DB2 on z/OS:

```
SELECT DEPT_ID FROM DEPARTMENT ORDER BY DEPT_ID ASC;
```

Sorted EBCDIC Data in DB2/zOS	Sorted ASCII Data in Oracle on Unix
105A1	10500
105C1	10503
10500	10505
10503	105A1
10505	105C1
20500	20500
20700	20700

Any application that depends on the sorted data returned from the database will have an incorrect order of results. This becomes a big issue when predicates like BETWEEN and GREATER THAN or LESS THAN are used in queries with alphanumeric keys. For example the following query will return data in Oracle where as it will not return data when executed against DB2 on z/OS:

```
select * from departments where dept_id between '10505' and '105G9';
```

Filtered EBCDIC Data in DB2/zOS	Filtered ASCII Data in Oracle on Unix
Now rows returned;	10505
	105A1
	105C1

Solution: The NLS_SORT and NLS_COMP parameters in Oracle database allow users to emulate the EBCDIC sorting and computational behavior even though the data is stored in the database in ASCII format.

The settings for these two parameters for EBCDIC-like behavior are:

```
NLS_SORT=EBCDIC (Default value is BINARY)
NLS_COMP=LINGUISTIC (Default value is ANSI)
```

As discussed earlier for case sensitivity issues, these two parameters can be set at the instance, session or query level as shown in the previous section.

Globalization

With increasing integration of global economies, it has become quite common for corporations to store, manage, present multi-lingual data to their users operating from different locations worldwide. To simplify their operations they need to be able to manage the data from around the globe represented in multiple languages and dialects in an effective manner. To support this requirement, Unicode Consortium which is a non-profit organization devoted to developing, maintaining, and promoting software internationalization standards and data, has come up with the Unicode Standard. This specifies the representation of text in all modern software products and standards and provides the basis for handling text data in all known languages in the world. All databases support globalization in a variety of ways such as database character sets or code pages, collation sequences, support for Unicode data in special data types and support for multi-byte characters with special data types for character and large objects (LOBs).

Here is a list of equivalent Unicode character sets supported by SQL Server, DB2, Sybase and Oracle:

Oracle	DB2	Sybase	SQL Server	Informix
AL32UTF16 (default)	UTF-8,UTF-16	UTF8, UTF 16	UTF 8, UTF-16	UTF 8(1252)
ALT32UTF8				

In Oracle Unicode data can be handled in multiple ways. Oracle supports handling Unicode just as regular data by specifying the AL32UTF16 as the database character set during the database creation. Once the database is created with AL32UTF16 character set, Unicode data can be stored in regular fixed length character data type (CHAR), varying length character data (VARCHAR2) and large object data type (CLOB). The data in these columns can be of mixed type also—Unicode data mixed with ASCII data.

The other option is to use NCHAR/NVARCHAR2/NCLOB data types that are specifically meant to store multi-byte characters required by many languages such as Asian, Arabic, and European. These data types require at least two bytes to store a single character even if the data is ASCII format. They are useful when there are very few tables/columns that store Unicode data in the database.

Sybase supports special data types for storing Unicode data such as Unichar, Univarchar and so on in addition to supporting NCHAR/NVARCHAR data types.

In Oracle, when using Unicode string literals in SQL Statements, the string needs to have the prefix N:

```
Insert into department (department_name) values (N'Finance');
```

For viewing data in another language than the default local language using Windows console applications (MS DOS executables like Oracle SQL*Plus utility or COBOL/C/C++ Programs), it is necessary to perform the following steps:

1. Supplemental language support packages need to be installed on the Windows operating system (Windows XP, Server and so on). In some environments, these are installed by default, but it is worthwhile to make sure they are installed.

   In Windows XP, **Start | Control Panel | Regional & Language** options (**Languages** tab)

2. Set the Oracle environment variables for the intended character set such as, to display Japanese data in US based users the following needs to be set in DOS command prompt:

```
SET NLS_LANG=AMERICAN_AMERICA.JA16SJIS
SET ORA_NCHAR_LITERAL_REPLACE=TRUE
```

The second parameter ORA_NCHAR_LITERAL_REPLACE is required for inserting multi-byte characters into an NCHAR/NVARCHAR2/NCLOB column in Oracle.

Database migration case studies

The following sections are few case studies showcasing successful database migrations from different types of databases such as DB2, Sybase, and Legacy Mainframe databases to Oracle, as well as data integration projects executed by Oracle and partners over the years. These case studies highlight the tools and technologies used in these migration projects and also the business problems that they tried to solve with migration to Oracle. These case studies highlight Oracle partner eco-system proficient in database migrations that have the necessary skill sets and expertise, not only to manage the migration project, but also have subject matter expertise in migrations in general.

Case Study #1: DB2/400 migration to Oracle using Oracle DRDA Gateway for DB2

Customer: Leading business and financial management solutions company for individuals, small businesses, and finance/tax professionals.

Source Environment: IBM system i (AS/400) with DB2.

Challenges: The legacy platform was expensive to maintain as data volume was constantly increasing. At the time of migration the DB2 database size was 6 Terabytes (approximately).

Tools used for data migration: Oracle DRDA Gateway for DB2 was used to migrate and query the data residing in DB2/400 to Oracle RAC database.

Duration: From January 2008 to December 2008.

Benefits: In addition to the benefits of simplified administration and superior performance, the following additional benefits were realized:

- Reduced reporting costs
- Promoted better business intelligence with real-time data warehousing
- Improved availability and scalability through the use of Oracle database clustering technology

Case Study #2: Sybase migration to Oracle

Customer: Leading Bank and financial services company in North America

Challenges: Due to the growth of data resident in the reporting database tables and the limitations of the Sybase product for such large tables, the performance of the processes that load data to the reporting database tables, and the reporting applications that access data from those tables, has degraded to an unacceptable level. To address this issue, the reporting database tables and associate processes are to be converted from Sybase 12.5.3 to Oracle 10g. At a future date, the Sybase reporting database was to be decommissioned.

System Integrator: Tata Consultancy Services, India

Source/Target Environment:

- Frontend: PowerBuilder, Oracle Stored Procedures
- Backend: Unix, C++, Sybase Stored Procedures, Oracle Stored Procedures
- Reporting: Business Objects XIR2 freehand SQL calling Stored procedures
- Direct Connect: Used for connecting Sybase to Oracle

Project Duration: 12 Months + (December 2007 – December 2008)

Business Benefits:

- Short time-to-market
- Better performance of the Oracle procedures – Almost 20 fold increase in performance for ER Scatter Graph result (20 minutes in Sybase and less than a minute in Oracle)
- Quick response time
- Solution to the difference in CT-lib behavior in C++ is implemented in architecture layer, thus avoiding changes to the application

Lessons learned:

- Tool-based testing
- Tool based migration for schema and data
- Difference between Sybase and Oracle behavior
- Sybase Open Server Technology and Sybase Direct Connect
- Performance tuning of the Oracle procedures with the help of Oracle partners
- Oracle and Sybase environment data should be in sync to do complete migration testing

Case Study #3: Mainframe data migration/ archiving from various databases such as DB2, IDMS, and VSAM

Customer: Leading Bank and financial services company in North America

Customer Challenge: Leading Utilities Company servicing customers in Mid-west region of United States

Customer Challenge:

- Replace core legacy applications such as Metering, Billing, Accounting, Supply Chain and Work Management with a modern packaged application

- As a result of implementation of the new packaged application, the historical data was required for compliance and reporting purposes

- 6 TB+ historical data on mainframe needed to be migrated to Oracle 11*g* from various mainframe databases e.g. DB2, IDMS, and VSAM

System Integrator: PracTrans, South Bend, Indiana, USA

Source/Target Environment:

- Mainframe Databases to be migrated:
    - ° 147 IDMS record types
    - ° 1072 DB2 tables
    - ° 3397 Sequential tape files
    - ° 109 VSAM files

- Target Database: Oracle Database 11*g*, 4725 tables, 6 Terabytes (approx.) data

Project Duration: 12 Months (September 2009 – September 2010)

Migration Tasks: PracTrans won a competitive bid for performing this data migration/archival project. Following tasks were executed by PracTrans to successfully complete the project on time.

- Inventory analysis to identify / validate all files that require conversion

- Design, creation, and load of Oracle tables from IDMS, DB2, sequential tape files, VSAM files

- Determine the amount of storage needed for Oracle databases and the temporary storage on the mainframe

- Assist in finalizing hardware and software requirements

- Define and develop the mapping, extracted data and transferred all of the data from the identified systems
- Developed/documented relational database design constructs and standards for Oracle 11*g*
- Customized PracTrans Data Transformation Toolset (DTT) for the customer's environment
- Developed a detailed project plan including detailed tasks, duration, predecessors, successors, all resources, usage, and assignments
- Led customer in the development of test plan and acceptance of the test process

Summary

Regardless of how standards-compliant/database-independent an application is, when the underlying database is migrated, changes need to be made to the application. In this chapter, we covered common challenges that come up during database migrations and how best to address them. Sufficient time needs to be allocated for the analysis and design phase in a database migration project, especially for schema design, issues such as null values handling, case sensitivity, and globalization requirements as they affect the application. Having a good understanding of all these issues will prepare you for challenges that may come up in a migration project. It is worth noting that all database migration efforts may not run into all the challenges mentioned earlier, but readers can have peace of mind knowing that they can anticipate challenges that may lie ahead.

Careful planning and awareness of potential issues and challenges go a long way in executing a database migration project successfully. In the next chapter, the focus will be on addressing data consolidation to avoid duplication and enable master data management.

6
Data Consolidation and Management

I need a single version of the truth. We hear that all the time. This is symptomatic of the growing amount of data on an ever-increasing number of platforms being managed by many different applications, database engines, and hardware infrastructures.

In this chapter, we will lay down the groundwork for the hands-on chapters that follow. Before we do that, we need to introduce some concepts and products to support the notion of data consolidation, what is driving it, and an approach to solving these problems with Oracle products. We will explore this from an application perspective with **Oracle Master Data Management (MDM)** strategy, as well as core technology products like RAC, TimesTen, and Coherence. Also, we will cover some topics regarding **Information Lifecycle Management (ILM)**, data archiving and what that means for heterogeneous data sources. **Software as a Service (SaaS)** and Cloud Computing are growing in momentum and we will discuss some practical strategies for delivering Oracle as a service on the cloud. Finally, this chapter will touch on hardware consolidation options and what that can mean for the enterprise.

What is enterprise data?

Enterprise data. *What does that really mean?* Much has been written on this subject, but for the sake of this discourse, let's try to define this in discrete terms and usages. At Oracle, we view data in one of three ways: **analytical**, **transactional**, and **master**. Analytical data drives decision-making. Transactional data supports the applications, and master data represents the business objects and points upon which transactions are performed and how analytics are built. We can see this model described in the following figure:

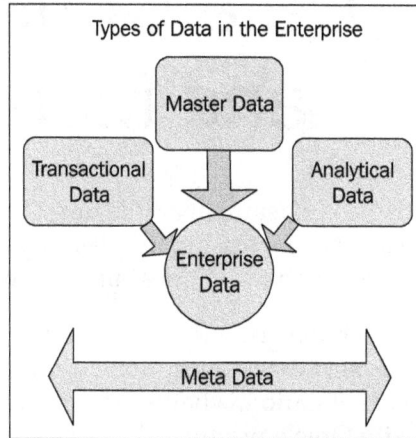

When an organization moves and uses data, it is transformed, changed, and stored in different ways. Incidentally, this introduces some ideas around ILM such as active and passive data archiving, but we are jumping ahead a bit. The description of the data and its characteristics represent a fourth conceptual type of data, called metadata. This will become important as we look at MDM strategies in the coming section. Before we move on to MDM, let us take a moment to dive deeper into these concepts.

Transactional data

A company's operations are supported by applications that automate key business processes. These include areas such as sales, service, order management, manufacturing, purchasing, billing, accounts receivable, and accounts payable. These applications require significant amounts of data to function correctly. This includes data about the objects that are involved in transactions, as well as the transaction data itself. For example, when a customer buys a product, the transaction is managed by a sales application. The objects of the transaction are the Customer and the Product. The transactional data is the time, place, price, discount, payment methods, and so on, used at the point of sale. The transactional data is stored in Online Transaction Processing (OLTP) tables that are designed to support high-volume, low-latency access, and update.

Analytical data

Analytical data is used to support a company's business decision-making, and underpin 'Business Intelligence'. You can examine customer, supplier, and product behaviors in its entirety. This is especially useful when looking into supply chain or value chain issues. Customer buying patterns are analyzed to mark churn, profitability, and market segments. Suppliers can be organized, based on many different attributes which can leverage better supply chain decisions. Product behavior is analyzed over the long term to identify various patterns in performance and quality. All of this data is stored in a data warehouse with structures designed to support heavy aggregation, ad hoc queries, and data mining. Organizations usually store this type of data in very large fact tables surrounded by key dimensions such as customer, product, supplier, account, and location. Fact tables are the centralized table in a 'star schema'. Though this isn't a book on data warehouses, it is important to understand them when looking at analytical data.

The following figure is an example of a fact table on Units, with some added dimensions for product, shipping, and location.

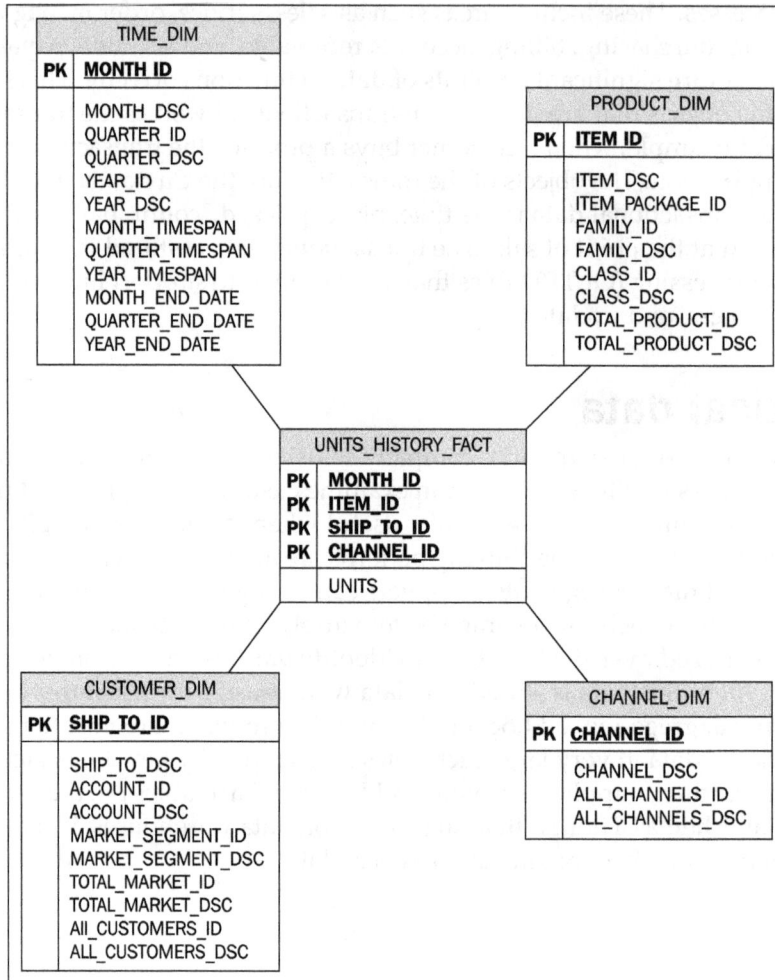

```
┌─────────────────────────────────────────────────────────────────────────────────────┐
│  ┌──────────────────────────┐                                                          │
│  │        TIME_DIM          │                                                          │
│  ├────┬─────────────────────┤                                                          │
│  │ PK │ MONTH ID            │              ┌──────────────────────────┐                │
│  ├────┴─────────────────────┤              │       PRODUCT_DIM        │                │
│  │  MONTH_DSC               │              ├────┬─────────────────────┤                │
│  │  QUARTER_ID              │              │ PK │ ITEM ID             │                │
│  │  QUARTER_DSC             │              ├────┴─────────────────────┤                │
│  │  YEAR_ID                 │              │  ITEM_DSC                │                │
│  │  YEAR_DSC                │              │  ITEM_PACKAGE_ID         │                │
│  │  MONTH_TIMESPAN          │              │  FAMILY_ID               │                │
│  │  QUARTER_TIMESPAN        │              │  FAMILY_DSC              │                │
│  │  YEAR_TIMESPAN           │              │  CLASS_ID                │                │
│  │  MONTH_END_DATE          │              │  CLASS_DSC               │                │
│  │  QUARTER_END_DATE        │              │  TOTAL_PRODUCT_ID        │                │
│  │  YEAR_END_DATE           │              │  TOTAL_PRODUCT_DSC       │                │
│  └──────────────────────────┘              └──────────────────────────┘                │
└─────────────────────────────────────────────────────────────────────────────────────┘
```

TIME_DIM
PK	MONTH ID
	MONTH_DSC
	QUARTER_ID
	QUARTER_DSC
	YEAR_ID
	YEAR_DSC
	MONTH_TIMESPAN
	QUARTER_TIMESPAN
	YEAR_TIMESPAN
	MONTH_END_DATE
	QUARTER_END_DATE
	YEAR_END_DATE

PRODUCT_DIM
PK	ITEM ID
	ITEM_DSC
	ITEM_PACKAGE_ID
	FAMILY_ID
	FAMILY_DSC
	CLASS_ID
	CLASS_DSC
	TOTAL_PRODUCT_ID
	TOTAL_PRODUCT_DSC

UNITS_HISTORY_FACT
PK	MONTH_ID
PK	ITEM_ID
PK	SHIP_TO_ID
PK	CHANNEL_ID
	UNITS

CUSTOMER_DIM
PK	SHIP_TO_ID
	SHIP_TO_DSC
	ACCOUNT_ID
	ACCOUNT_DSC
	MARKET_SEGMENT_ID
	MARKET_SEGMENT_DSC
	TOTAL_MARKET_ID
	TOTAL_MARKET_DSC
	All_CUSTOMERS_ID
	ALL_CUSTOMERS_DSC

CHANNEL_DIM
PK	CHANNEL ID
	CHANNEL_DSC
	ALL_CHANNELS_ID
	ALL_CHANNELS_DSC

Master data

Master data represents the key business objects that are shared across multiple applications within the enterprise. This data represents the business objects around which the transactions are executed and holds key information around customers, transactions, products, employees, and so on. This data also represents the conformed dimensions components, around which analytics are executed. Master data creates a single version of the truth about these objects across the operational IT landscape.

I was recently working with a law enforcement agency in the United States. In this situation, the various enforcement agencies and courts systems had a very difficult time flagging and identifying offenders when they were apprehended due to multi data types, storage facilities, and methods to integrate. In one situation, an offender was released before the various systems were able to determine that this individual was wanted on an existing arrest warrant. This was because there was no single Master Data Hub. As a result, this person went on to commit some major violent offenses, instead of being detained. This is an example where we see the absence of data integration and the management of master data can affect public safety.

A MDM solution should to be able to manage most of the master data objects. These include account, assets, customer, product, supplier, and site data. Other objects can be stored as well. For example, we often see things like invoices, campaigns, and service requests, which need to be maintained across applications and need the consolidation, cleansing, and distribution services. Of course, this will all depend on which industry you are in and which objects are core to your business operations.

It is also important to note that since MDM supports transactional applications, it must support extreme volume transaction rates. *What does that mean, really?* If you are going to have a performant master data, it must reside in data models designed for OLTP environments and thus running on a backbone of infrastructure that can support that. We will examine the Exadata 2 Database Machine in later sections of the chapter to see how these types of applications can be supported.

True business value is derived from managing both transactional and analytical master data. We call this type of solution Enterprise MDM. If we can gain efficient operational data across all applications and create meaningful analysis dimensions; we can gain true insight into our operations, markets, and potential.

We believe that Oracle provides the most dynamic and versatile Enterprise MDM solutions on the market. The next sections will cover some of the key concepts that Oracle defines around MDM with respect to the customer, product, supplier, and site data management hubs.

We see companies spending millions of dollars buying, integrating, and maintaining business applications of all types. However, executives often have a very limited aggregate view of what this means to the business, both operationally and physically. Achieving a 'single source of truth' is a challenge in any company and a rationalized view of applications is even harder to achieve. Executives are making critical business decisions on intuition rather than on credible information. The financial risks of this all-too-common scenario are startling. Further, federal regulations like Sarbanes-Oxley have essentially created a mandate for complete and accurate data.

From marketing activities, to supply chain operations, to the financial department, all aspects of an organization rely on customer data at some level. This is often the most disparate view, however. The result is an enterprise with extremely silo'd data that do not collaborate across the organization. This is exacerbated by the lack of standardization for data within the organization, so that when sharing does happen, it is quite difficult to rationalize which data is correct or the most current.

What can we do about that? Of course, through the enterprise data hub model we can provide a comprehensive and efficient single version of truth solution. With the Master Data Hub, we can aggregate both legacy and third-party data, along with active data and put it centrally in an online repository. The elegance of the hub environment is that the single version of truth can be achieved without disrupting existing business processes or requiring costly reinvestments. In addition, all data quality and data maintenance services can be centrally maintained and managed, with the clean and standardized data flowing throughout the organization and available to all users across all departments.

The true value in an enterprise data hub is grasping the idea that key data can be shared, with integrity, across the entire organization rather than kept departmentally and hidden. Think of the analysis time saved simply in trying to go cross departments to gather and rationalize data. With this, we now truly have a single version of the truth.

Enterprise data hub

Our walk through the hub world takes us to the idea of creating an enterprise data hub to actually manage these types of data concepts. Practically speaking, the enterprise data hub is an operational system working in a real-time manner. When data comes into the hub, we can automatically standardize it through cleansing, deduplication, and transformation. This is how we can create a unified view of data across the enterprise.

Oracle Master Data Management

Now that we have covered some key concepts and definitions around data management, we can build upon that with the MDM process.

Let us look at the following figure:

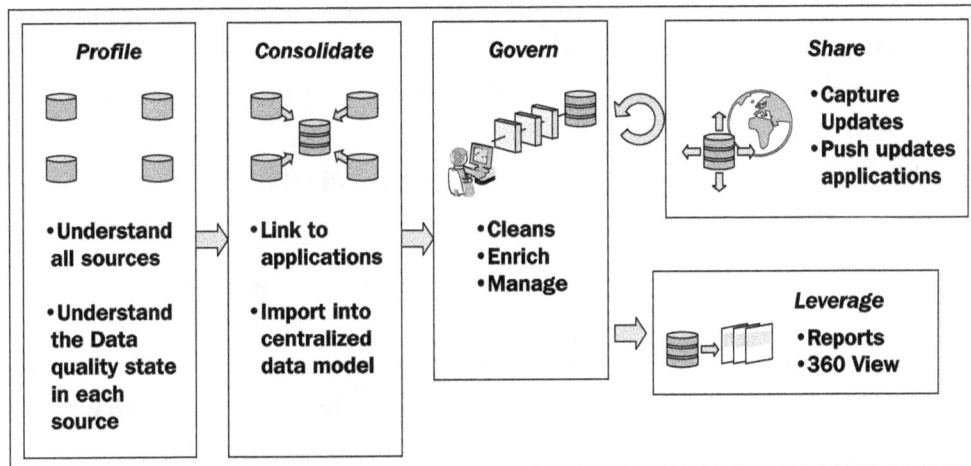

This model demonstrates the key processes of the MDM process.

- **Profile the master data**: This stage allows us to rationalize where all of the data is coming from and the state of the data
- **Consolidate**: Consolidates data into a central repository
- **Govern the master data**: Here, we clean up the data, run it through a deduplication process, and possibly augment it with information from third-party applications
- **Share it**: This is where an organization can expose this single version of truth across the entire organization
- **Leverage it**: This means that we can do something meaningful with the data

Now that we have a high-level approach to the MDM process, we will dive into some of the key hubs in the MDM product suite.

Oracle Customer Hub

The **Oracle Customer Hub (OCH)** is Oracle's lead Customer Data Integration (CDI) solution. OCH's comprehensive functionality enables an enterprise to manage customer data over the full customer lifecycle—capturing customer data, standardization, and correction of names and addresses; identification and merging of duplicate records; enrichment of the customer profile; enforcement of compliance and risk policies; and the distribution of the single source of truth best version customer profile to operational systems.

OCH is a source of clean customer data for the enterprise. The primary roles are:

- To consolidate and govern unique, complete, and accurate master customer information across the enterprise
- To distribute this information as a single point of truth to all operational and analytical applications just in time

To accomplish this, OCH is organized around the five MDM pillars:

1. Trusted customer data is held in a central MDM schema.
2. Consolidation services manage the movement of master data into the central store.
3. Cleansing services deduplicate, standardize, and augment the master data.
4. Governance services control access, retrieval, privacy, audit, and change management rules.
5. Sharing services include integration, web services, event propagation, and global standards-based synchronization.

These pillars utilize generic services from the MDM foundation layer, and extend them with business entity-specific services and vertical extensions.

While a Customer hub can make the IT organization more agile, the major benefit is realized in the business side by enabling business growth through enhancing operational efficiency and improving the organizational standardization. Businesses can obtain revenue growth by building a customer spending model and thus creating product cross-sell opportunities. Improvements in operational efficiency can be avoided and realized through the reduction of human errors and B2B information sharing. Risk and compliance are major concerns for organizations, and a customer hub solution enables organizations to reduce its compliance risks and credit risk costs. One final point is that the IT agility of the organization increases by reducing integration costs and time to take new applications to market.

Oracle Product Hub

The Oracle Product Hub (OPH) is an enterprise data management solution that
enables organizations to centralize all critical product information from different
types of systems, thereby creating a single view of a product, giving managers
a unified view of product information available across the enterprise. The OPH
helps customers eliminate product data fragmentation, which is a problem, that
can form disjointed supply chains, legacy systems, and disparate processes that
often arise from growth or acquisition. The OPH, along with Oracle Product Data
Synchronization, are a part of Oracle's Product MDM solution. Oracle's Product
Information Management (PIM) solution helps companies manage business
processes around activities such as centralizing their product master, managing sell-
side or buy-side PIM catalogs, and integrating their structure management. These
tools are not specific to any one industry or foundational architecture, meaning, it
can be integrated with legacy systems in any vertical. The key here is that it is an
enabling technology for a well-managed value chain.

Oracle Supplier Hub

The Oracle Supplier Hub (OSH) is the application that unifies and shares critical
information about an organization's supply base. It does this by enabling customers
to centralize all supplier information from heterogeneous systems, to create a single
view of supplier information that can be leveraged across all functional departments.

Oracle Supplier Hub capabilities

The Oracle Supplier Hub delivers:

- A pre-built extensible data model for mastering supplier information at the
  organizational and site levels–both for buyers and suppliers
- A single enterprise-wide 360-degree view of supplier information
- Plug-ins to allow third parties to enrich supplier data
- A unlimited number of predefined and user-defined attributes for
  consolidating supplier-specific information
- Web services to consolidate and share supplier data across disparate systems
  and processes

The complexities of global supply chains, extended supplier networks, and geopolitical risks are forcing organizations to gain more control and to better manage their supplier data. Moreover, companies today are hard-pressed to govern and to maintain their supplier data in a way that helps them sufficiently understand it. From process-related issues like on-boarding, assessment and maintenance, to data- related issues such as completeness and deduplication of information, there has been no trusted solution in the market to address these two sides of the supplier information management problem until the arrival of the Oracle Supplier Hub and Oracle Supplier Lifecycle Management combination.

Together, these applications provide tremendous business advantages — chiefly, they enable spend tracking and supplier risk management. Without the Supplier Hub, supplier information sits in different procurement systems across different geographies, divisions, and marketplaces. Senior-level management has a better window into enterprise-wide spend when all that information is consolidated into one repository. Simply put, centralized, clean data creates visibility into spend. Spend visibility creates opportunities for cost reduction. Once data becomes centralized, decision-makers are better equipped to see which suppliers cost more and which have been performing better. Furthermore, they can create opportunities by running reports on particular attributes. For example, if a user consolidates their data and then sees they have been procuring computer monitors in different regions from three different suppliers, they may opt for a sole-source contract with just one of them in order to drive their costs down.

Beyond that, supplier management enables supplier risk management. According to AMR research, it costs companies between $500 and $1,000 to manage each supplier annually. Employing a technology solution can reduce that cost by upwards of 80 percent. By enabling suppliers to manage themselves, not only does the streamlined process cut costs, but by reducing their barrier to entry into the user's business, supplier management creates opportunities to do business with an expanded set of suppliers. Furthermore, buyer administrators mitigate their risk of engaging in business with suppliers who fail to comply with corporate or government-set standards when users can track that information with a rich data model.

Oracle Site Hub

Oracle Site Hub is a master data solution that enables organizations to centralize site and location information from heterogeneous systems. The key concept here is that with site location information put into a single or aggregated view, all departments within an organization can look at data, processes, and analysts in concert. Business users can eliminate stale, duplicated, and fragmented data that comes from silo'd applications and data stores. More importantly, this can be collected and managed from multiple data stores and platforms. Entropy and disorganization comes rapidly to any organization of a large size as a result of growth, management change, and mergers.

The Oracle Site Hub key capabilities include (Think MDM concepts here):

- **Trusted site data**: Creates and maintains unique, complete, clean, and accurate master data information across the enterprise, maintains cross-references to source data track historical changes
- **Consolidate**: mass import site information into a trusted global single source of truth master repository; cleanse, normalize, cleanse, validate, and enrich master data, leveraging trusted sources for master information (sites, addresses, and so on)
- **Govern**: Manages the Overall Site Lifecycle and fully automates the Organization Data Governance process; defines and executes security
- **Share**: Deploys a 360-degree view of sites and related information, distributes master data information to all operational and analytical applications just in time

Oracle Site Hub delivers a competitive advantage in site-driven business decisions. Site Hub provides a complete repository for all site-specific data throughout the entire lifecycle of a site. Site Hub leverages web services and integration with Oracle E-Business Suite applications to provide a holistic data hub for site data.

Oracle RAC

The core enabler for Oracle's Data Management capabilities revolves around Oracle **Real Application Cluster (RAC)** technology. There have been many discussions about RAC, so we don't have a lot of new things to say here, but it is certainly worth a mention at a high level. The following figure shows a typical RAC implementation. We can use this model to describe what RAC technology is.

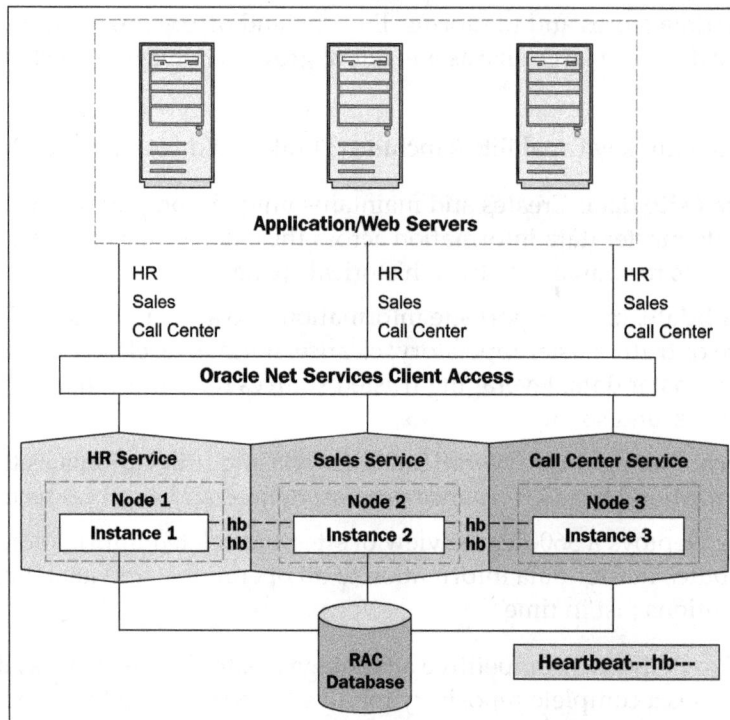

Oracle RAC databases differ architecturally from single-instance Oracle databases in that each Oracle RAC database instance also has:

- At least one additional thread of redo for each instance
- An instance-specific undo table-space

The combined processing power of the multiple servers can provide greater throughput and Oracle RAC scalability than is available from a single server.

Traditionally, an Oracle RAC environment is located in one data center, but you can configure Oracle RAC on an extended distance cluster. This is an architecture which provides fast recovery from a site failure and allows for each node at all of the sites to actively process transactions as part of single database cluster.

Oracle RAC is a singularly differentiating technology that provides high availability and scalability for any kind of application. Oracle RAC is an integral component for implementing the Oracle enterprise grid computing architecture. Having multiple instances of access to a single database prevents the server from being a single point of failure. Oracle RAC enables organizations to build smaller commodity servers into a cluster to create scalable environments that support mission critical business applications, or with Exadata (more on that later) deploy a database and an online transaction processing (OLTP) machine that outperforms even the mainframe.

Data grids using Oracle caching

Data does not have to be limited to storage and management in a fixed stored source, but also within a data grid. With data grids, we can leverage in memory data caches with either a real-time database like TimesTen or a data object cache like Coherence. Both of these technologies are key aspects of data management and consolidation. With TimesTen, we can take legacy data sources from say, Sybase, Band put them in a highly accessible in-memory data grid. In addition, we can make heterogeneous data accessible from say, the mainframe, to Java applications through Coherence in-memory database cache. This allows us not only to make data accessible across the enterprise, but also creates a low cost platform, reducing Millions of Instructions Per Second (MIPS) consumption on the mainframe to access data. As the data is cached in Java objects, the application is not concerned where the actual data source is, and thus has achieved a level of heterogeneous data consumption. This is not meant to be a tutorial on Coherence and TimesTen, though it is helpful to cover these topics as components needed for any integrated data environment.

An in-memory database cache grid provides horizontal scalability in performance and capacity. A cache grid consists of a collection of Oracle In-Memory Database Caches (IMDB Cache) that collectively manage an application's cached data. Cached data is distributed between the grid members and is available to the application with location transparency and transactional consistency across all grid members. Online addition and removal of cache grid members are performed without service interruption to the application.

Applications using IMDB Cache may choose to configure a combination of caching options:

- Read-only caches where updates are performed in the Oracle database and refreshed to the cache
- Updatable caches where transactions are performed in the cache and then propagated to the Oracle database

- Cache data may be loaded on-demand or preloaded, and may be shared across the cache grid members or reside in a specific cache node

Depending upon data access patterns and performance requirements, an application may choose to allocate specific data partitions to some grid members for locality optimizations, or it may choose to make all data available to all grid members for location transparency. The cache grid software manages cache coherency and transactional consistency across the grid members.

Data synchronization with the Oracle database is performed automatically. Updates to the in-memory cache tables are asynchronously or synchronously written to the Oracle database, depending upon the desired trade-off between performance and consistency. Synchronous write-through will ensure that, if the Oracle database cannot accept the update(s), the transaction is rolled back from the cache database. In contrast, asynchronous write-through leverages the speed of Oracle TimesTen by first committing the transactions locally, and then using asynchronous write-through to send the updates to the Oracle database. Asynchronous write-through cache groups provide better application response time and transaction throughput.

For read-only cached groups, incremental updates in the Oracle database are asynchronously refreshed to the in-memory cache tables in the application tier, at user-specified intervals.

IMDB Cache is designed to continue running even after the Oracle database server or network connection has been lost. Committed transactions to the cache tables are tracked and, once the connection is restored, they are propagated back to the Oracle database. Similarly, committed transactions to the cached tables in the Oracle database are tracked and refreshed to the TimesTen in-memory database, once the connection to the Oracle database is re-established.

Availability is an essential requirement for most real-time applications. High availability for in-memory cache tables is provided through real-time transactional replication.

TimesTen gives a data-centric focus and Coherence gives us an application-centric view of the data. Let us look at these a bit more and unpack this idea.

Database-centric—TimesTen

As we discussed earlier, we pointed out that Oracle TimesTen IMDB is a memory-optimized, relational database that provides applications with extremely fast response times and very high throughput, as required by many applications in a wide range of industries. What does this mean for data consolidation? By abstracting from applications the assumption about where data runs (IE, in memory for this case), we can start to look at bringing different data stores together and pinning the needed data in memory and archiving legacy data in more efficient means. With TimesTen as a consolidation platform, architects can have the needed data faster, as it is in memory, and archival data stored, thus saving storage costs while increasing availability.

Application-centric—Coherence

Coherence provides replicated and distributed (partitioned) data management and caching services on top of a reliable, highly-scalable peer-to-peer clustering protocol. Coherence has no single point of failure; it automatically and transparently fails over and redistributes its clustered data management services whenever a server crashes or is disconnected from the network. When a new server is added, or when a failed server is restarted, it automatically joins the cluster and Coherence failover services to that node, transparently redistributing the cluster load. Coherence includes network-level fault tolerance features and transparent soft restart capability to enable servers to self-heal.

Again how does this help for consolidation and integration? Much like TimesTen, we can look at data more as a commodity rather than something tied to a particular DMBS system. Where TimesTen is an in-memory database store, Coherence is an in-memory object cache of data. The source of the data doesn't matter to the cache and thus to the application. So, as we begin to look at bringing data stores from SQL Server, DB2 even older versions of Oracle into one version of the truth, we can just modify our object cache to pull from the needed source. This strategy enables a cleaner and more transparent transition for the applications and thus the business.

Oracle as a service

In the cloud computing space, there is a growing demand for a database as a service. The industry has moved from the Application Service Provider (ASP) to a multi-faceted cloud model including, **Software-as-a-Service (SaaS)**, **Platform-as-a-Service (PaaS)**, and **Infrastructure-as-a-Service (IaaS)**. With the growing trend for private clouds, we have seen an increase in demand for the Oracle database to be delivered as a PaaS model. There are several cloud providers, including the Amazon Cloud that provides Oracle as a database on demand.

Oracle as a Service (**OaaS**) allows large enterprises to consolidate disparate data sources and leverage underutilized cycles. We see this implemented on every type of hardware infrastructure from commodity-based services, Linux on Z to Exadata (more on Exadata later in the chapter). In each of these situations, database owners would consolidate heterogeneous data sources such as DB2, Sybase, and SQL Server to an Oracle platform. In some situations, such as in governments, the central IT office would provide a hosted database environment so that each supported agency or ministry did not have to have its own infrastructure and database administrators. Though not a formal definition in the cloud, we can introduce the OaaS design pattern that has been applied as a number of strategic customers has delivered significant business benefit. It is typically deployed as follows:

- Construction of one, or more, clusters consisting of standardized commodity hardware components that hosts these shareable Oracle instances

- Establishment of procedures for project and application support teams to engage with the Oracle shared services team and to have their database applications hosted in this environment

- Definition of a cost, funding, and operational model for the shared Oracle environment and the organization's IT operations team

Reasons to consider Consolidation

In the current economic climate, keeping recurring operational costs down is imperative. Consolidation will assist the reduction of total cost of ownership (TCO) in several ways, including envisaged savings in hardware, software, and hosting, as follows:

- **Reduced administration**: By standardizing and reducing the number of servers, businesses reduce the complexity of the infrastructure they must administer. Fewer support staff can therefore manage the same service demands. This standardization also facilitates the provision of 24/7 support using worldwide support resources.

- **Reduced operational costs**: Increase in service capacity and growth are achieved with better utilization of resources. Typically, fewer servers are required, resulting in hardware and power savings.

- **Reduced data centre costs**: Site space formerly used for IT services can be returned to the business, and existing facilities can be used more efficiently.

- **Reduced data centre hosting costs**: Typically, hosting contracts are based on infrastructure under management — the less infrastructure under management, the less the cost.

- **Reduced revenue loss through higher uptime/availability**: Consolidation reduces the cost of implementing high-availability solutions, which reduces revenue losses due to downtime.

- **Improved service management**: By standardizing and reducing the complexity of the service infrastructure, organizations facilitate more effective service management processes, tools, and automated system administration.

- **Simplified contingency planning solutions**: A simpler service infrastructure means that more services can be restored when a site failure occurs.

- **Improved quality of service (QoS)**: Consolidation will facilitate improvement in application uptime and will deliver higher systems performance.

- **Increased reliability and availability**: Server consolidation makes it more economic to provide high-availability configurations and dedicated support staff. Organizations also benefit from implementing better storage management and service continuity solutions.

- **Improved performance**: Standardized systems deliver more predictable performance, and proprietary technologies such as data compression can improve query response times.

- **Improved infrastructure agility**: In uncertain times, flexibility and the ability to respond quickly to changing needs of the business can help to maintain the competitive edge. Consolidation results in a more standardized, centralized, and dynamic infrastructure, which makes it possible for systems to be more responsive to change and to quickly adapt to business needs.

- **Improved consistency**: Consolidation improves interoperability, and makes systems more productive and easier to manage.

- **Better integration**: A consolidated platform provides for easier, and cheaper, systems integration, which improves data consistency and reduces the complexity of tasks such as extract, transform, and load (ETL) operations.

- **Centralized management**: As consolidation facilitates centralized management, it becomes easier to implement standard policies across your systems.

- **Reduced carbon footprint**: With greater emphasis on sustainability, many organizations are striving to reduce the environmental impact that their activities have. Consolidation enables organizations to reduce their energy consumption by using less hardware, as well as by using the hardware more efficiently.

- **Improved resource utilization**: Most applications that utilize Oracle elect to provision the server/s with capacity that will exceed their maximum peak load. It is a global phenomenon that many database servers run at low utilization rates. In a consolidated deployment model, idle capacity across this infrastructure can be reclaimed by reducing the total number of required servers while not affecting application performance or availability.

Information Lifecycle Management

As we look at managing data with MDM and data hubs, we often have to deal with aging data and database management platform systems. This is where we can introduce the notion of Information Lifecycle Management (ILM). ILM enables practitioners to save money and resources by managing where old data lives, how to get it, and when. To further complicate the issue, ILM strategies have to incorporate aging platforms and RDMS systems, and even pre-relational data. In the world of ILM, we introduce the idea of active data archiving and passive data archiving. Which option to use depends upon when and how you need the data.

Active data archiving

Active data archiving is where the data has been archived and partitioned away from the current application data, but is available quickly to the live application. This type of archiving can be maintained through an appliance or legacy data retrieval system.

Passive data archiving

Passive data archiving is data that is stored and not accessible in real-time by currently used applications. Often, this data and its reports are stored and retrieved in a remote location and access to the data can take some time to retrieve. It is cheap to store, but can be time-consuming to acquire. This is mostly used for legal storage reasons as is the case for financial records or government storage.

Oracle Exadata

The Oracle Exadata Database Machine is an easy to deploy, pre-configures configured solution for hosting the Oracle database that delivers the absolute highest levels of database performance available today. Benchmarking studies have shown that queries can execute 10 times faster, and we have some antidotal stories of even more performance. It is important to note that we are not talking about a 10 percent to 20 percent increase, but actual multiples of 10. This is not just marketing speak, but actual experience we have had in the field.

So, what's so special about the Exadata Database Machine? Think of it as a cloud in a box composed of database servers, Oracle Exadata Storage Servers, an InfiniBand fabric for storage networking and all the other components required to host an Oracle database.

Further, there is onboard smart flash cache that is specially configured and controlled to run the database. It delivers outstanding I/O and SQL processing performance for OLTP, data warehousing (DW), and consolidation of mixed workloads. Extreme performance is delivered for all types of database applications by leveraging a massively parallel grid architecture using Real Application Clusters and Exadata storage. Database Machine and Exadata storage delivers breakthrough performance with linear I/O scalability, is simple to use and manage, and delivers mission critical availability and reliability. Queries are actually executed on the storage device in extremely efficient ways so that some queries that take hours can be reduced to seconds, and that–again–isn't just marketing speak.

We could write an entire book on Exadata, it's features, benefits, and influence on the cloud, but we will touch on one key technology advancement, which is offloading SQL Query parsing. This is where a lot of the performance gains are found. SQL Query Offloading means that the storage servers can apply filters within the storage layer, instead of shipping every possible result set back to the database server. Additionally, the volume of data returned can be reduced by column projection. For example, if you select one column from a 200 column table, the server will not return or process the other 199 columns.

What we are seeing is a movement toward the consolidation of Oracle data stores as well as non-oracle data to the Exadata platform. There is nothing special about how to migrate non-Oracle data to Exadata, the steps and processes explained in this book will work just as well with Exadata. It is 11*g* after all.

Data management at IHOP, a case study

The restaurant chain IHOP perfectly illustrates the 'on the ground' financial potential of the enterprise data hub model. IHOP's corporate headquarters realized that the organization lacked a view into its franchises and wanted better visibility into the day-to-day operations of each of its locations. Unfortunately, each franchise maintained its own data such as legal, finance, operations, marketing, and so on. Each franchise also had its own resources devoted to managing that data. As a result, poor business decisions were being made and operational errors were occurring too frequently. In short, executives and managers could not vouch for the very data they were relying on to make key business decisions.

IHOP has begun to deploy its version of a data hub—a franchise data hub to collect all the different 'silos' of information. In doing so, the company not only eliminated the need for multiple data managers, but also ensured that every department could see every interaction that had taken place with every customer. The second phase of the deployment will focus on gathering customer data and feedback from its frequent diner programs and complaint cards to better service customers and improve targeted marketing campaigns.

This unified view will impact IHOP's operations at every level. At the service level, customer interactions will become more efficient. From a strategic standpoint, IHOP will be better equipped with real-time access to critical data on customer spending habits and regional trends that it hasn't had before. The hub will also collect data from the restaurant's point-of-sale systems and various business applications (which will manage finance, human resources, and so on.) to get a clear, accurate view of all the information that is coming out of each restaurant.

Enterprise data can only reveal so much. While sales numbers may tell how much business was done in Europe for the last fiscal quarter, they won't reveal that only 25 percent of deals were closed, or that a major customer broke off negotiations and subsequently signed a contract with a competitor. Marketing totals also will not explain local purchasing trends, average lead generation costs or how effective a national marketing campaign was in targeting a specific audience.

These and countless other business answers can be extracted from a centralized Customer Data Hub. With built-in analytic tools, managers can model customers in all their complexity and look at customer data consolidated from across all operations, rolled up into hierarchical structures (such as a family of companies or households), or graphically segmented for analysis. This real-time visibility allows fact-based decisions to drive change and increase efficiency. The financial picture is dynamic, and can be adapted to reflect sudden market changes or windows of opportunity, such as spikes in supply or demand.

To be meaningful, customer data must be up-to-date and fit to be reported. With scores of data silos around the world, companies today operate with huge information blind spots. It can take weeks or even months to collect, reconcile and analyze corporate performance data. And at a time when corporate accountability is under intense scrutiny, corporate and financial officers need current, enterprise-wide business intelligence. This need is driving adoption of the data hub model, which offers several distinct advantages.

With built-in integration and data management, information from across the enterprise can be centrally located and stored. With access to this customer data, companies can analyze information across multiple product lines, geographies, departments, and applications. Third-party content can be leveraged to augment and verify customer information, as well as to keep abreast of changing corporate relationships. As a result, hub users can improve business operations and strategies by enriching the quality of their data, without having to replace their IT infrastructure. And as businesses grow, they can scale their current systems without sacrificing integration.

Summary

In this chapter, we have opened the book, as it were, on many topics in the sphere of integration and migration of data. We began the chapter laying the foundation by addressing some of the reasons that propel an organization to tackle this problem, while addressing some of the unique challenges that one will face both from a technical and business perspective. Next, we began to unpack some of the approaches to integration, which will provide the foundation in the coming chapters when we get more hands-on. Finally, we explored an example of a real-world firm that has dealt with migration and integration issues. In the upcoming chapters, we will begin to get more hands-on training and look into specific tools and techniques, as well as more in-depth case studies.

7
Database-centric Data Integration

Database-centric data integration involves data interchange between different databases, either in asynchronous or on-demand in the context of active transactions, or bulk data merges between source and target databases. The earliest information integration techniques involved exchanging data between different databases/applications through flat files. This data interchange using flat files made the data integration processes a batch process. This approach is in use even today, due to its technical simplicity and lower cost in terms of use of native database utilities. Organizations do not need to buy expensive proprietary tools or technologies.

However, the need for access to data in real-time, that is, when executing a transaction such as checking the current stock level for an item, current account balances, confirmation of address, ascertaining credit scores while processing loan applications, and so on, has increased with the advent of internet computing. These types of requirements have forced database vendors to come up with solutions that can provide direct access to the other databases using database-specific or standards-based tools and technologies. These solutions provide the technology for a seamless interaction between two databases leveraging native features, SQL Translation, and so on. Today, with all the available technologies, database-centric data integration is possible in following ways:

- **Exchange of flat files (delimited)**: This approach is typically used for batch applications where data changes from one database are propagated to another database during off-peak hours or at regular intervals. But this method also has drawbacks, such as the data changes in the source database are not immediately visible in the target databases, making the data in the target database stale.

- **Online data access using gateways/adapters**: As the name suggests, gateways/adapters allow databases to access data from other databases in real-time. In addition to real-time data access, gateways/adapters also increase developer productivity by supporting native SQL Translation capabilities as well as data type mappings and enabling integration at the database layer in stored procedures, triggers, and SQL Statements. A major downside to these tools and technologies is that they are proprietary and are not free for use.

- **Online data access using ODBC/JDBC drivers**: There are gateways that leverage ODBC or JDBC drivers instead of proprietary gateways as a mechanism to connect to different databases. This provides the best of both worlds, that is, it uses standard interfaces for integration and it is able to leverage native Oracle SQL semantics. There are, however, restrictions in terms of the level of support for different databases that can be accessed through ODBC and also less support for native database features (target) compared to the database gateways/adapters.

- **Data replication**: Data replication tools have been around for quite some time. Data replication removes the complexity of accessing different databases from the application by making the changes in data of other databases available locally. However, setting up data replication between two or more databases can be a cumbersome task as restrictions are placed on what management tasks can be performed on objects that are participating in data replication, and they may put constraints on the system resources under heavy load. Data replication features in databases typically support both the asynchronous or synchronous mode. The synchronous mode of data replication is usually implemented to distribute load across multiple database servers in distributed architecture ensuring data availability at all sites, if and when a transaction occurs. The asynchronous mode of replication on the other hand is used to replicate data for reporting, data aggregation, and so on. Data replication is implemented in two ways:

    ○ **Using triggers**: Since most RDBMSs support triggers, they are the earliest mechanisms used for data replication between databases. Typically, triggers were used to write data changes in a log table that was used later to replicate changes to another database. This approach also requires the creation of triggers for every table in a database that needs to participate in data replication.

- ○ **Using log mining**: Almost all databases (especially relational databases) support the notion of transaction logs where all transactions occurring in databases are recorded for backup, recovery, and archival purposes. Use of log mining as a foundation for data replication became quite popular due to the low impact on the databases from where data was being captured and replicated to other databases.

- **Changed data capture**: The changed data capture (CDC) method also depends on either triggers or log mining as the principal mechanism to capture data changes occurring in a database. Unlike the data replication method where data can be replicated either in synchronous or asynchronous mode, the CDC method can only support asynchronous data replication, that is, only after the changes are committed on the source database. This is a very good option for data propagation to data warehouses, reporting databases, and data consolidation from transactional databases by providing a continuous stream of data changes piped to the target databases. CDC tools/technologies are also becoming quite popular for data extraction, especially from mainframe/legacy environments from where data extraction was typically performed through flat files.

Architects and DBAs frequently wrestle with the selection process to choose the right solution for their data integration needs. This problem gets compounded because of the overlapping features/functionalities offered by many of the data integration products/technologies. This issue can be best resolved by understanding the requirements first and picking the right approach. The following is an analysis of the most common requirements and corresponding approaches that can be adopted to meet those requirements.

Data integration requirements	Data integration approaches
Once or twice daily data exchange in bulk	Data exchange using flat files
On-demand access from database applications to data sources such as FoxPro, Dbase, Excel, and so on	Gateways/adapters potentially leveraging ODBC drivers
Near real-time data synchronization for load balancing/reporting/auditing purposes	CDC solutions
Database integration with TP monitors such as CICS/IMS, messaging systems such as MQ, JMS	Gateways/adapters
Significant data transformation requirements along with data integration	CDC solutions and ETL solutions

Oracle offers a wide array of data integration solutions that fit into these categories. The Oracle offerings for database-centric data integration can be summarized as follows:

Data integration method	Oracle products/technologies
Data exchange using flat files (delimited)	Oracle SQL*Loader, External Tables feature in Oracle database
On demand, synchronous access to disparate data sources	Oracle Heterogeneous Services and Oracle Database Gateways for SQL Server, DB2, Sybase, Teradata, VSAM, IMS, Adabas, CICS/IMS, MQ, APPC, and so on
Data replication	Oracle Streams, Oracle GoldenGate, Oracle Data Integrator
CDC	Oracle GoldenGate, Oracle Database Gateway Adapters for CDC, Oracle Data Integrator

These products have some overlapping functionality, but they also complement each other in many ways. For example, Oracle Data Integrator and Oracle GoldenGate can truly complement each other in high-volume, high-performance data warehousing environments by using Oracle GoldenGate to replicate the transactions and using Oracle Data Integrator to transform these transactions before making them available in the data warehouses.

The availability of in-house tools/technologies and the potential cost of the data integration solution also play a big role in the selection of the right solution.

In the earlier chapters, we discussed in detail how SQL*Loader can be used to load data from flat files (ASCII delimited or EBCDIC fixed length files) as a means for data migration between different databases. The same technique can also be used for data integration between multiple databases. We also discussed how Oracle GoldenGate can be used in database migration upgrade projects.

In the following sections of this chapter the focus will be more on Oracle products such as Oracle GoldenGate, Oracle Data Integrator, Database Gateways for SQL Server, Informix, Sybase, Teradata, DB2, VSAM, ISAM, Adabas, and so on. Then we will take a look at how the CDC adapters, Oracle GoldenGate, and Oracle Data Integrator enable data integration.

For more information on SQL*Loader refer to *Chapter 2, Oracle Tools and Products; Chapter 4, Oracle Database Migrations to Oracle;* and *Chapter 5, Database Migration Challenges and Solutions.*

Oracle GoldenGate

Simply put, Oracle GoldenGate allows data exchange and manipulation between heterogeneous data sources such as Oracle, Sybase, SQL Server, and DB2 at a transaction level. Oracle GoldenGate facilitates replication of transactional data, changes to table/index definitions through **DDL (Data Definition Language)** across many databases by providing a low-latency high-performance modular solution.

Typical business requirements supported by Oracle GoldenGate, including data integration, are:

- High availability solution for databases
- Initial data load and migration between different databases
- ETL functionality in a data warehousing/reporting environment

Oracle GoldenGate supports many deployment topologies such as peer-to-peer, unidirectional, bidirectional, broadcast, cascading, and so on. A graphical image of the supported topologies by Oracle GoldenGate is shown in the following screenshot:

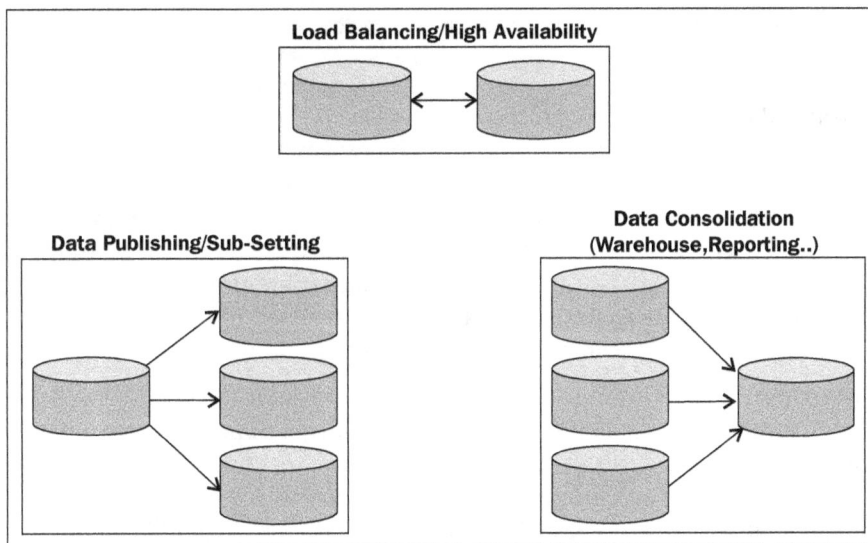

Oracle GoldenGate is comprised of seven modular, lightweight, loosely coupled components. Architecturally, Oracle GoldenGate operates in a stateless manner, that is, each component is independent of the working status of the other. Together, these seven components ensure rapid extraction, transmission, and delivery of transactional data among different databases.

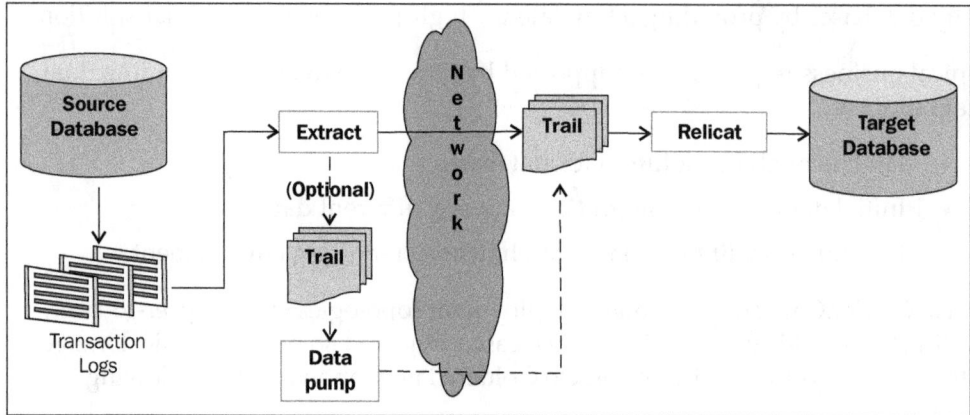

The following is a short description of each of the seven components that Oracle GoldenGate is comprised of:

- **GoldenGate Software Command Interface (GGSCI)**: is a Command Line Interface to set up the GoldenGate environment and perform all configuration steps. It can be used to configure **Extract** and **Replicat** processes, start and stop all GoldenGate processes, and so on. In addition to managing GoldenGate processes, it can be used to interact with databases to execute configuration tasks such as enabling logging on tables, setting up checkpoint tables, and so on. It can also be used to reset the database log checkpoints before restarting the Extract process.

- **Manager**: It is the monitoring or control process for the Oracle GoldenGate environment on servers where source and target databases are in operation where either the Capture or Extract processes are configured to run. It is the first process that needs to be started before starting the Extract or Replicat processes. It performs the following functions in a GoldenGate environment:
  - Monitors and restarts Oracle GoldenGate processes
  - Issues threshold reports, for example when throughput slows down or when synchronization latency increases
  - Maintains trail files and logs
  - Allocates data storage space

- ○ Reports errors and events
- ○ Receives and routes requests from the user interface

- **Extract**: As the name suggests, this component is responsible for extracting data from the source database (depicted in the previous screenshot on the left-hand side). It can be configured to extract data directly from source database tables as part of an 'Initial data load' operation or extract data changes from transaction logs (redo logs in Oracle). The Extract process captures changes for objects configured for extraction from the transaction logs and puts the data in a file called `Trail` in a sequentially-ordered transaction unit. It is possible to configure multiple Extract processes to capture changes for multiple objects with different characteristics such as predefined intervals, and so on.

- **DataPump**: This is an optional component of the Oracle GoldenGate product. Its primary purpose is to write the contents of the trail files on the source database system to the trail files on remote database servers, where the changes will later be applied. It can also perform data filtering, mapping, and transformation functions. Its primary purpose is to shield the Extract process from performing network activity (TCP/IP). In case of a network or remote system failure, the Extract process can continue to work without any interruptions. In the absence of a data pump process, the Extract process is responsible for writing the changes from the source database to a trail file on the remote database server.

- **Replicat**: This process runs on the target database server and its primary job is to apply the changes from trail files to the target database. Similar to the Extract process on the source database server, it can be configured for initial data load function or change synchronization modes. It can use either ODBC or native database interfaces for connecting to the target databases and applying the changes. Users can configure multiple Replicat processes to speed up the apply process on the target database server.

- **Trails**: These are files that contain the extract data ordered in a sequential transaction unit. They enable both the Extract and Replicat processes to run independently of each other, as well as serve as a mechanism for fault tolerance. Trails on the source system where the Extract process is running are known as extract or local trails and ones on the server where Replicat processes are running are known as remote trails. Trails are written in a canonical format and the files are written in append mode. By default, the size of a trail is 10 MB and they roll over automatically to avoid interruption due to file maintenance operations. Extract files are created when an initial load or change synchronization in batch mode is run to store the data extracted from the source database.

- **Checkpoints**: These files store the current read and write positions of a process to disk for recovery purposes. They ensure that data that is marked for extraction is indeed extracted and replicated to avoid duplication. In case a process needs to be restarted, checkpoints help in positioning the correct starting point. Using the guaranteed message delivery technology of Oracle GoldenGate, checkpoints work with inter-process acknowledgements to avoid data loss due to an outage in system, network or software layer. They can also be stored in a database table instead of a file on the disk.

- **Collector**: A Collector is an optional process that is started by the Manager process when the extracted data is being sent across the network to a trail file. Collector processes are required only if a network connection is required to write the trail.

- **GoldenGateDirector**: This is the Graphical User Interface (GUI) version of the GoldenGate Software Command Interface (GGSCI tool. It provides a rich interface to manage and monitor all GoldenGate processes.

In high transaction volume environments, multiple Extract and Replicat processes can be used to reduce sync latency and improve throughput performance. For good throughput performance, data changes can also be applied to the target database in batch mode.

> GoldenGate requires enabling transaction logging on all databases where the Extract processes are configured for capturing data changes. It uses transactions logs as the primary source for extracting data changes for configured objects.

Configuring GoldenGate for IBM DB2 to Oracle data replication

The goal of this example is to familiarize readers with the configuration steps of critical GoldenGate processes. This example only covers one scenario where data is being replicated from DB2 to Oracle.

Prerequisites

This exercise assumes that you have already installed the Oracle GoldenGate software on both the source IBM DB2 server and the target Oracle Database server; all DB2 and Oracle databases are configured and are running normally; a sample DB2 database has been migrated to Oracle; and the initial data load has been completed. Oracle SQL Developer can be used for DB2 schema migration (tables, indexes) and data migration. This example demonstrates a simple setup with no requirements for data pump, and Collector processes. Let us take a look at steps required to configure GoldenGate to replicate data between DB2 and Oracle in detail. Please note that this exercise only demonstrates the process to replicate data from IBM DB2 to Oracle, and not from Oracle to DB2 (bidirectional replication is supported by GoldenGate).

Before proceeding with the actual configuration steps for setting up replication from DB2 to Oracle, the GoldenGate environment needs to be set up on both the source and target server. The source and target databases that is, DB2 and Oracle, can also be set up on one server for the sake of convenience. When using the GGSCI command line utility, editing all parameter files and so on, requires usage of the `vi` command line editor on Unix/Linux platforms. Having knowledge of the `vi` editor or any text editor is essential in performing the tasks outlined in this section.

Configuration overview

To set up the GoldenGate environment after installing the software, the following actions need to be taken:

1. Run the command shell and change the directories to the new GoldenGate directory.

2. From the GoldenGate directory, run the GGSCI program.

    `./GGSCI`

3. In GGSCI, issue the following command to create the GoldenGate working directories:

    CREATE SUBDIRS

4. Issue the following command to exit GGSCI:

    EXIT

These commands create all the necessary sub-directories required by GoldenGate under the GoldenGate installation directory such as `dirrpt`, `dirdat`, `dirprm`, and so on. The configuration parameter files for processes such as Manager, Replicat, and Extract are stored in the `dirprm` directory.

To set up changed data replication from an IBM DB2 database (source) to an Oracle database (target), the following actions need to be performed:

1. **On the DB2 database server (source) configure DB2 for** `logretain` **and** `userexit`: This step is essentially the first step required to configure the DB2 database to set up logging on tables that are required for migration. Use the following commands to enable logging on DB2 using the DB2 CLI utility for database db2ora:

   ```
   db2 => update db cfg for db2ora using logretain on

   db2 => update db cfg for db2ora using userexit on
   ```

   These two commands ensure that the active logs are retained and they also become available as archive log files.

   ° Stop and start the DB2 database manager.

   ```
   db2 => stop database manager force

   db2 => start database manager
   ```

   ° **Mandatory step**: Back up the db2ora database after restarting the database manager and configuration changes.

   ```
   db2 => backup db db2ora
   ```

   ° **Optional**: Set the archive log path in case required. Omit the node name from the path.

   ```
   db2 => update db cfg using overflowlogpath "<Path>"
   ```

2. **On the DB2 database server (source) configure GoldenGate Manager process for source database (DB2)**: This step involves configuring the Manager process of GoldenGate on the DB2 server for the first time. This step can be performed using the GoldenGate utility GGSCI launched from the GoldenGate installation directory after logging on to the server as GoldenGate user:

   `./ggsci`

   Issue the following command to create a parameter file for the Manager process:

   `EDIT PARAMS MGR`

   Specify a port number 7809 for the Manager process:

   `PORT 7809`

3. Save the file using the 'vi' editor commands such as : wq or x and a file called mgr.prm will be created under the dirprm directory on the server where the parameters for the Manager process are stored.

2. To start the Manager process, issue the following command at GGSCI command prompt:

    ```
    START MANAGER
    ```

3. To check the status of the Manager process, issue the following command:

    ```
    INFO MANAGER
    ```

4. The output from the above command will be as follows:

    ```
    Manager is running (IP Port <Hostname>:7809)
    ```

    Add supplemental logging for tables that need to be migrated in DB2: Using GGSCI utility, tables can be configured to enable capture of changes on the table. The command for this purpose accepts wildcards to make database/schema wide-changes. At the GGSCI command prompt the following commands can be used to connect to a DB2 database and enable changed data capture:

    ```
    DBLOGIN SOURCEDB sample, USERID demoi, PASSWORD demoi
    ```

5. Issue the following command, you can use a wildcard to specify multiple table names:

    ```
    ADD TRANDATA DEMOi.*
    ```

> Do not log out of the GGSCI command prompt after issuing this command. It will be required to perform the next step to generate the source database definition parameter files.

6. The previous command will list out all the tables for which changed data capture is enabled as a result of this command. This command internally executes the following DB2 command to enable desired changes, which can be directly executed from DB2 CLI utility also:

    ```
    ALTER TABLE <name> DATA CAPTURE CHANGES INCLUDE LONGVAR COLUMNS;
    ```

    ° **Create DB2 database definitions file**: The database definition files are basically parameter files that contain information on the DB2 database and tables such as the database name, username/password, tables whose data changes will be captured by the Extract process of GoldenGate, and so on. Again, this file will be created in the `dirprm` directory by default, which will be created as a result of the steps executed in the prerequisite section of this example. To create the source database definitions file, issue the following command at the GGSCI command prompt:

    ```
    edit params db2src
    ```

7. This command will open a file named `db2src.prm` in `vi` editor with the following set of parameters in it:

```
DEFSFILE ./dirdef/source.def, PURGE
SOURCEDB db2ora, userid demoi, password demoi
TABLE DEMOI.*;
```

8. Save the file without making any changes to the parameters in `vi` editor. We then need to generate the definitions for the tables in the `db2ora` database in DB2 by issuing the following command:

   defgen paramfile ./dirprm/db2src.prm

9. The previous command will generate definitions for all tables in the `db2ora` database in `source.def` file under the `/dirdef` directory.

   ◦ **Configure GoldenGate Extract process for DB2**: Now we are ready to configure the Extract process for the DB2 database and start it. To do that, execute the following commands in GGSCI command prompt:

   Add extract extdb201, tranlog, begin now

10. The previous command configures an Extract process named `extdb201` whose source of information is `tranlog` and it immediately starts extracting data from transaction logs due to the directive `begin now`. To perform the initial data load (not change synchronization) substitute `tranlog` with `sourceistable` clause.

11. The status of the `Extract` process thus created can be verified by the following command:

    Info extract extdb201

12. Create a parameter file `extdb201.prm` for the newly created `Extract` process by issuing the following command:

    Edit params extdb201

13. A file named `extdb201.prm` will be created under `./dirprm`. Add the following parameters and save the file in `vi` editor.

```
extract EXTDB201
sourcedb db2ora, userid demoi, password demoi
rmthost v-1q, mgrport 7809
rmttrail /u01/app/ggora/dirdat/rt
table demoi.*;
```

○ **Create remote trail on DB2 database server**: This is necessary when writing directly to a remote trail for the target server from the source server using the Extract process. To create a remote trail on the source database server, issue the following command:

```
add rmtttrail /u01/app/ggsora/dirdat/rt, extract extdb201,
megabytes 10
```

On the Oracle database server (target)

1. Configure the GoldenGate Manager process for Oracle by executing the commands illustrated in step 2 for the source database configuration tasks (DB2). Do not forget to start the Manager process on the target server.

2. Copy the DB2 source definitions file from the DB2 database server (source) located under the ./dirdef/ directory to the dirdef directory located under the GoldenGate installation target server using the copy command from the operating system. Make sure all read/write permissions for the GoldenGate user are preserved when copying the files over.

3. Configure the GoldenGate Replicat process for Oracle. Since we are replicating data from a DB2 database to Oracle, we do not need to configure the Extract process for the Oracle database. We only need to configure the Replicat process, which will apply the changes replicated from DB2 to the Oracle database. To configure a Replicat process for the Oracle database on the target server, issue the following command:

```
Add replicat replora01, exttrail /u01/app/ggsora/dirdat/rt
nodbcheckpoint
```

4. Create a parameter file for the Replicat process on the target server with the following command:

```
Edit params replora01
```

5. This command will open a file named replora01.prm under the dirprm directory. Add the following parameters to this file and save it:

```
REPLICAT REPLORA01
userid ggs@orcl, password ggs
SOURCEDEFS /u01/app/ggsora/dirdef/source.def
discardfile /u01/app/ggsora/discard/replora01_discard.txt,purge,
megabytes 10
handlecollisions
MAP DEMOI.EMPLOYEE, TARGET DEMOI.EMPLOYEE
```

These commands can be interpreted as follows:

- ○ **Discardfile:** This parameter tells the Replicat process to store the data that is rejected when applying them to the Oracle database for any reason. It is recommended to have this parameter set to keep track of any kind of failures in the replication process.

- ○ **MAP**: The MAP parameter basically maps the source table to the target table. It is possible to map columns with different names where required.

- ○ **Handlecollisions**: This parameter is used for instructing the Replicat process to handle duplicate, as well as missing, table row data when applying the SQLs on the target server. In case of an initial data load operation, this clause is not required, but when performing change synchronization on a regular basis it is advisable to have this clause in the Replicat process definition.

6. Now start the Replicat **replora01** process by issuing the command:

```
Start replicat replora01
```

- ○ **Execute transactions on DB2 and verify the data replication to Oracle**: Once all the components are configured and started, we can test the system to see if the data is being replicated or not. This can be done by issuing some INSERT/UPDATE commands on the DB2 database and issuing, SELECT statement on the same table in Oracle database after waiting for few seconds due to the lag.

Oracle Database Gateways

Introduced in Oracle 9*i*, the Heterogeneous Services component of the Oracle database and the database gateways enables synchronous data integration between Oracle and non-Oracle databases in a transparent manner. The main advantage of this Oracle solution is that the database developers do not need to customize the applications based on the databases they are trying to access from an Oracle database-based application, in terms of using different APIs for different databases. Oracle enables the use of the same SQL dialect for all non-Oracle databases as Oracle. These gateways are optimized for the databases that they connect to and provide an end-to-end solution for integration with non-Oracle systems.

There are many benefits of an Oracle heterogeneous connectivity solution, including:

- Consistent set of APIs (Oracle) for access to non-Oracle systems
- Access to objects from non-Oracle systems in SQL Statements, views, triggers, stored procedures, and so on, without the need for access management tasks
- Reduced development effort in terms of customization for database-specific access routines/APIs
- Leveraging Oracle application development and reporting tools
- Increased agility due to less customization
- Performance optimization specific to a non-Oracle system

Oracle heterogeneous connectivity solution architecture

The architecture of this solution primarily consists of two components—**Heterogeneous Services**, which is common for all non-Oracle systems, and **Heterogeneous Services Agent–Oracle Database Gateway**, which is a target-specific component. The benefit of the two component architecture is that if for some reason Oracle decides to use a different technology to connect to a non-Oracle system or add support for another non-Oracle system, then the application written for an Oracle database need not be changed. In that case, the main Heterogeneous Services layer stays the same and only the Heterogeneous Services Agent layer is different. Both of these components are discussed in detail later in this chapter.

Non-Oracle systems are primarily accessed from an Oracle database by using the Oracle database link objects. Database links traditionally provide connectivity between different Oracle databases. The heterogeneous services component extends that feature to include access to non-Oracle systems through database links, leveraging the database gateways.

Architecture for heterogeneous connectivity to other relational databases and data sources such as Excel, dBase, and so on, can be visualized as follows:

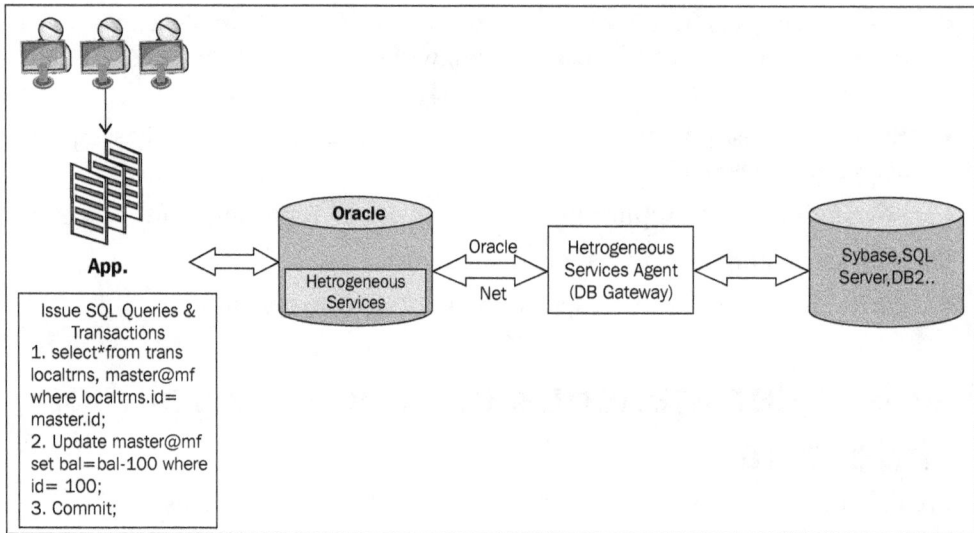

The architecture of gateways for mainframe data sources and TP monitors differs somewhat from that of other relational databases because, for mainframe data sources, there is a third component known as **Oracle Connect** (a mainframe adapter) that is installed on the mainframe. So, the architecture for the heterogeneous connectivity for mainframe data sources can be visualized as follows:

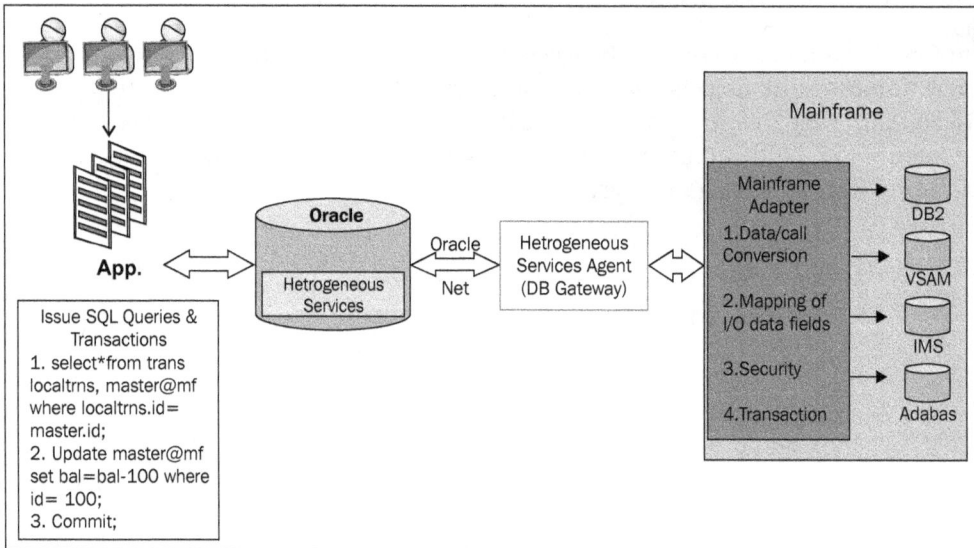

Some of the key features of Oracle database gateways are:

- **SQL and PL/SQL support**: As discussed earlier, the database gateways provide access to remote database objects in SQL Statements and PL/SQL objects such as triggers, procedures, views, and so on.

- **Heterogeneous replication**: Data can be replicated between a non-Oracle system and Oracle using materialized views. There are however restrictions associated with this feature:
  - ° Only a non-Oracle system will be the master site
  - ° Only a complete refresh of materialized views is supported

- **Pass-through SQL**: This is a very powerful feature by which a SQL Statement can be directly executed on the remote system without first being parsed by Oracle database. Such a feature may be useful when trying to execute a SQL Statement with a feature set that is not available in Oracle but is only available on the remote system. The PL/SQL package DBMS_HS_PASSTHROUGH provides the necessary interfaces to execute a pass-through SQL Statement.

- **Result set support**: Support for accessing result sets from stored procedures in non-Oracle systems where possible. This is similar to the support for result sets in Oracle PL/SQL stored procedures/functions.

- **Oracle's Query Optimizer and Heterogeneous Services**: A Heterogeneous Services component provides input on tables and indexes in the non-Oracle system to Oracle Query Optimizer, which uses the input to build better query execution plans.

Heterogeneous Services

The Heterogeneous Services component is a part of the Oracle database software and as such gets installed with the rest of the database software. Customers do not have to license this component separately or perform additional steps to configure it. A Heterogeneous Services component provides two main services when interacting with a non-Oracle system:

- **Transaction service**: A Transaction service enables support for sessions and transactions when there is interaction between an Oracle database and a non-Oracle system. When a non-Oracle system is first accessed from an Oracle database, a session is first established with the non-Oracle system by the Heterogeneous Services component. This session remains active until the Oracle session stops. The Transaction service also enables non-Oracle systems to participate in a distributed transaction initiated by Oracle. When an application commits a transaction, then Oracle's two-phase commit protocol accesses the non-Oracle system to co-ordinate the distributed transaction.

- SQL service: As the name suggests this service handles all tasks related to the processing of SQL operations. Important tasks performed by this component are:

  - Translation of SQL Statements (Oracle dialect) to non-Oracle system SQL dialect
  - Translation of queries that access Oracle's data dictionary tables to queries that extract information from the non-Oracle system's data dictionary objects
  - Conversion of data from non-Oracle system data types to Oracle data types
  - Where there is a functionality mismatch, it issues multiple queries to the non-Oracle system to extract the needed information

As discussed earlier, the Heterogeneous Services component plays a very important role in data integration by isolating users from tasks such as establishing a connection to the non-Oracle system, transaction co-ordination, using database-specific SQL dialects, and so on.

Database Gateways (Heterogeneous Services agent)

The Database Gateway is the component that interacts with the non-Oracle system on request from the Heterogeneous Services component of an Oracle database. The gateway is comprised of two components, namely agent generic code and the system-specific driver for connecting to non-Oracle systems. The agent generic code (or simply the agent) shields the Oracle database from any failure occurring on the remote non-Oracle system. In case of a fatal error in the remote system, only the agent process crashes without affecting the Oracle database.

There are two types of gateways. The first type is the gateway for non-Oracle systems where Oracle provides both the agent generic code as well as the database specific driver. The other is the Database gateway for ODBC (Open Database Connectivity), which only contains the agent generic code. The customer is responsible for providing the appropriate driver for the gateway to connect to the non-Oracle system, that is an ODBC Driver for the target database such as Sybase, DB2, SQL Server, and so on. Database gateways are database-specific, which means that multiple gateways need to be installed and configured based on the number of non-Oracle databases that are being accessed from Oracle. They are also licensed individually for each non-Oracle system. Although it is possible to install all of the desired gateways on one server, they still need to be configured individually.

Overview of Database Gateway installation and configuration

For configuring Heterogeneous Services, no additional tasks are needed as everything is configured out of the box when installing Oracle database software. Database Gateways, however, needs to be installed separately on a new server or on the same server where Oracle database is installed. This section is by no means intended to be a substitute for the Oracle Database Gateways installation guide for specific platforms, but rather an attempt to illustrate the configuration steps clearly with sample configuration files. After installation of the Gateway software, some tasks need to be executed to enable the Oracle database to communicate with the non-Oracle system through the Database Gateway software. In the following steps, these configuration steps and sample configuration information are provided as a reference.

1. Install Database Gateway software. The Oracle Database Gateway 11*g* R2 software is available as a separate downloadable package from the Oracle Technology Network (OTN): `http://www.oracle.com/technetwork/database/enterprise-edition/downloads/112010-win32soft-098987.html`

2. Database Gateway software needs to be installed in a separate `ORACLE_HOME` directory, an `ORACLE_HOME` directory for an Oracle database installation cannot be used for this purpose.

3. During the Gateway software installation process, users will be provided with an option to choose the gateways they are interested in installing. All gateways chosen for installation will be installed under the same `ORACLE_HOME` directory. A separate directory will be created for each gateway installed under ORACLE_HOME such as. `C:\Oracle\Gateways\dg4sybs[Sybase]`, `C:\Oracle\Gateways\dg4mq[MQ Series]`, `C:\Oracle\Gateways\dg4db2[IBM DB2]\` and so on.

4. After software installation, the next step is to configure the Gateway initialization parameter file. These initialization files follow the naming convention `init [SID].ora` where `[SID]` represents a unique identifier for a gateway that is, `initdg4db2.ora` may represent the gateway initialization file for IBM DB2. A sample initialization parameter file is provided under `ORACLE_HOME/[Gateway]/admin` directory for example, `ORACLE_HOME/dg4db2\admin`

5. In the initialization parameter file for most non-Oracle database gateways, the main parameter that needs to be set is the HS_FDS_CONNECT_INFO, which typically needs the input about the target database host name, port number, and the database name for example, for the DB2 database the input may be as follows:

```
HS_FDS_CONNECT_INFO=[mvs09]:8899/myudb,ZOS

HS_FDS_TRACE_LEVEL=OFF

HS_FDS_RECOVERY_ACCOUNT=RECOVER

HS_FDS_RECOVERY_PWD=RECOVER
```

6. The syntax for this information is provided in a sample initialization parameter file for each gateway under the admin directory, which can be modified as needed.

7. The second most important parameter in the initialization parameter file is the HS_FDS_TRACE_LEVEL which accepts the values ON, OFF, and DEBUG. Setting this parameter to DEBUG may result in generation of great deal of trace information, which ultimately affects performance. By default this parameter is set to OFF. Based on the target non-Oracle system (messaging system, database, TP monitor, and so on) there will be several other parameters in this file, each of which is described in detail in the corresponding user guide.

8. The next step is to configure a Listener for the gateway. The Oracle database server interacts with the Gateway software via the Listener. The Listener is responsible for starting up the Gateway process when it receives the request from an Oracle database for the first time. If both the Oracle database and Gateway software share a single physical server, then a single Oracle database Listener can be configured to handle requests for Gateway (from the Oracle database) as well as users trying to connect to the Oracle database. It then becomes a matter of picking either one of the installations as a starting point for configuring the database Listener. Assuming that the Listener for the Gateway is different than the Oracle database, the following is a sample configuration for Gateway Listener:

```
LISTENER =
  (ADDRESS_LIST=
      (ADDRESS=(PROTOCOL=tcp)(HOST=localhost)(PORT=1521))
  )

SID_LIST_LISTENER=
  (SID_LIST=
      (SID_DESC=
          (SID_NAME=dg4db2)
          (ORACLE_HOME=D:\OracleDB\11.2.0\tg1)
          (PROGRAM=dg4db2)
```

```
       )
     )
   #CONNECT_TIMEOUT_LISTENER = 0
```

9. In case the Oracle database Listener is also running on the same server, the parameters LISTENER, SID_LIST_LISTENER will need to be changed to a different name such as LISTENER_GATEWAY, SID_LIST_LISTENER_GATEWAY, respectively and the default port number used, for example 1521, also needs to be changed because the default Listener port number for an Oracle database is also 1521.

10. After configuring the Listener, the Oracle database software installation needs to be updated by creating an alias in the TNSNAMES.ORA file under the ORACLE_HOME/network/admin directory. This is because the Oracle database passes requests to the Gateway through database links. Database links in Oracle use a Transparent Network Substrate (TNS) alias for obtaining the connection information to remote systems. A sample TNS alias for a Gateway is as follows:

```
dg4db2   =
  (DESCRIPTION=
    (ADDRESS=(PROTOCOL=tcp)(HOST=localhost)(PORT=1521))
    (CONNECT_DATA=(SID=dg4db2))
    (HS=OK)

  )
```

11. Now we need to create database links pointing to the TNS alias in the Oracle database. A public database link can be created in Oracle with the following command using SQL*Plus utility:

```
CREATE PUBLIC DATABASE LINK <dblink> CONNECT TO
 "user" IDENTIFIED BY "password" USING 'tns_name_entry';
```

12. Gateways for some data sources such as Sybase, DB2, and so on, require additional scripts to be run on those data sources to create certain views/tables for the Oracle Gateway to function properly. These scripts typically create Oracle equivalent views/tables on these databases.

13. Finally, test the connection from the Oracle database to the non-Oracle system via the gateway using a simple SQL Statement such as, for most databases:

```
SELECT * FROM DUAL@<DBLINKNAME>;
```

14. Alternatively, each gateway installation has some sample scripts that can be run to test the configuration. The sample scripts can be found under ORACLE_HOME/[Gateway]/admin directory. For some databases these scripts can be found under the ORACLE_HOME/[Gateway]/demo directory.

Oracle Data Integrator

Oracle Data Integrator (ODI) is Oracle's primary data integration and ETL platform as discussed in *Chapter 2, Oracle Tools and Products*. It supports a variety of data integration needs such as batch data loads, event-driven data integration feeds, as well as SOA-enabled data integration services. ODI provides high performance data integration and transformation capabilities with its lightweight architecture and the ability to leverage native features/functionality offered by various databases as well as an extensible framework for incorporating data integration rules, sources, and targets in a declarative manner. With its declarative design feature, it is easier for users to redesign legacy batch processes and integration processes into modern, modular, reusable business processes, eliminating dependencies on legacy code. ODI also provides a robust security framework by separating project-specific metadata repositories from the data that defines enterprise data sources, security roles, and user information, giving administrators the ability to control access to critical information.

The following screenshot is an illustration of the component architecture of ODI:

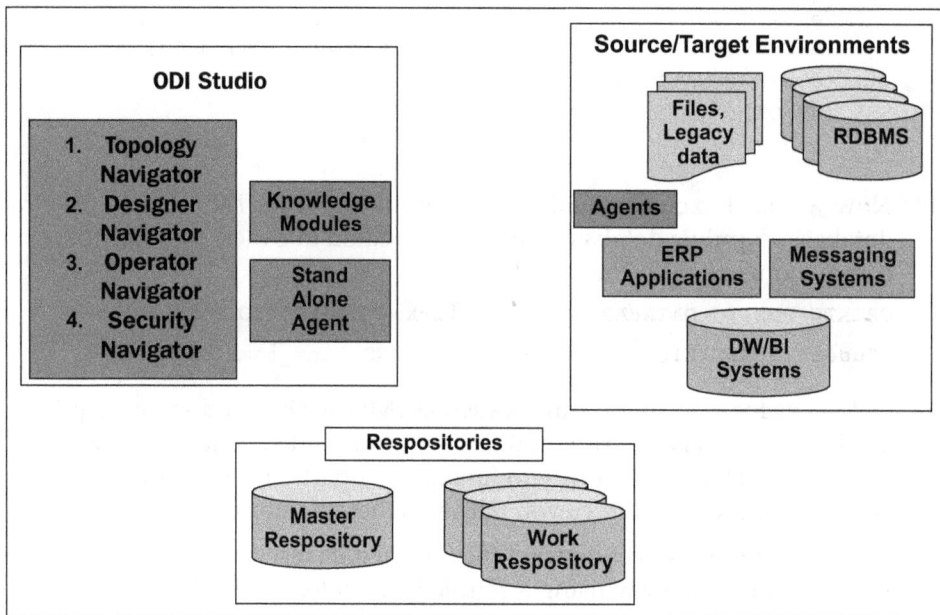

The key benefits of using ODI are:

- **Easier, quicker development and maintenance**: A declarative rules-driven approach reduces the learning curve for developers, as well as eases the maintenance efforts in an ODI environment. This approach also separates the process definition from process execution and various business rules governing that process such as source, target, transformation/validation rules, data loading technique, and so on. This is made possible in ODI by breaking down a data integration process into many tasks such as reverse-engineering source database, loading data into the target database, enabling changed data capture on a data source, validating in-flight data with existing data on the target, and so on, which leverages predefined code templates known as **Knowledge Modules (KM)**. The many KM data sources such as RDBMSs, flat files, LDAP, and messaging systems are included in the ODI distribution media. So, a typical data integration process will make use of knowledge modules such as reverse-engineering a database, loading data into a target database, and data validation based on the integration steps involved. Also, in any data integration project, a KM can be customized to meet a specific requirement if that functionality is not available out of the box.

- **Data quality**: ODI ensures that data gets verified before being loaded into the target server without requiring any coding. This is accomplished using the rules and data constraints in ODI as well as the target database.

- **Optimized architecture**: ODI supports both the Extract-Load-Transform(E-L-T) and Extract-Load/Transform(E-LT) architectures. By supporting the ELT architecture, ODI can perform staging/transformation activities on either the source database or on the target database instead of requiring a separate server. Using the ELT architecture eliminates the need for deploying/managing a separate server. It is also possible to dedicate a separate server for staging operating in ODI, which in some cases can be beneficial, for example distributing data to multiple targets after staging/transformation operations.

- **Better performance**: ODI delivers increased performance by leveraging the ELT architecture versus the traditional ETL architecture to perform set-based transformation. By using the set-based data transformation and leveraging target database features and SQL, it can perform much better than other competitors.

- **Reduced cost**: By eliminating the need for separate hardware and software for ETL servers, it reduces the overall cost of deployment in a new environment.

ODI primarily consists of repositories, a GUI design studio, runtime agents and a web-based console to monitor various tasks in this environment in real-time. These tasks/processes can also be monitored in the Design Studio, which is discussed in more detail in this section.

ODI repositories

In ODI, the repository plays an important role in managing metadata information about the IT infrastructure, business processes, databases, business rules, and so on. The ODI metadata repository also allows for the existence of different environments such as Development, Test, and Production. ODI supports two types of repositories, the Master and Work repository. Metadata such as topology information, data source definitions, technology used for integration, users, roles, and so on are stored in a master repository. In every ODI environment, this is the first repository that needs to be created. Metadata information pertaining to projects and data model objects used in a project such as tables, columns, constraints, data lineage and also execution/job logs, are stored in work repositories. In any environment, it is very common to find multiple work repositories under a single master repository to cater for different projects and also different versions of a single project (test, development, production, and so on).

ODI Studio

ODI Studio is a Java-based GUI that allows administrators, developers, and operators to access the relevant repositories, administer the infrastructure (security and topology), and perform project management tasks such as the design, development of packages and procedures, scheduling, monitoring, and so on.

The ODI Studio provides four different navigators for usage by administrators, designers, and developers. Let us take a closer look at these four navigators:

- **Topology Navigator**: It is used to define the infrastructure topology such as the source and target servers, databases, schemas, users, and associated technologies for data access. It also allows the definition of physical and logical architecture. Usually this component is used by administrators to define various databases and servers for later use in development of integration interfaces.

- **Design Navigator**: As the name indicates, this component is used for the design and development of different data integration and transformation processes (interfaces) in the form of packages, procedures, and development of associated components such as schemas, reverse engineering of source databases in some cases, and so on. This component can also be used for the generation of documentation, testing of developed interfaces, as well as customization of generated code.

- **Security Navigator**: Mostly used by administrators, this component allows the creation of users and profiles, privileges for methods (edit, create, and delete) on generic objects such as data types, data servers, instance specific rights for users such as server 1, server 2, and so on.

- **Operator Navigator**: This component allows operators/administrators or other users to manage and monitor integration tasks. It allows the monitoring of in-flight integration interface execution, restart, modify parameters, and so on.

ODI runtime agent

The **runtime agent** is responsible for the execution of different integration tasks created by the ODI Studio. The agent connects to the repository and retrieves all the metadata information pertaining to a task and executes the code. It is responsible for orchestrating the code execution on both source and target servers. It also reports any error messages returned from the tasks executed during runtime and also returns useful information such as the number of rows processed, the execution time, and step-by-step status information such as failure, success, and so on.

The runtime agent is Java-based so it can be deployed as a web application leveraging all the features of an enterprise application server, or can be run as a standalone Java program which can be deployed anywhere. It is also multi-threaded and supports load balancing. In ODI Studio, the agent can be scheduled using a built-in scheduler or from an external scheduler as needed. An agent can also act as a job scheduler by executing job schedules setup and is maintained within ODI Studio. It can also be accessed from a Java API or web service.

ODI console

ODI also provides a web-based UI that can be deployed to an application server such as Oracle Weblogic Server, where users can manage/monitor most of the ODI operations. There is a plugin available to manage ODI repositories and an agent that integrates with the Oracle Fusion Middleware console.

ODI supports various deployment environments such as test, development, and production by providing a mechanism to differentiate between where a particular data integration task can be executed. This mechanism is known as a CONTEXT. The first step in creating a project to implement a data integration task is to establish the CONTEXT in which it will be executed. A CONTEXT can also be password protected, so that users cannot change the CONTEXT to run a specific task in different environments. There is also a default CONTEXT provided which is named GLOBAL.

Support for most platforms and almost all databases make ODI an ideal choice as an Enterprise data integration platform. Knowledge modules are the most important component of ODI. They generate executable code when a task is run. Most commonly used KMs use substitution methods provided by ODI, however it is possible to extend/customize a KM using Jython/Java. Each KM is leveraged for executing a specific step in a data integration process. There are six types of KMs available in ODI. Each KM is highly configurable and can be customized to suit the needs of a specific task. It is quite common to create a totally new KM by copying an existing KM and customizing it as the situation dictates. Many KMs are in fact created on-demand during a data integration project. ODI ships with dozens of KMs out of the box that are data source specific and some also leverage native features/tools made available by data source vendors. It is not mandatory to use all the KMs in any data integration task. Users can choose which KMs they need based on their requirements. The following section is a brief description of different types of KMs available in ODI.

- **Reverse-engineering Knowledge Module (RKM)**: This KM can connect to a data source and reverse-engineer an object to extract all the metadata information about it, such as column names, data types, indexes, and so on. This metadata can be later used in the project for data extraction or creation of the object in the target database. Typically, this KM utilizes a JDBC Driver to connect to a source database

- **Load Knowledge Module (LKM)**: This KM assists with the loading of data from a source to a temporary staging area or directly to the target database for further transformation/validation. ODI provides standard LKMs for reading flat files using native tools such as `SQLLDR` for Oracle, JDBC Driver-based flat file access, and so on. There are also data source-specific LKMs available for DB2, Sybase, SQL Server, and Teradata.

[An LKM is not needed when only one technology is being used.]

- **Check Knowledge Module (CKM)**: This knowledge module is responsible for validation of in-flight data as well as data that is already in the target data store by using the declared constraints on the data source. CKM provides two configurable parameters to enable/disable validation of data against the constraints. These two parameters are:
  - `FLOW_CONTROL`: Setting this parameter to `Yes` causes the CKM to enforce the constraints defined on the target data store for the incoming data before it gets written to the target data store.

○ STATIC_CONTROL: Setting this parameter to Yes causes the CKM to validate the data while at rest in the target table, once again using the constraints defined in the data store.

- **Integration Knowledge Module (IKM)**: It is responsible for writing to the target data store after all data transformation activities are complete. Most KMs also provide an option for simply appending the incoming data to the existing data stores, while others can perform incremental updates or update slowly changing the dimensions. There are two types of IKMs available for use. These IKMs differ on the location of the staging area, that is, staging area is on the same server as the target data store or on a different server than the target data store.

- **Journalizing Knowledge Module (JKM)**: This type of KM is responsible for setting up the CDC infrastructure at the source data server to periodically gather transactional changes. By default, ODI uses a database trigger-based mechanism to implement CDC for non-Oracle databases and supports using Oracle Streams, Oracle GoldenGate for Oracle databases. So data sources that support triggers can leverage this KM to have the CDC infrastructure.

- **Service Knowledge Module (SKM)**: This type of KM is responsible for web service enablement of a model defined in ODI. It generates the complete set of objects required for accessing the data model through a web service. Typically, these objects get deployed to a Java Application Server instead of being executed by ODI, as in the case of other KMs.

Since KMs can be customized or created from other KMs, here are some guidelines on managing KMs:

- It is better to avoid hardcoding any database-specific information such as username/passwords or values for particular fields in a command. Doing so restricts the reusability of KMs across many data integration processes, usage of the KM, and can lead to developing numerous KMs, which ultimately results in a management headache.

- KMs should be developed leveraging configurable options or flex fields, so that any values that need to be passed to it can pass from the interface making it more reusable instead of using variables in the KM.

- Writing the full code template in a KM using languages such as Java and Jython only makes it more difficult to manage, just like regular application programs. It is better to make use of SQL Statements, which are more readable and understandable.

- Including a detailed note about the purpose, acceptable inputs/outputs, and process flow information in the KM is useful for maintenance later on.

- Code indentation is a must when writing in Jython. It also makes the executable code more readable. So care should be taken when formatting the generated code in the KM.

Implementing a typical data integration task in ODI involves the following steps:

- Creating data servers or physical schemas for source and target data servers under appropriate technology providers in the Topology navigator.

- Creating a project in ODI studio using the Designer navigator.

- Importing appropriate KMs that are required for the task at hand.

- Creating a model for both the source and target data objects.

- Building the actual interfaces to tie the source and target data models using the KMs.

- Packaging the interface(s) in a package and creating a schedule for it for recurring execution.

- Verification of execution results in the Operator navigator in ODI Studio.

Data management case study

The following case study was showcased to the public during a large international conference. Here, we will recount the success story of Overstocked.com and the challenges and success they had in building an enterprise data integration framework. Overstock.com is on online retail marketer that serves the liquidation marketplace, which is a very large, yet fragmented industry. Some estimates put the total liquidation market at $60B+. This story is how Overstocked.com could increase their the fragmented supply flow and consolidate the target market and increase their revenue through better integration internally, and externally.

Company overview

Overstock.com (NASD:OSTK) is one of the top five online retailers on the web today. Founded in 1997 by Robert Brazell, they have led the industry in selling surplus and liquidation production online. Overstock.com was initially founded as D2: Discounts Direct and was acquired by Patrick Bryne and relaunched as Overstock.com. They yearly have over 18 million unique visitors and boast of over 2 million online products over the years. They generated over $US1.09B in revenue in 2010 and experience consistent revenue growth.

Company challenges

Liquidation retail is different from traditional online retail. There are challenges in both the supply and demand side. Supply is not constant, pricing is unpredictable, and there is no regular supply source. Further, lots tend to be small and highly seasonal. On the demand side, consumers are looking for extreme discounts and the transactions are small, which is difficult in the liquidation marketplace with an increased level of competition from Amazon and eBay.

As a result there are a few consequences that pose business challenges:

- Small and varying lots are difficult and costly to acquire and manage
- Limited ability to distribute
- Unpredictable supply for consumers
- Poor customer service
- Shopping in difficult economic climate

`Overstock.com` believed the Internet is an efficient and cost-effective channel for stripping out information cost, which allowed the firm to efficiently and effectively match up this fragmented supply with the fragmented demand. This is the core of their business strategy for execution.

Initially, there was a prevailing thought that the Internet is a great way to strip out the distribution costs of retail. However, unlike traditional retailers, `Overstock.com` incurred friction cost from bringing in the inventory into the warehouse, stocking it, and then picking, packing, and shipping it to their customers after they placed an order.

Overstock.com's value proposition

`Overstock.com` believed that with the intelligent application of real-time data integration, they could provide a huge value to consumers and manufacturers, while turning out a profit.

To do this, `Overstock.com` recognized that manufacturers may wish to have a separate channel for their liquidated goods and their in-line products. As a result, `Overstock.com` built a reliable and effective channel for the liquidated goods. They did this by assisting manufacturers to discreetly sell off liquidation inventory. In some cases, the liquidated goods may also be the brand new products of the season, and the reason why it ended up having to be liquidated is because of a cancelled order.

In the following figure we can see what this proposed value model looks like:

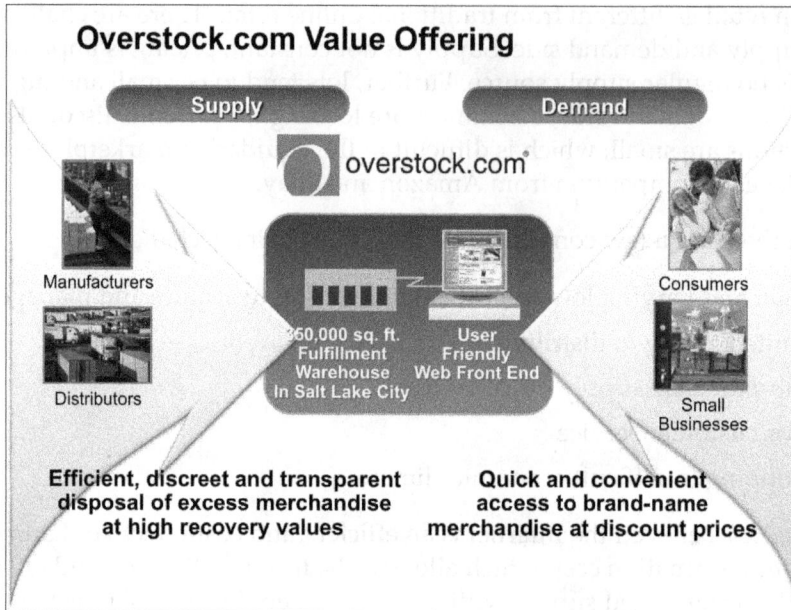

Overstock.com Value Offering

Integration framework

`Overstock.com` invested in two frameworks to deliver business value. The first was the traditional, batch-based information framework. The second was based on real-time data feeds and integration data stores. They discovered that a huge challenge was getting data feed extracts from various data warehouses and integrating it with live core systems. The following chart outlines the characteristics of each option:

Comparing Data Integration Frameworks

Traditional Framework	Emerging Framework
• Batch extracts/feeds from operational systems	• Near real-time feeds from operational systems
• Transformations in ETL engine on the middle tier- Heavy CP	• Lightweight middle tier
• Bulk load to the data warehouse	• Transformations on the database plateform
• Large nightly batch, user online day	• Small mini-batches throughout the day

As a result of the analysis, they determined that ODI and OGG would be able to provide near real-time data integration and a lightweight, but powerful data transformation mechanism.

The following image shows how `Overstock.com` used ODI and OGG together to achieve this:

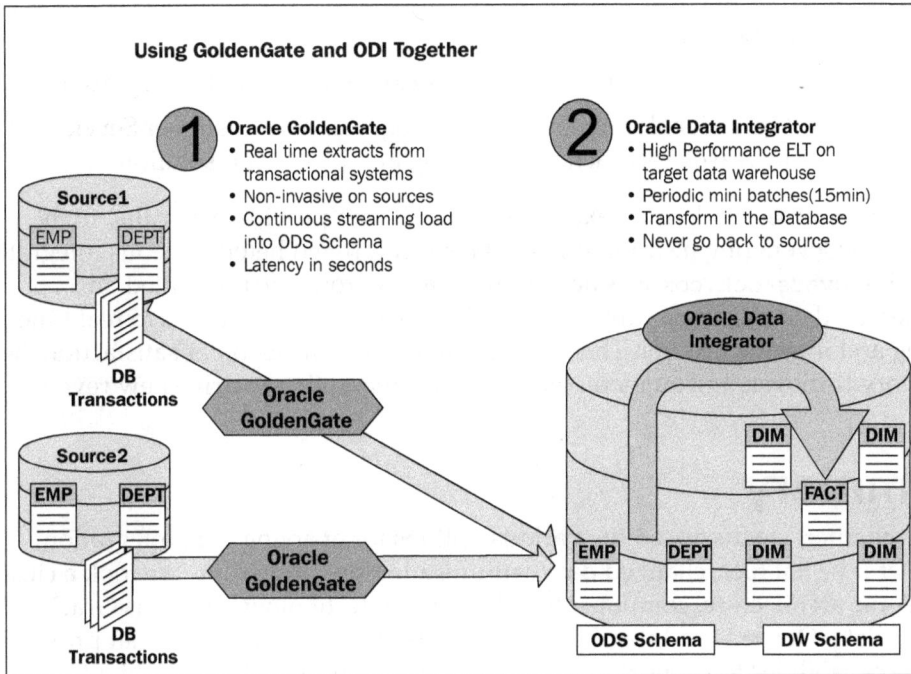

Active data with high availability gave `Overstock.com` many key benefits. One of the key benefits was related to the batch window. In some cases, it was totally eliminated, based on the source data warehouse. The low-latency access to near real-time data gave the marketing and sales channel the ability to create more personalized campaigns and cross-sell opportunities based on inventories as they became available. Many divisions in the organization realized hard dollar benefits, for example:

- Marketing
    - Reduced marketing spend in a smart way
    - Increased contribution margin
    - CRM improvement

- Merchandising
  - Increased gross margins
  - Decreased carrying inventory
  - Increased inventory turnover
  - Increased return on investment
- Customer Service
  - Applied the consistent scoring to every operational department
  - Operational improvements in Logistics and Customer Service led to increased satisfaction, shipping, and problem resolution

This snapshot case study is an example of how IT can provide true value to the business by leveraging near real-time data and improved heterogeneous integration strategies. Overstock.com was able to move away from batch-oriented and fragmented data to a more fully integrated environment with access to real time pricing and inventory levels. This leads to an increase in customer satisfaction, better inventory turnover, and an increased ability for marketing to drive new revenue.

Summary

In this chapter, we discussed the various options for enabling data integration, whether it be flat files, changed data capture, adapters, and so on. We took a closer look at the architecture, components of key Oracle technologies such as Oracle GoldenGate, Oracle Data Integrator, and Oracle Database Gateways that provide unique capabilities to support most data integration needs. Oracle GoldenGate is well suited for transaction replication to achieve high availability, load balancing between databases, maintenance of reporting databases in near real-time, and so on. Oracle Data Integrator provides powerful transformation capabilities for enterprise data warehousing in a declarative manner. Oracle Database Gateways on the other hand enables data federation in a unique way at the database tier, that is at SQL, and PL/SQL level, isolating developers from the complexities of the SQL Semantics, configuration, and so on in a heterogeneous environment.

Finally, the snapshot case study is an example of how IT can provide true value to the business by leveraging near real-time data and improved heterogeneous integration strategies. Overstock.com was able to move away from batch-oriented and fragmented data to a more fully integrated environment with access to real time pricing and inventory levels. This led to an increase in customer satisfaction, better inventory turnover, and an increased ability for marketing to drive new revenue.

8
Application and Process Integration

Application integration focuses on exposing the application components or leveraging the application outputs to integrate applications with each other. Process integration focuses on integrating by combining business processes into a business flow that encapsulates a business transaction or combines a set of transactions into one unit of business work. Process integration is used along with application-integrated components to control the flow, message handling, security, business rules, and transformations of the newly integrated applications. Applications are integrated using standards based Web Services Definition Language (WSDLs), J2EE Connector Architecture (JCA), or Java Messaging Service (JMS). The integration could also use the newer lightweight style of web-based integration which is a Uniform Resource Identifier (URI) with an XML file communicating over Hypertext Transfer Protocol (HTTP). This less robust, but quick and easy, method is referred to as Representational State Transfer (REST).

Used together, process and application integration can integrate any resource, whether it is a web service, data persisted in a database, data located in a flat file, business logic in a C application, or a transaction on a mainframe system. The advantage that application integration has over data based integration is that you leverage the extensive business logic in the application. This is the main reason some customers chose application integration over a data-centric approach to integration. The business rules, transaction management, security, and other business logic in the application are not bypassed.

In this chapter, we will start by covering the history of application and process integration. Actually, most of it is not history as many organizations still use flat file transfer, FTP, point-to-point hand-coded application integration, custom-coded workflow engines, and maybe even socket-based communication. Oracle also has its own legacy application and process integration products and tools such as Oracle Interconnect, Oracle Process Connect, and Oracle XML Gateway, which are the foundation of many companies' application integration solutions.

As discussed in *Chapter 2, Oracle Tools and Products*, Oracle **Application Integration Architecture (AIA)** is a SOA-based integration architecture that removes the developer from having to build the integration infrastructure and lets the developers and end users focus on application integration. AIA raises the bar from working with point products and process integration solutions like Oracle BPEL, Oracle Service Bus, and Oracle SOA Adapters to business process integration across Oracle and non-Oracle-based applications. However, the Oracle SOA Suite products like Oracle BPEL Process Manager, Oracle SOA Adapters, and Oracle BAM can be used without using AIA. If you are not using Oracle applications, you will probably integrate using Oracle SOA Suite instead of AIA. The information in the AIA section is just as useful even if you don't use the AIA foundation packs or other technologies specific to AIA. This is because it describes the technologies your organization could use to build pure SOA-based enterprise application architecture. These technologies include enterprise business objects, web services, and business flows all stored in a common repository.

The last part of the chapter covers two Oracle application integration projects. Since AIA is fairly new, neither case study covers using AIA. The case studies do show how Oracle Fusion Middleware, Java EE, XML, SOAP, and web services can be used to build a flexible architecture for SOA-based application integration.

History of application integration

Application integration as discussed in this book can most easily be understood as the exchange of transaction data and the synchronization of master record data across business applications. As such, application integration has been around in some manner since the beginning of computerized business applications; it has always been one of the most complex, costly, and error-prone aspects of business applications. The holy grail of application integration technology has been and continues to be the simplification, ease, reduced cost, and improved accuracy of application integration.

Application integration started as a set of **Object Management Group (OMG)** standards and vendors attempts at creating defacto standards. One of the first standards from the OMG was the **Common Object Request Broker Architecture (CORBA)** introduced in 1991. Other standards like the **Distributed Component Object Model (DCOM)** emerged from Microsoft. These standards, APIs, and transaction processing platforms required too much investment, changed rapidly, and cost a lot to maintain. In many cases, you could not find many application integration standards from OMG adopted by software vendors, or the standard was really only supported by one vendor (DCOM from Microsoft), so it was not an industry standard at all and only worked for companies that only used one vendor's software products for all IT application integration software needs.

Point-to-Point API-based integration

For most of the history of business computing, application integration has been implemented as Point-to-Point integration between individual applications. Point-to-Point integration involves each of the two applications that are sharing information to have a dedicated communication channel. Additionally, to pass transactions or synchronize master records from one application to another required custom coding. This customer code was typically written in the native language of one or both of the applications. Implementing custom-coded Point-to-Point integration required a careful understanding of the data structures in the two applications, and a detailed mapping of fields between the two. The programmer typically had to convert data formats from the sending application to the receiving application—a painstaking task. Whenever a data or file format changed in either of the two applications, the integration code would have to be modified to ensure the integration still worked correctly. Over time, if that code was not well documented in the organization, the integration programs would become fragile and required high maintenance costs. It's safe to say that integration code has long been the bane of IT departments, because of its complexity, tight coupling of integration, and business logic, and the need to recompile, test and redeploy applications after a simple change to an integration data stream.

Over time, organizations began to architect application integration to be easier to develop and maintain. **Application programming interfaces (APIs)** evolved to standardize the way in which data is staged in one application, transferred to another, and imported into it. Well-architected applications came to have standard APIs, making it easier for integration developers to design, build, and maintain integration more flexibly and productively. Moreover, application packages also evolved to contain standard APIs for integration with other applications, particularly those that commonly required interchange with other applications, both within the organization and across businesses.

Some early application integration APIs were based upon the Open Software Foundation's (OSF) **Distributed Computing Environment** (DCE) specification. The goal of the DCE specification was to create multi-vendor infrastructure support for distributed computing. DCE provides the key services required for supporting distributed applications, including:

- Support for remote procedure call (RPC) between clients and servers
- A directory service to let clients find servers
- Security services to ensure secure access between clients and servers

Remote Procedure Call (**RPC**) technology is based upon the Open Software Foundation's (OSF) Distributed Computing Environment DCE) specification. Remote procedure calls RPC provide the foundation of application integration as it is based on the client-server model, where multiple client computers may connect to a server and retrieve data from it. This is achieved using inter-process communication, where one computer can execute a procedure or sub-routine on another computer. Most operating systems support RPC—Windows, Unix, and Linux.

Common Object Request Broker Architecture (CORBA) produced by OMG is a set of standards for interfaces to various distributed services. Much like DCE, the CORBA specifications aim at defining a multi-vendor solution for building a common distributed infrastructure. Unlike DCE, however, CORBA is explicitly object-oriented, and the various CORBA standards only define interfaces and not how to implement a CORBA integration engine or product. Microsoft's Distributed Component Object Model (DCOM) defines the remote procedure call that allows DCOM objects to be run remotely over the network. Simply stated, DCOM uses RPC to allow DCOM objects on one Windows machine to talk to DCOM objects on another Windows machine. DCOM began shipping with Windows NT 4.0 and was Microsoft's answer to CORBA.

You could do application integration all through RPC. However, RPC is a low-level coding-based solution. It also ties the application integration to the operating system implementation of RPC. Taking application integration another layer up (less low-level coding), CORBA and DCOM could and were used more than 10 years ago to do just that. CORBA never achieved industry acceptance and there are limited numbers of application integration solutions based upon CORBA. CORBA also suffered from a lack of IT infrastructure vendors offering CORBA engines. Companies are hesitant to adopt technologies that are not widely accepted by the IT vendor community. DCOM was more popular then CORBA, but it is a technology only offered by Microsoft. Being a Windows-only solution from Microsoft, the product was confined to customers with an all Microsoft IT infrastructure, or a significant investment in Microsoft technology.

EDI

The first significant step in the standardization of application integration across businesses was **Electronic Data Interchange** (**EDI**), which first appeared during the mid-1960s (by a group of US railroad companies), and became a significant mechanism for business-to-business application integration. A variety of EDI standard bodies evolved to define EDI standard transactions and data sets for common transaction types, such as purchase orders, purchase receipts, orders, invoices, and master records, such as customers and vendors. EDI took much of the effort out of defining these standard data sets in applications, and mapping them to applications requiring integration. A significant software industry grew up around EDI, with vendors specializing in pre-built EDI transaction formats and transport mechanisms, reducing the effort needed for IT departments to build standard integration.

Nevertheless, companies who adopted EDI in a big way to handle business-to-business integration found EDI to be costly and cumbersome. The very detailed nature of EDI transactions, often requiring many data elements to be defined in a transaction, proved to make them fragile and costly to maintain. Moreover, EDI transactions were typically defined as Point-to-Point between two applications, and were subject to the constant changes that typically occur in business applications, resulting in frequent EDI errors and maintenance to fix them. Also, the complexities of business applications meant that standard EDI transactions could typically be defined only for say, 80 percent of the most common data elements, requiring customization in every case for the remaining 20 percent. As a result, EDI itself proved to be a sub-optimal solution to application integration among businesses. Nevertheless, EDI still exists today, particularly in supply chain management solutions, and will undoubtedly die a slow death.

Message and integration brokers

Addressing the problems of building and maintaining Point-to-Point solutions became the next evolutionary focus of integration technology. The concept underlying this next stage of EDI involved defining standard integration interfaces for common business transactions, similar to the way EDI works, and combines them with a generic transport mechanism to any other business application, both inside the enterprise and across business partners. The first such transport mechanism to gain market traction was the Teknekron Information Bus, which became a highly successful standard in the brokerage industry for communicating financial transactions and information feeds like stock trades. Teknekron Information Bus later became the foundation for TIBCO's product offerings, which evolved into one of the leading integration brokers in the market.

The information bus concept became an effective transport mechanism for generic application integration, but, as was the case for EDI, did not solve the real problem of transaction standardization to achieve efficient multi-application integration. The next stage of integration technology, integration brokers, tackled that problem in the mid-1990s. The first company to popularize the integration broker was Crossworlds, which focused on application integration at the business process level, and tackled the major business processes addressed by the leading ERP packages in the market at the time—SAP, Oracle Applications, PeopleSoft, and a few others. Crossworlds tried to define generic business transaction interfaces for major accounting and supply chain processes, and set about defining the touch points for these ERP packages. Shortly thereafter, several other companies, including Active Software, SeeBeyond, webMethods, BEA, and TIBCO itself, entered the integration broker market, and these products became quite popular for the next decade. They all developed a range of connectors for the leading application packages, as well as toolkits for building custom application interfaces, and enjoyed varying levels of market acceptance through the mid-2000s. Ultimately, the market began to consolidate, such that only TIBCO today remains an independent integration broker company, signaling that this generation of integration technology did not drive the cost of building and maintaining integration enough to be truly successful.

The search for the holy grail of seamless application integration continued with the advent of service-oriented architectures (SOA) that followed, and quickly evolved with the use of the Internet as the predominant transport mechanism for business-to-business integration through web services. By making the definition of integration services more discrete and elemental, SOA and web services quickly became a successful mechanism for less complex Internet-based application integration transactions, such as bank transfers, calendaring events, and so on, such that SOA has now become the dominant integration architecture and standard for application integration in IT departments. Making it the most dominant current approach does not mean it's the most widely used. This is because organizations take time to adopt new integration technologies and is burdened with large investments in legacy application and process integration solutions. All the major ERP vendors have now adopted SOA as their integration architecture, and the cost of integration continues to come down. While the holy grail of seamless application integration is still a way off, progress is clearly being made.

Messaging queuing systems are often used in large organizations for data and application integration. As most of these large organizations run IBM mainframe systems and have a relationship with IBM, frequently the messaging queuing systems in place at Fortune 500 companies are IBM MQSeries. MQSeries is used to send and receive data between applications or database systems.

MQSeries is effective but in many cases a very expensive way to perform application integration. Microsoft and Oracle also offer message queuing-based systems that are popular solutions for exchanging data and messages between applications, systems, databases, and even cloud-based SaaS implementations.

XML over HTTP or FTP

You cannot discuss SOA without a discussion of XML as the underlying technology of SOAs is based upon XML. XML in the late 1990s as the next big thing, just like DCE, CORBA, and DCOM were also given the title of the next big thing in the 1980s, to solve all application integration needs. There was an uptick in XML usage in the early 2000s. The Gartner Group in October 2000 predicted that XML for integration: "By 2003, 80 percent of application-to-application traffic passing over public networks will be in XML format". We are in 2011 and very far from even a 20 percent adoption of XML. One of the biggest issues with 'XML everywhere integration' was that XML is simply a standard for encoding documents and messages on the Internet. XML does not define a standard way to send these messages, a message protocol, or an API for applications to send and receive these XML-based messages and documents. Another big issue is that most organizations have relationships with many trading partners and even internal organizations that are based upon file formats established over twenty years ago and are not easy to change, because of application, internal standards, and product dependencies. What is great about XML is, unlike other application messaging approaches, it provides a standard message format, and the message content is readable as easily by humans or computers. Missing a standard protocol interface, most XML traffic occurs over HTTP and FTP. Using XML with FTP is not much unlike using a proprietary formatted flat file message or document over FTP. In fact, most early implementations of SOA application integration architectures that used XML were nothing more than customers and vendors sending and receiving XML formatted messages. Many IT organizations considered this their SOA application integration solution.

History of Oracle integration products

Oracle introduced several products in the late 1990s/early 2000s to address the needs of application and process integration. None of these products caught on in the industry. The early products were database-centric, and SOA industry standards which were still evolving were not web services friendly. It was not until the release of the Oracle Enterprise Service Bus in 2005 did Oracle begin to make inroads into the application and process integration space.

Given the long list of Oracle application and process integration products that have come and gone, Oracle customers have a right to question whether the current offerings will be around in three to five years. The number one reason that customers should not be concerned is that Oracle is building its entire Oracle Fusion Middleware Application software stack on these technologies. Some other reasons that the current set of products have longevity are:

- **Market leading products that were acquired**: Most of the products in the current application and process integration stack were acquired from other companies. These products are installed at hundreds or thousands of customer locations and oftentimes market-leading products before being acquired by Oracle.

- **Oracle is a leading middleware company by virtue of BEA WebLogic**: Oracle is no longer scrambling to catch IBM and BEA, as Oracle now owns BEA. This scrambling caused Oracle to launch new middleware products to attempt to catch IBM and BEA. Oracle now has a solid application server in Oracle WebLogic and suite of SOA products with the Oracle SOA Suite.

Oracle InterConnect

Oracle InterConnect was first released under version 3.1.2 in 1999. With the release of the Oracle **Enterprise Service Bus** (**ESB**) in 2005, this product went into maintenance mode in 2006. Oracle InterConnect is a data and application integration product, and really Oracle's first attempt at a true application and process integration product. The product used the Oracle9i Database, Oracle **Advanced Queuing** (**AQ**), and the Oracle9*i* Application Server as foundation technologies. The focus of the product was to offer high-speed, reliable, and scalable messaging. It provides a canonical view of enterprise messages using a hub and spoke architecture. The metadata repository and all messages are stored in an Oracle Database. This makes it a database-centric integration solution; something that prevented it from being well received by the middleware developers and IT organizations that often feel that a database is just a file system to persist application data. It is not based upon web services/SOA standards, but later versions of the product offered interoperability with Oracle BPEL and the Oracle Enterprise Server Bus ESB. All design and development is done in iStudio. iStudio is a standalone development tool that allows you to model the integration logic.

Oracle ProcessConnect

Introduced in 2003, Oracle ProcessConnect, as the name implies, was designed to add process integration to Oracle's application integration product line. Oracle ProcessConnect had a shorter life than Oracle InterConnect as it no longer exists at all and went into maintenance mode in 2005. It provided application integration just as Oracle InterConnect did, but also added process and B2B integration. It had a cleaner internal architecture than Oracle InterConnect, being a pure J2EE application, as well as using the Java Connection Architecture (JCA) for all adapters and XML for all internal messages. The acquisition of Collaxa BPEL Server in 2004 meant that ProcessConnect was no longer a required Oracle product.

ProcessConnect was a metadata-driven system with all the integration defined in one repository schema. All development and testing was done against one repository and new application versions were deployed to an identical schema in a runtime repository.

Oracle Enterprise Service Bus

ESB was introduced in 2005. Just as Oracle ProcessConnect was superseded by Oracle BPEL, Oracle InterConnect was superseded by Oracle ESB. Oracle ESB is a multi-protocol fabric to separate integration concerns from applications and business logic. Oracle ESB and Oracle BPEL serve as the application and process integration foundation for Oracle Fusion Middleware. It runs as a J2EE application and supports web services and SOA standards such as Xpath, XSLT, SOAP, JMS, and JCA. All artifacts in Oracle ESB can be exposed as a web service. The product is also hot pluggable as it runs on application servers like IBM WebSphere.

Oracle ESB was the first Oracle application integration product to be managed and monitored by Oracle Enterprise Manager. It was also the first application integration product that did not have its own standalone design and development tool, but instead all development is done in Oracle JDeveloper.

The acquisition of BEA in 2008 was the starting point of a de-focus of Oracle ESB and a focus for Oracle on Oracle Service Bus and Oracle SOA Suite for application and process integration. After the BEA acquisition, Oracle ESB, and the BEA AquaLogic Service Bus were merged into the new **Oracle Service Bus** (OSB). OSB, however, has inherited functionality from ESB; it, however, is not based on ESB and is based more on what was BEA AquaLogic.

Oracle Workflow – process integration

Oracle Workflow delivers a complete workflow management system that supports business process-based integration. Its technology enables modeling, automation, and continuous improvement of business processes, routing information of any type according to user-defined business rules.

Oracle Workflow was originally part of Oracle E-Business Suite and also embedded in the Oracle Warehouse Builder. Oracle Workflow was the main product, Oracle BPEL is taking its place, for process integration in the Oracle E-Business Suite. There are hundreds of pre-defined E-Business workflows in Oracle Workflow. The workflow engine and workflow processes are all stored in the Oracle Database. The product uses Oracle Advanced Queuing, which is a part of the Oracle Database. Oracle Workflow Builder provides a graphical drag-and-drop process designer. Using Oracle Workflow Builder, you can easily evolve a business process to incorporate negotiated business practices with your customers or suppliers. The Oracle Workflow Builder supports a type of function activity called an **External Java Function Activity**. External Java Function Activities lets you model workflow processes that include Java programs executed on the middle tier.

Oracle commercial off-the-shelf (COTS) application integration history

With the history of Oracle integration products as a backdrop, it is interesting to note how Oracle Applications, and later Oracle E-Business Suite and the Oracle-acquired application package portfolio, have evolved in their approach to application integration.

Oracle Financials first entered the market in 1998 as the first of a new generation of packaged applications using open standards—character-mode user interfaces deployed on the Oracle relational database supported by Unix operating systems. The first modules, General Ledger, Accounts Payable, Purchasing and Fixed Assets, had no integration features in the early releases, aside from tight integration among them, at the database level. Over time, customers demanded integration capabilities in Oracle Financials, Manufacturing and Human Resources, and an architecture evolved called **Open Interfaces**. Initially, the Open Interface architecture involved staging tables, called **Open Interface Tables**, which were used to populate transactions to be imported into Oracle Applications. Supporting each Open Interface Table was an import process run under the Oracle Concurrent Manager that used business rule validation logic identical to the validation rules used within the Oracle Forms for each transaction.

In addition, an error table was used to insert transaction errors that failed the validation, and documentation described in the manual processes, which were needed to fix errors and resubmit transactions to completion. While this architecture worked acceptably, it was somewhat fragile and failed easily due to the error handling requirements and the need for both sides to be up and running for consistency.

A similar architecture was used for outgoing transactions from Oracle Applications to external applications through Open Interface Tables and leveraged database views extensively. This architecture was later supplemented and enriched with the use of PL/SQL to encapsulate business rules in the Oracle database that were called during the integration process, and provided the first real-time validation capability, complementing the batch nature of Open Interface Tables.

In the mid-1990s, Oracle leveraged this integration architecture with an interesting market strategy. Oracle's major applications competitor was SAP, which entered the market for open applications a few years after Oracle, but executed a highly-successful strategy fueled by the Y2K phenomenon to become the dominant package application provider, ahead of Oracle. SAP employed a 'build-it-all' strategy, promising customers that it would be the single supplier for all their application needs. At the time, SAP had a much broader application footprint than Oracle; so to compete against SAP's monolithic approach, Oracle developed a best-of-breed strategy by partnering with niche application providers across a wide range of horizontal, vertical, and infrastructure software products. Named the Cooperative Applications Initiative (CAI), the program recruited partners under the Oracle umbrella to compete with SAP. Oracle packaged its open interfaces along with partner-enabling services and marketing support to develop Point-to-Point, out of the box integration with over 150 partners. Partners would build and package the integration, get 'approved' by Oracle, and go to market with Oracle co-marketing support.

The CAI program received positive analyst support and sustained well into 2000s. It's important to note that all of these packaged integrations were entirely Point-to-Point, utilizing Oracle-published Open Interfaces (and a few unpublished ones), and never supported the integration brokers that evolved in parallel. Customers who bought integration brokers needed to retrofit CAI integration to interoperate with them.

It's also interesting to note that Oracle attempted its own 'CAI' strategy with its Consumer Packaged Goods (CPG) initiative, by pre-integrating Oracle Applications with IMI, Manugistics, and two other package vendors into a very complex application set for large customers. It actually sold the solution to several customers, and struggled mightily to deliver and support during the late 1990s and early 2000s – again a Point-to-Point solution that was very costly to build and support. Ultimately, the solution was too unwieldy and unsustainable, and Oracle discontinued it.

Another interesting development began in parallel. Among the leading application vendors, Siebel took the most aggressive approach with its **Universal Application Network (UAN)** strategy. Its idea was to pre-build application integration for its products architected to support all the major integration brokers out of the box. In fact, Siebel had intended entering the packaged integration market with this strategy — a sort of updated Crossworlds strategy. Unfortunately, UAN received disappointing market acceptance prior to the Siebel acquisition by Oracle, so Siebel's strategy did not advance any further. Interestingly, though, the UAN architecture and development team was recognized as a real asset by Oracle as part of the acquisition, and has since become the foundation of Oracle's Application Integration Architecture product strategy. UAN was a true SOA architecture, and represents Oracle's integration solution for its application family of products.

Many customers and partners still have Oracle E-Business Suite integration architectures in place that use the Open Interface Tables or the PL/SQL packages exposed as 'integration services'. Just as it was difficult for customers to move away from thousands or tens of thousands of lines of FTP legacy integration code, it is just as difficult for E-Business Suite customers and partners to part ways with their heavy investment in Open Interface and PL/SQL API integration architectures.

Oracle application and process integration software stack

Oracle Fusion Middleware and the Oracle SOA Suite are the foundation of the Oracle Application and Process Integration solution. You cannot do application or process integration without Oracle Fusion Middleware. You can do application and process integration without the Oracle SOA Suite, but this would mean you are using the Oracle Java EE standards that Fusion Middleware is built on. By choosing to not use Oracle SOA Suite, you are building your own application and process integration from scratch using Java EE and are 'reinventing the wheel'. This is not much different then writing your own integration solution using flat files, FTP, and custom scripts.

In *Chapter 2, Oracle Tools and Products* we introduced the Oracle SOA Suite and AIA, but did not go into detail on either solution. That is because we are going to cover them in detail here. You can use the Oracle SOA Suite without using AIA to integrate both Oracle Applications and non-Oracle-based applications. However, when using AIA, it implies that you are using Oracle SOA Suite. This is because Oracle AIA is an architecture built on top of Oracle Fusion Middleware and the SOA Suite. The SOA Suite Adapters, which have thousands of integration interfaces to Oracle Applications and other non-Oracle applications, can be used without using AIA.

The Oracle SOA Suite application adapters provide you with the capability to integrate applications without having to use a generic SOA Suite database, flat file, JMS or other technology adapters. Oracle AIA in fact uses the SOA Suite application and technology adapters for its application integration.

Oracle Business Process Analysis

The first step in defining your application integration and business processes is to define the functional flow of your business. In the mainframe days, this was done using pencil and paper, drawing data flow diagrams and flow charts. Newer methods to define business flows include Microsoft Visio and UML modeling. These new tools are still restricted to use by developers or DBAs.

Oracle Business Process Analysis Suite (BPA) allows the business and IT community (process owners, business analysts, and architects) to perform process modeling and analysis, simulation, and publish business processes. Oracle BPA supports enterprise architecture, process improvement and change management projects, and provides for alignment of BPM and SOA initiatives. In addition, the suite is integrated with Oracle SOA Suite, BPEL Process Manager, and BAM. This allows your company to model your business processes using Oracle BPA and deploy them to the Oracle BPEL Process Manager and BAM.

Oracle BPA suite is composed of four components:

- **Oracle Business Process Architect**: This is a standards-based tool for process modeling. It uses various standards-based notations and templates such as BPMN, EPC, and so on.

- **Oracle Business Process Simulator**: Tool for simulating the process models based on a set of discrete events to do 'what if' analysis. This helps you evaluate process feasibility (such as endless loops), process performance (such as lead time), process cost, and resource utilization.

- **Oracle Business Process Server**: Server component for sharing the process repository across multiple users in a collaborative environment.

- **Oracle Business Process Publisher**: Publishes process models to a large audience outside of the core team designing the process models.

Oracle Business Process Analysis Suite not only provides tools for modeling your business, but also helps bridge the gap between business process design and implementation, resulting in IT systems that are more responsive to changing business needs.

Oracle Business Process Management

The Oracle Business Process Management (Oracle BPM) Suite enables collaboration between business and IT, as it provides both process modeling and design capabilities in one tool. The Oracle BPM Suite enables business users to drive process modeling with minimal IT involvement. The Oracle BPM Suite is intended for human-centric use cases that require flexibility and collaboration.

Specifically, the Oracle BPM Suite contains the following components:

- **Oracle BPM Studio**: Oracle BPM Studio provides a modeling tool for both business analysts and IT to build and test processes. It supports both **Business Process Modeling Notation (BPMN)** and **XML Process Definition Language (XPDL)** standards. The BPM Studio tool within JDeveloper can also be used to deploy and manage business processes.

- **Oracle Business Process Composer**: Oracle Business Process Composer is a web-based application that enables business users to collaborate with developers and designers. A catalog of services, tasks, and rules can be created in Studio and this catalog can be included in project templates, which can then be used to create new projects within Business Process Composer. Here business rules can be edited at run time.

- **Oracle Metadata Service (MDS)**: The MDS repository used to store information about deployed applications is used to share projects and project templates.

- **Oracle BPM Engine**: The Oracle BPM engine runs BPMN and BPEL processes, which are separate components but they share the same process core (that is, security, audit trails, invoke services, and persistence).

- **Oracle Human Workflow**: This component contains functionality for task routing to users, groups or application roles, management of deadlines, escalations, and notifications related to a task, task forms (including workspace and portals), and organization, filtering, prioritization, and dispatching rules.

- **Oracle Business Rules**: This component lets you automate policies, computations, and business logic in a flexible and reusable fashion.

- **Oracle BPM Dashboard**: Oracle BPM Dashboard provides process visibility into the processes that are running in the Oracle WebLogic Server or IBM WebSphere.

- **Oracle BPM Server**: Oracle BPM Server provides execution of BPMN and XML Process Definition Language XPDL processes. It also enables the import and export of XPDL processes to BPEL process for use with Oracle BPA Suite.

- **Oracle BPM User Interaction**: Oracle BPM User Interaction provides user interface options for end user interaction with processes, including the BPM Workspace (which is a web-based UI), extensions, or portlets that integrate with Oracle's portal solutions, and lastly, options that enable process interaction through Microsoft Office.
- **Oracle BPM Workspace**: Workspace gives you the opportunity to view running process instances, Work/View task lists, access out of the box dashboards, build custom-made dashboards, and manage organizations and roles.
- Oracle BPEL Process Manager and Oracle Business Activity Monitor (BAM).

All components of the Oracle BPM Suite provide a set of loosely-coupled facilities and services that can be utilized in any useful combination to build new processes; refine and change existing processes as the needs of the business move on; improve new and existing processes for operational efficiency purposes; to store and retain process information for future reuse.

Although there are some overlaps between Oracle BPA Suite and Oracle BPM Suite, such as BPMN modeling and simulation, the two suites address distinct use cases. While the Oracle BPA Suite supports top-down modeling starting from business objectives and strategies down to BPMN models, Oracle BPM Suite provides BPMN modeling and implementation and not the higher-level modeling features of Oracle BPA Suite.

SOA Adapters

The authors have seen companies that have purchased an ESB suite, BPEL Process Manager product, or **Message Orientated Middleware (MOM)** solution and believe that they now have everything they need for application integration. These products are all a solid foundation for application and process integration, but leave out one of the most important aspects of application integration—*how do you connect to all the disparate applications, database systems, e-mail servers, web sites and other system components?* This is the work of a gateway, adapter, connector, or whatever other name you have for it. In this chapter, we will refer to it as the adapter. Without adapters, you cannot connect to or communicate with any other application, business process or resource such as a SAP application, Salesforce web service, database or flat file.

The Oracle SOA Adapters can be used with Oracle BPEL, OSB, and BPMN. This makes the adapters useable across all components in your SOA integration architecture. The key adapters offered from Oracle include:

- **File Adapter**: File Adapters enable the user to read from, write to, and monitor flat files. These adapters can be used to integrate distributed applications that involve accessing the local file system. The File Adapter service category consists of the following prebuilt services:

  ○ **File Reader service**: The File Reader service reads data from the specified file and sends it to its output port. This service can be plugged into any application and enables you to read data from any file existing in the file system.

  ○ **File Writer service**: The File Writer stores the data received by it, in the specified output file. This service can be plugged into any application, enabling you to persist data into a file for future reference.

  ○ **File Receiver service**: The File Receiver service reads files of a specified type from a directory and sends it to the output port. By default, the service reads the files, sends its content to the output port, and then removes the files. It can be configured to move the files it reads to a backup location also.

- **FTP Adapter**: The FTP Adapter is used for getting or putting any file into the server.

  ○ The FTPGet component is used for downloading files from the FTP server. It can be used for downloading a single file or all files in a directory to a desired location.

  ○ The FTPPut component is used for uploading files to the FTP server. It can be used for uploading one or more files in a directory.

- **Oracle AQ Adapter**: The Oracle AQ Adapter handles the en-queuing (posting of messages) and de-queuing (removal of messages) to or from a queue, based upon what has been specified using the adapter commands.

- **Database Adapter**: The Database Adapter is a partner link in BPEL which is used to interact with the database for read, write operations. Using the Database Adapter you can perform the following functions:

  ○ Call a Stored Procedure or Function
  ○ Perform DML operations like insert, update, delete on a table
  ○ Perform SELECT operation
  ○ Execute custom SQL Statements

Some of the most commonly used database adapters are for Oracle, Sybase, SQL Server, DB2, Teradata, and Informix. There are also adapters for mainframe data sources like IMS and VSAM.

- **JMS Adapter**: The Oracle Fusion 11*g* JMS Adapter provides an interface that can work with any JMS provider. The adapter has been certified against Oracle AQ JMS, TIBCO JMS, IBM MQSeries, Weblogic JMS, and Apache Active MQ. The adapter supports global transactions (two-phase commit) as it is XA compliant. An inbound JMS Adapter service listens on a Java Message Service (Oracle and non-Oracle) destination and forwards incoming messages to the Oracle OSB or BPEL. An outbound JMS Adapter service writes messages from Oracle OSB or BEPL to a Java Message Service external to Oracle OSB or BPEL.

- **Oracle Applications Adapter**: An inbound Oracle Application (OA) Adapter sends XML messages to OSB on receiving messages from an Oracle E-Business Suite interface.

    ° An outbound OA Adapter inserts data from OSB into OA using interface tables, APIs, web services, concurrent programs.

    ° Oracle provides adapters for Oracle Applications, PeopleSoft, JD Edwards, and Siebel. Oracle also provides out of the box application adapters for the mostly commonly used SAP R/3 and mySAP modules. Third-parties provide application integration adapters for Clarify, Arbia, I2 Technologies, Microsoft CRM, Salesforce, Lawson, and other commonly used COTS application software.

- **IBM MQSeries Adapter**: The IBM MQSeries allows for bidirectional MQSeries integration. An inbound Native MQSeries adapter service sends an XML message to Oracle Enterprise Service Bus when new XML message is received by a queue. An outbound Native MQSeries Adapter service writes messages from OSB to a message queue.

Other technology adapters exist for TIBCO Rendezvous Socket, MSMQ, HTTP(s), e-mail, SOAP, and other common technologies.

Choosing the SOA Adapter to use is a matter of what technologies you have in-house, whether you have direct access to the database you are integrating with, your current application integration infrastructure, and many other business and technology variables. Here is a generic look at what adapters to use, in order of the recommended adapter first down to the least desirable, but perhaps most viable, in your environment:

1. **Application adapter**: This is always the first choice. There is no coding (input and output results mapping or transformations) required. When applications are updated, new out of the box adapter will be upgraded. These adapters utilize all the business logic, data transformation, and data cleansing embedded in application logic. There is nothing more elegant than an application adapter which has business logic encapsulation, database access, transformations, data cleansing, business rules, and marshalling and de-marshalling of messages all out of the box.

2. **Database**: Going directly to the data source is great if you have access to the database of the application you wish to integrate with. Database adapters can typically be used when the integration is being done within the same organization or intercompany. It is usually not possible to perform database process integration with a trading partner, vendor or other outside organization. Using a database adapter does not necessarily mean you are bypassing business logic as you can call stored procedures or issue complex SQL using the database adapter.

3. **Web services**: It could be argued that web services should be an option used before the database adapter. This would be the case if web services are available for the custom or ISV application you desire to integrate with. Although web services have existed for a number of years, there are still many custom and ISV applications that do not have web services interfaces. Web services also have the overhead of HTTP-based communication, which may not be a desirable choice if you are integrating applications within your own IT infrastructure. Web services also have limited support for two-phase commit and can be more difficult to secure.

4. **JMS**: JMS is the best choice if you are building an ESB where typically asynchronous communication is preferred. JMS supports both common messaging models: queuing and publish-subscribe. This allows for either Point-to-Point message communication or a hub and spoke where a number of clients subscribe to receive the same messages. Messaging-based systems like JMS are called **Message Orientated Middleware (MOM)**. MOMs can be used to integrate intra-or intercompany operations as it allows separate business components, written in any language, to be combined into a reliable, yet flexible, system.

5. **MQSeries**: The biggest reason for using IBM MQSeries is that MQSeries is already embedded in the enterprise. This is often the case in large enterprises. Using the MQSeries adapter allows you to keep your entire MQSeries integration infrastructure in place and add process integration to the mix using Oracle BPEL.

6. **Flat file**: Although flat file adapter integration is listed sixth out of the top seven options, it may be the first adapter you use as you move to a SOA-based application and process integration platform. This is because most organizations already have a significant investment in legacy flat file based integration and the flat file adapter is non-disruptive to this architecture.

7. **FTP**: FTP is considered legacy application integration but there are still a lot of custom FTP-based application integration solutions that exist in corporations. Therefore, it may make sense to simply use the FTP-based integration infrastructure that currently exists. Using FTP because '*it is the way we have always done integration*' can lead to a situation where you lock yourself into this legacy way of integration. For this reason, as well as it is not an efficient way to perform application integration, it should be your last resort.

Oracle Business Rules

Oracle Business Rules (OBR) can be used to store business logic and business rules for BPEL processing. The OBR engine can also be used to store business rules for any Java EE application. Business rules can be as simple as customer credit rating logic, for example, what is the credit limit based upon the customer's credit rating? Since business rules play a more significant role in an enterprise, the ability to store them in a central repository in the OBR product lets your company use the same business logic across all of your application and process integration products.

Oracle BPEL

Open systems business automation processing is typically achieved through the BPEL Process Manager product. BPEL Process Manager lets you orchestrate web service implementations, human interactions, and system workflows quickly and easily using graphical, drag-and-drop techniques. The tools are end user focused, allowing users to orchestrate their own systems. The execution language for orchestration is BPEL, and the runtime engine is Java EE. BPEL supports human and automated orchestration. Enterprises typically use BPEL Process Managers to streamline and rethink existing business processes.

Oracle BPEL Process Manager consists of the following:

- A mark-up language for composing multiple services into an end-to-end business process
- A workflow and process flow language
- An engine for executing synchronous and asynchronous interactions
- A BPEL Process Manager for parallel processing of business processes
- An embedded exception management engine
- A method to integrate a set of heterogeneous services to implement business processes
- Interfaces to the OSB using **Service Component Architecture (SCA)**

Oracle Service Bus

OSB is a lightweight and scalable messaging platform that delivers standards-based integration for high-volume, mission critical enterprise service bus deployments. It is designed to connect, mediate, and manage interactions between heterogeneous services, legacy applications, packaged applications and multiple ESB instances across an enterprise-wide service network. OSB provides built-in management and monitoring capabilities and supports out of the box integration with SOA Governance products.

The functional features of OSB can be categorized into the following functional layers:

- **Messaging layer**: This feature reliably connects any service by leveraging standard web service transports, traditional messaging protocols, and configuration of enterprise-specific custom transports.
- **Security layer**: This is a rapid service configuration and integration environment that abstracts policies associated with routing rules, security, and service end-point access.
- **Composition layer**: It's a metadata driven feature-rich configuration interface for service discovery and validation capabilities for automatic import and synchronization of services with UDDI registries. It allows message flow modeling, transformations, third-party service callouts, and a test console.
- **Management layer**: This is a service management environment that includes dynamic service and policy configuration, centralized usage and performance monitoring, and management of services — not just web services, but also Java, .Net, messaging services, and legacy end points.

Oracle Mediator comes up in Oracle discussions involving OSB and application integration. Oracle Mediator is an internal component in a composite application and can be used to mediate between the components, or the component and the outside world. OSB is a standalone fully-functioning, powerful, stateless ESB which is an intermediary between heterogeneous clients and services and is not embedded in either the client or server like Oracle Mediator is.

Mediator is primarily targeted to composite developers. OSB is primarily targeted to a system integrator using a development console for drag-and-drop development. Mediator is geared at being used to broker messages between components that complement each other and form a composite application. Although performs similar tasks to Mediator–IE brokering, validation, transformation routing and delivery, OSB is geared at brokering information company-wide and serves to decouple inter application communication.

Oracle Complex Events Processing (CEP)

Organizations can use CEP to coordinate business processes that work across numerous heterogeneous information systems and applications. CEP is often not considered an application and process integration platform, but as the business world becomes more real-time and event based, it is beginning to gain traction in this area. Business processes are often triggered by one event, or sometimes by a complex series of events. A CEP application can easily detect these events or complex series of events. The CEP application can then trigger the appropriate actions in other applications, BPEL processes, OSBs, or business rules in a business rules engine like OBR. For example, the selling of stock event might trigger a BPEL process flow in an internal customer validation application (where the business logic is stored in OBR) and an external request to New York Stock Exchange (NYSE) to get the current stock price. At the same time, the CEP application's analysis of the stock sell causes it to initiate, through a message, a process flow in a fraud application. The CEP application could then 'wait' for completion of the customer validation event, current stock price request, and a fraud clearance event before triggering a process to confirm the sell in yet another application. This entire flow certainly has all the characteristics, events, messages, process flows, and multiple applications, of an application and process integration system.

Oracle CEP is a Java-based middleware framework for event-driven applications. It is a light weight application server process, which connects to high volume data feeds and has a CEP engine to match events based on user-defined rules. Oracle CEP has the capability of deploying standard Java code, which contains the business logic for the event processing.

Oracle Business-to-Business (B2B)

Oracle B2B provides the secure and reliable exchange of documents between businesses, such as retailers, suppliers, and manufacturers. This type of e-commerce, B2B, represents mature business documents, classic business processes and industry standard messaging services, and requires a graphical interface to manage the complete end-to-end business process. As a component of the Oracle SOA Suite, Oracle B2B provides an architecture enabling a unified business process platform, end-to-end instance tracking, visibility, auditing, process intelligence, governance, and security. Oracle B2B has the following capabilities:

- Document management
- Transport and exchange management
- Partner management
- Reports and monitoring
- System management using the Oracle Enterprise Manager Fusion Middleware console and the Oracle Web Logic Administration console

Oracle B2B is much more than a business communication and document exchange standard like EDI and Swift. In fact, Oracle B2B supports EDI and Swift documents and communication. Oracle B2B provides reporting, monitoring, management, auditing, and other enterprise features that are not present in B2B standards such as EDI and Swift.

The Oracle acquisition of the **ART Technology Group** (**ATG**) means Oracle is serious about e-commerce. However, the ART COTS e-commerce solution is a Business-to-Consumer (B2C) platform. It includes capabilities for merchandising, marketing, automated recommendations, live services, and content personalization. Therefore, Oracle ATG and Oracle B2B are complementary solutions.

Oracle Service Component Architecture (SCA)

Building end-to-end SOA-based applications has been a challenge given the products, technologies, and languages that most organizations have across their enterprise. There are many standards defining how services should be invoked, interact, managed, and monitored; but there are few standards defining how services should be developed. SCA provides a standard for defining components and how those components interact, independent of their underlying implementation technology, product, or infrastructure. Therefore, a business process defined by a business analyst using Oracle PBMN deployed as an Oracle BPEL process can be represented and described in the same manner as a web service defined by a software architect.

The software developer creating a component in Java, C, C++, COBOL, or another programming language can use the same component definition language. Another great example of SCA in action is an OSB process that you defined is now able, with a few clicks of a button in JDeveloper, to be integrated with a complex BPEL process. SCA enables traditionally standalone applications or SOA Suite components to be easily integrated. Until SCA, MOMs such as an OSB and process flows using Oracle BPEL were difficult to get to talk to each other.

Oracle Web Services Registry

Oracle Web Services Registry is an industry standard UDDI-compliant web services registry. When you first start building your SOA-based enterprise application integration platform, the limited number of services you will have, and the fact that these services will mostly be consumed internally, usually make the use of a Web Services Registry overkill.

Oracle Web Services Manager

Oracle Web Services Manager (WSM) is a solution for securing and managing SOA components such as web services. It allows IT managers to centrally define policies that govern web service operations such as access control (authentication, authorization), logging, and content validation, and then attach these policies to one or multiple web services, with no modification to existing web services required. In addition, Oracle WSM collects runtime data to monitor access control, message integrity, message confidentiality, quality of service (defined in service-level agreements (SLAs) and displays that information in graphical charts. Oracle WSM brings to the enterprise better control and visibility over SOA deployments.

Metadata Services (MDS)

In general, a metadata repository is a central place in which to store and manage software assets and their metadata. This includes anything from complex services to applications to simple components. A repository maps and manages the relationships and interdependencies that connect the various assets. This results in your organization having a visible and traceable entire enterprise software asset portfolio. Therefore, reducing infrastructure complexity, reducing duplication of components across departments and organizations, and increasing business agility by leveraging existing IT assets.

The Oracle MDS stores business events, rulesets for use by Oracle Business Rules, XSLT files for Oracle Service Bus and Oracle Mediator, XSD XML schema files for Oracle BPEL Process Manager, WSDL files, and metadata files for CEP. It also stores the settings and deployment composites of the SOA Suite, security policies for OWSM, Enterprise Object Library, configurations and other AIA components, and customizations for ADF. The repository can be database-based or file-based; most components (such as WebCenter, SOA Suite, and OID) require a database-based repository. The components in the MDS can be leveraged at both design time and runtime.

AIA—Going beyond the Oracle SOA Suite

AIA takes application and process integration to a higher level of abstraction than Oracle SOA Suite. Just like using Oracle SOA Suite, instead of handcoding your own solution using Java EE, JCA, JMS, and JAXP relieves you from coding in Java using JCA and JMS, and reading and writing XML using JAXP. AIA relieves you from building BPEL process flows or OSB messaging flows so you can focus more on your business needs and more quickly move new integration points into production. As AIA is an architecture that has a strict framework associated with it, it may take some training and hands-on trails for developers and business users to get comfortable with it. Like any framework, the more you use it, the easier it is to work with and the more time it saves.

AIA does have a framework associated with it so you must use the tools, configuration files, and associated Java classes that are part of AIA. Although AIA runs on top of Oracle Fusion Middleware and SOA Suite, it has its own unique configuration files, XSD and WSDL files, and Java classes which are part of the AIA framework. It has its own error messaging and handling framework, XSLT style sheets, and, of course, security framework. Most of this is hidden from you when you use the frameworks, web-based development environment. Because the framework is extensible, you can use the underlying framework components for adding extensions for transformations, security or other custom functionality.

AIA—fundamentals

To fully understand and appreciate the benefits that AIA provides, you need to understand the building blocks and key software the makes up AIA. At its core, AIA is an out of the box library of reusable business services for cross-application process automation. It provides a common semantics foundation to easily build, change, and optimize business processes. This provides your organization with the building blocks and methodology to build your Enterprise Business Services.

Before you can create your process integration, you start by building enterprise business objects, business services, and messages. These components can then be used in the predefined integration patterns. These integration patterns can be deployed, through the framework user interface to Oracle BPEL Process Manager or OSB. These integration patterns have the transport built-in and can be synchronous or asynchronous in nature. AIA integration patterns also have built-in error handling for end-to-end error resolution of both integration components (BPEL, OSB) and participating applications.

Enterprise Business Objects

Enterprise Business Objects (EBOs) are standard business data object definitions used in the canonical data model. EBOs contain components that satisfy the requirements of business objects from participating application data models. EBOs are built from three types of components:

- **Business components**: Business concepts are specific to a business object. Business components are dependent business concepts that do not exist independently. They exist only within the context of another business concept.

  Examples of dependent business concepts are: SalesOrderLine, PurchaseOrderLine, InvoiceLine, InvoiceLineAllowance, and so on.

- **Common components**: Common concepts are shared across business objects. Common components do not exist independently. Common components are schema modules for containing components and business data types that are applicable to all EBOs and EBMs.

  Examples of common component EBOs are: Address, Note, UnitPrice, Attachment, CreditCard, and so on.

  The benefits of common component EBOs are: promotion of reusability and a common schema module is imported into each of the EBO schema modules.

- **Reference components**: They provide references to other EBOs (any EBO may have a reference component). References to other EBOs act as a foreign key. A group of attributes could become part of the reference structure depending on the business need. Reference components share the same namespace with common components.

  The benefits of reference components are: reduced overhead, the entire payload is not carried across the network, and you can easily associate an EBO to other EBOs.

Enterprise Business Messages

The Enterprise Business Message (EBM) is the payload that is paired to an EBS. The response returned by the EBS will also be an EBM. EBMs use structured XML messages for message interchange between applications/services. An EBM is comprised of: data area, action, and an EBM header (message metadata).

Enterprise Business Service

The Enterprise Business Services (EBSs) are application-agnostic web services that are used by calling applications to interface with different applications. This helps the cross-application processes to be participating-application unaware. The EBM containing the canonical object is the payload of the enterprise service and contains business-specific messages. These foundation blocks are generally coarse-grained in nature. The purpose of the EBS is to:

- Receive the request from the calling application
- Identify the implementation, as well as the deployment that is responsible for providing the requested service
- Delegate the requested task to the right implementation
- Receive the response and return the EBM to the calling application

There are two types of EBS:

- **Entity Services**— Entity Services expose a set of operations acting on the Business Object, that is the Enterprise Business Object (EBO)
- **Process Services**—Process Services expose the operations related to the business processes

Enterprise Business Flow

An Enterprise Business Flow (EBF) is a cross-functional BPEL flow used to coordinate the flow of a single EBS operation that is complex, potentially long-lived, and spans multiple services. These flows only interact with EBSs to keep them agnostic of participating applications.

Application Business Connector Service

Application Business Connector Service (ABCS) is the name for APIs developed to transform application business objects into enterprise business objects, and vice versa. Components of this service include the ABC implementation service and the ABC interface service. ABCSs facilitate the exposure of core business transactions, as well as data access as web services. They essentially serve as a glue to integrate applications with Enterprise Business Services. They also allow for participating applications to become service providers as well as service consumers without disruption to code. ABCs also allow for applications having a non-standard connectivity to expose their functionality as services. Most ABCSs are deployed to Oracle BPEL, but can also be deployed to the OSB.

There are two types of ABCSs:

- **Requestor ABCS**: These types of ABCSs are the interfaces between requesting/source application and the EBS. The Requestor ABCS is provided by requesting applications to interface with an EBS for performing a single business task.

- **Provider ABCS**: These types of ABCSs are the interfaces between the EBS and provider/target applications. The Provider ABCS is a service provided by the provider application to interface with an EBS for servicing a single business task.

The key responsibilities of ABCs are establishing connectivity with the participating application (web services-based and non-web services-based), message transformation from application-specific format to application-independent format and vice versa, invocation of EBS and/or Application Services and managing cross-referencing of instance identifiers. They also perform internationalization and localization of message content.

Tools—development environment

There are a number of tools for the AIA environment. These tools include a service repository, project lifecycle workbench, XSL mapping reporter, PIP auditor, validation system, and diagnostics framework.

The Oracle Business Service Repository (BSR) is a database repository and UDDI registry with a web-based UI for administration. The BSR contains all the AIA SOA Suite artifacts. The BSR provides end-to-end lifecycle support including: design time asset development and runtime services. The BSR can also be accessed through JDeveloper.

Project Lifecycle Workbench is an Oracle **Application Development Framework (ADF)**-based web application. It formalizes and orchestrates SOA development lifecycle activities. It is the business-focused process development environment for AIA and provides the following functionality:

- Facilitates business user or Subject Matter Expert (SME) process definition, decomposition, and service reuse during the functional analysis phase of the project

- Automatically associates implementation artifacts with their respective functional definitions during the implementation phase

- Supports installation developers' deployment plan generation activities by autogenerating a bill of material for a given development project

The **XSL Mapping (XMAN)** and **Process Integration Pack (PIP)** Auditor are tools for AIA SOA governance. SOA governance is all-controlling, centralizing, measuring SLAs, and promoting reuse within your SOA architecture. The XMAN reports provide content level governance. This is done by analyzing and showing mapping information that exists in hard-to-read ABCS XSLT files in a more readable manner, so that existing connector mappings can be considered for reuse in other applications. The PIP Auditor provides technical level governance. This is done by checking your AIA services for compliance to programming best practices and patterns found in the AIA Integration Developers Guide.

The Oracle AIA **Composite Application Validation System (CAVS)** validates integrations of individual services, end-to-end flows across silos, and backward compatibility of business flow. The CAVS Simulator is used to emulate service behaviors, predefined inputs to probe services, output definition options, and test assertions with XPath. It offers a layered approach by allowing developers and QA resources to test different portions of the integration in isolation.

The AIA Diagnostic framework is a script-based execution on an operating system level. It allows batch mode, single test, and selected single testing (such as test a particular BPEL process for modifications). You can trigger CAVS for initiating some of the diagnostic tests. The diagnostic output is available on a system level and through Oracle Enterprise Manager logging features. The AIA Diagnostic framework is used to validate the AIA integration landscape after changes and is used by Oracle Support Services to identify issues.

Oracle AIA Foundation and Process Integration Packs

One of the most common challenges in application integration is inconsistent business semantics across applications. AIA addresses this challenge by providing over 130 standards-based Enterprise Business Objects and over 1,200 Enterprise Business Services that form the basis for a common vocabulary across all your Oracle and non-Oracle applications. The AIA Foundation and PIPs provide packaging of Oracle standard AIA components to prevent duplication of business objects, business services, and business processes across the enterprise. The AIA Foundation and Process Integration Package (PIP) include:

- **Reference Process Models (RPM)**: This is an extensive collection of Reference Process Models that have been decomposed to four levels of detail, to help you see and understand how Oracle Applications can be used to optimize your business processes.

- **Process Integration Packs (PIPs)**: They optimize processes; they are prebuilt composite business processes across enterprise applications. They allow companies to get up and running with core processes quickly.

- **Direct Integrations (DI)**: These are prebuilt integrations that manage data flows and data synchronizations between applications.

- **Predefined Reference Architecture and Methodology**: This is Oracle's documented approach to implementing a proven SOA.

Oracle JDeveloper

Oracle JDeveloper is a free, integrated, development environment that simplifies the development of Java-based SOA applications and user interfaces with support for the full development life-cycle. Oracle JDeveloper enables you to develop Java enterprise applications as well as desktop applications. Oracle JDeveloper is packaged with Oracle Application Development Framework (ADF), which provides a rich set of templates for developing business applications. Oracle ADF is the framework being used to develop Oracle Fusion Applications. Both Oracle BPEL and OSB development is done through JDeveloper. You also have access to all Oracle SOA Adapters, including the E-Business Suite and other COTS application adapters, along with all their web service interfaces in JDeveloper.

Eclipse

Eclipse is an open source community tool whose projects are focused on providing a vendor-neutral open development platform and application frameworks for building software. The Eclipse platform is written in Java and comes with extensive plug-in construction toolkits and examples. It has already been deployed on a range of development workstations including Linux, HP-UX, AIX, Solaris, QNX, Mac OS X, and Windows-based systems. While JDeveloper is the development environment recommended by Oracle to use when developing SOA and SCA-based solutions, it is also well-known that many Java developers use Eclipse for standard Java or Java EE development.

Because of the large community of developers contributing to Eclipse plugins, the tool also has plugins for everything from reporting (BIRT), web services, BPM, BPEL, SOA repository management to Enterprise Server Bus development. Therefore, Oracle is a member of the Eclipse Foundation. As a member, Oracle offers the Oracle Enterprise Pack for Eclipse (OEPE) 11.1.1.7 for Eclipse Helios for developing standard Java EE and web services applications for Oracle WebLogic. In addition, Oracle offers plugins for BPEL Designer so you can develop Oracle SOA Suite deployments using Eclipse and Oracle BPEL Designer. As can be expected, the Oracle AIA framework cannot be used in Eclipse as not all the components of the Oracle SOA Suite can be used with Eclipse.

Oracle SOA Suite integration best practices

One of the first questions customers have when they start building an application integration architecture is: *"Do I need to use a BPA or BPM tool or can I start with BPEL or OSB?"*. BPA and BPM tools are not required to develop a flexible, secure, scalable, performant application, system or IT integration architecture that meets the needs of the business. However, BPA and BPM tools get the business community involved early, increasing the chance of an integration architecture that is built for the present and future. These tools also increase the likelihood that you will have an SOA integration architecture that is usable across the enterprise (instead of point solutions being deployed in different departments), that has a shared metadata model, and uses a common set of artifacts such as XSLT, data types, and SOAP messages. Not using a BPM or BPA tool is like not using an **Entity Relationship Diagram** (ERD) when developing a database system. Instead, you simply design and generate the Data Definition Language (DDL) by hand or use a SQL database development tool.

The equivalent in the Java EE world, or more generally the object-orientated development world, would be to write an entire system without classes, objects, states, use cases, activities or sequence diagrams. Once again, this is possible as coders love to 'just start coding', but this approach may not give you the most object reuse, inheritance, or flexible system.

What is the best way to integrate with all my internal applications, as well as all of my customer and trading partner applications? This is often the next question. During the SOA Adapter discussion, we discussed all the adapters including database, FTP, file, and other non-application integration adapters. Now the question is much more specific, *out of all the application integration-based options, which one is the best to use?* This excludes options like FTP, flat file, database, and MQSeries adapters. The top three options for pure application-based integration are: web services using SOAP/HTTP, JCA adapter-based, and messaging-based. Of course, which one you use depends upon your SOA integration strategy, company standards, the best ROI you can achieve from the underlying vendor product, and even the strength of your resources. Generally, the recommended use of these technologies is as follows:

- JCA adapters should be the first choice for applications making an outbound interaction with an internal application or resource. The JCA adapter provides speed, XA two-phased commit transaction support, security, connection pooling, and clustering for synchronous integration.

- For asynchronous integration, it is highly recommended to use message queues for publishing the requests. Messaging and queues provide significant scalability advantages over JCA and web services. Messaging using JMS is also a great choice when the systems being integrated use a variety of languages.

- For synchronous integration with third-party applications outside your firewall, you should consider sending SOAP/HTTP requests using web services. Web services do not support XA, but there are standards like WS-Coordination and WS-Transaction for transaction support.

- For interactions where the transactions need to be guaranteed, such as crediting or debiting an account, use either JCA or JMS transport to ensure the interaction is reliable and transactional.

There were many Oracle product offerings discussed in this section: BPM, BPEL, OSB, Events, B2B, and AIA. The following table provides a brief description of the best time to use each of these Oracle application integration products.

Product	Best time to use
Business Process Analysis and Business Process Management	When you desire business involvement in development of your SOA-based integration architecture, BPA provides you with capability to model your current and future state integration architecture. Keep in mind that if you desire automated generation of your deployment environment, these products only generate BPEL processes.
BPEL	Process integration where you have to integrate using web services, JMS, JCA, direct database calls, FTP, file-based, or any other resource.
OSB	High-speed asynchronous messaging based-system.
CEP	When application(s) rely on real-time intelligence, by trapping events, from another application or applications. Financial trading systems or manufacturing line systems are just two examples of applications that need to make real-time decisions based upon events in other applications.
B2B	Of course, when you are sending and receiving documents (such as purchase orders) from your suppliers and customers. Really only makes senses if your trading partners are using B2B document transfer standards like EDI, ebXML, and SWIFT.
AIA	Consider this architecture first if your organization has a significant installation of Oracle E-Business Suite, PeopleSoft, Siebel, Retek, iFlex or another Oracle COTS application.

BPEL and service buses are two technologies that are so similar they deserve a more detailed comparison outside the context of other technologies or products. Of course, with SCA, you don't need to worry about making this decision as most SCA-compliant products can be easily integrated with each other. Oracle BPEL and Oracle Service Bus are both SCA-compliant and can invoke each other. You still need to use the tool that makes the most sense for your application integration needs:

Implementation scenario	BPEL	OSB
Message-based system—you are passing application messages, XML documents, payloads		X
Sophisticated message routing, publish and subscribe, or queuing		X
Publish and subscribe or message queuing		X
Message throttling and flow control		
Stateless		X
Orchestration	X	
Long-lived process OR chatty conversations	X	
Aggregation/disaggregation—splitting/consolidating payloads and/or making multiple invocations to applications	X	
XSLT limitations on content validation/augmentation that can be otherwise addressed	X	
Other scenarios such as (a) participating application supporting only XML/HTTP binding (b) WSDL operation having multi-part messages OR binary attachments, and so forth	X	

Oracle success stories

These success stories are two examples from Estuate Inc. which describe the customer situation, the solution, the Oracle products used, and the benefits the customer received. The success stores will not only show what companies have done, but also give you ideas on how the Oracle application and process integration software stack can be used in your company. These examples are not large, sophisticated integration solutions. The reason for showing less complex solutions is to emphasize that most companies have success when the strategy is not to spend years attempting to implement an enterprise-wide integration architecture. The most successful projects are those that can be completed in less than six months and require a staff of six IT developers, an architect, and a project manager. These quick wins keep the momentum, show progress to the business community, and eventually lead to a corporate-wide, completely SOA-based application and process integration architecture.

Estuate Inc. is a Silicon Valley-based IT services firm founded in 2004 by two ex-Oracle executives. Estuate specializes in services leveraging the full Oracle technology and applications platform, both for end customers and for **Independent Software Vendors (ISVs)**. Since inception, Estuate has executed 20+ application integration projects, many for ISVs who build out of the box integration between their products and Oracle applications—including Oracle E-Business Suite, Siebel, PeopleSoft and JD Edwards. Vendors rely on Estuate to guide them through the integration process using Oracle's SOA stack, including the Oracle validation process. Estuate's notable integration product successes include Salesforce.com, Citrix, Cisco, Radware, Blue Coat, Boomi, Arena Solutions, and Wells Fargo.

Success one—Saleforce.com and Oracle E-Business Suite

Salesforce.com is a worldwide leader in on-demand **Customer Relationship Management (CRM)** services. Its **Sales Force Automation (SFA)** application gives businesses the upper hand with their sales data. It is comprehensive, easy to customize, and empowers companies to manage people and processes more effectively, so that sales representatives can close more deals, spending less time on administration.

The closed loop marketing application empowers customers to manage multi-channel campaigns and provide up-to-date messaging to sales. Lead hand-off is automated to ensure that no opportunity is missed. Real-time analytics and reporting give marketers the tools to evaluate results and adjust campaigns to maximize them.

To get real value from company data, customers need a comprehensive, real-time view of their business. Salesforce.com empowers users to create and access marketing, sales, and service information without the need for IT. Customers can use packaged reports or create custom ones to instantly analyze and report on their on-demand CRM data.

Companies of all sizes use Salesforce.com Service and Support to handle everything from merchandise orders and product support inquiries, to internal help desk requests. Regardless of whether service agents are located down the corridor, at home, or on the other side of the world, you can manage their time and tasks with Salesforce.com Service and Support. This adds up to faster response times, increased first-contact resolution rates, and improved service agent productivity.

Solution

Integration is one of the most complex challenges in enterprise applications. There is potential for additional complexity due to customization of either system, as well as the need to support different version combinations at a particular customer site. There is a pressing need for a sustainable integration architecture, which allows data to be synchronized and shared between the Salesforce.com and Oracle E-Business Suite 11i. The Salesforce connector is designed to bridge this gap.

Designed with extensibility and plugability in mind, the connector was built on open standards using J2EE, XML, and web services, and functions within the standard operating environment of Oracle E-Business Suite 11i. As an out of the box, end-to-end integration solution, the connector includes pre-built packaged integration processes for the most common integration points between Salesforce.com and Oracle EBS, such as Account/Customer Master, Quotes, and Sales Orders.

The fastest way to develop the integration is to utilize the power of both applications. Estuate leveraged extensibility in Oracle EBS built-in functionality and Salesforce.com applications to achieve data transfer in seconds for normal business volumes. Estuate identified the necessary supported API or Interface Tables from Oracle EBS and used them for the integration. Estaute also provided a mechanism to notify users in case of integration errors. The end architecture consisted of Oracle APEX, Oracle E-Business Suite 11i, J2EE, XML, and web services.

Benefits

Open standards messaging using SOAP XML payloads; the SOAP standards are becoming more industry-known. The adapters communicate with the applications using SOAP XML payloads. With this architecture, extensions/changes to messages can all be done via attribute changes, no coding, just configuration of the SOAP XML payload in the metadata repository. This integration really is quick and cost-effective and supports integration in a strategic way.

The message-based integration allows for real time updates as well as batch processing. Combined with the fact that the integration from one-to-many applications can be achieved with the Hub/Spoke method allows Salesforce to have a single version of truth that is up-to-date. In the past this has only been achievable through a data warehouse, but not only is data not necessarily up-to-date, it is also not accessible as a customer-facing application in real time. With this integration, we overcome this issue of data fragmentation.

Success two—cross-industry Oracle eAM print solution

This is a cross-industry solution to be co-marketed by Oracle and Estuate. Oracle Enterprise Asset Management (eAM) customers are in industries that have heavy plant maintenance functions. Therefore, this solution will mostly likely be used in manufacturing, distribution, and heavy industry companies.

Oracle eAM creates an efficient way for companies to track and schedule ongoing maintenance of their assets. Oracle eAM provides two user interface methods to create work orders and view attachments—Oracle Forms and Self Service/Web **Oracle Application Framework (OAF)**. Both of these methods provide access to work orders. However, neither fully address the need for printing work orders with their accompanying attachments in the same print request. Customers using Oracle eAM create thousands of work order packets each year. The inability to print complete packages, with work orders and attachments, can cause a major disruption in business processes. This leads to productivity losses and the accompanying risks associated with printing and collating large volumes of work orders can lead to costly mistakes. This is especially true for companies in asset-intensive industries that rely heavily on printouts for maintenance.

Solution

Estuate's Work Order Print Service solves the work order printing challenge, consistently rated one of Oracle eAM customers' biggest challenges, by enabling work order reports to be easily printed and related attachments stored in eAM. The solution leverages Oracle AutoVue, and integrates AutoVue's document rendering capabilities with Oracle eAM.

The solution includes Oracle Application Framework OAF pages to manage all work order print services, enabling print jobs for single or multiple work order attachments. The OAF pages call a custom Java view link based on the parameters passed from the form. The custom Java view link calls the appropriate AutoVue web service, and the AutoVue web service prints the document.

Here is a list of print web services, and the descriptions, that were used in the Oracle eAM and Oracle AutoVue integration:

print	This printing web service sends a given file to a printer for printing
getPrinterNameList	This utility web service returns a list of available printers
getPaperList	This utility web service returns a list each printer's available paper size
ping	This utility web service echoes service response

The AutoVue **Document Print Service (DPS)** that is included with Oracle is a web services-based interface. It allows a wide range of file formats to be printed and is intended for third-party developers who want to build a print solution that integrates AutoVue's printing capabilities with their applications. Clients that consume DPS can be written in any language, such as Java EE or .NET.

Benefits

The business bottom line is that the solution eliminated the errors and reduced the risks of manually-assembled work order packets. The tangible benefits of the solution are time savings and increased accuracy in plant maintenance and work scheduling activities by the ability to assemble work order packages, including attachments of any kind, flexibly and easily, and print them in a packaged unit. Estuate's Work Order Print Service provides these benefits:

- Enables customers to leverage the full power of eAM by integrating it with Oracle AutoVue for flexible, powerful work order printing
- Provides the ability to schedule work order package print jobs, both manually and scheduled

- Provides the ability to manage headers and footers for printing
- Supports work order printing directly from Oracle eAM R11i and R12
- The solution adds the ability to view and manage the print job history

Summary

This chapter covered significant material around Oracle application and process integration. After reading this chapter, you should have understood all the Oracle application and process integration products and frameworks, and how these products complement, and in some cases overlap with, each other. You now have a clear idea of when each of the solutions may be appropriate and how they work together, or, as in the case of the Oracle SOA Suite, form the foundation of other Oracle solutions like AIA. AIA is an important topic to cover as it is only about four years old and there are not even many articles, let alone books, on this topic.

Twenty years ago, most IT organizations handcoded any application and process integration needs on an as needed, one-off basis. The IT industry has come a long way in the last ten years in terms of functionality, performance, and out of the box capabilities for application and process integration products, frameworks, and tools. Ten years ago, products in the market place consisted of TIBCO Software, SeeBeyond, (aquired by Sun in 2005 and now owned by Oracle) and webMethods (now owned by SoftwareAG). Oracle has come a long way in the last five years. A Google search on 'Oracle application integration' will return many hits, with links to Oracle AIA web pages, documents, and even books. An 'Oracle information integration' web search will lead to web sites on Oracle Streams, Oracle XStream, Oracle Gateways, and Oracle Replication. As we have seen in this chapter, using these database-centric products for information integration is a myopic and legacy view of Oracle information integration. Oracle Fusion Middleware and SOA Suite are mature, capable, and easy to use to integrate information at the application and process tiers.

Still today, 'roll your own' integration, write the infrastructure themselves, is often an approach used by companies. Architects and developers read about REST, XML, Java messaging, TCP/IP connects to mainframes, and message queues and ask *"Why can't we just build something?"*. Developers are energized and impassioned by writing solutions using the latest technologies. Using J2EE CA, JAX-PRC, and other APIs, a developer could build a protocol connector, or an application that calls a C++ program and gets XML results back from this 'called application'.

The developer could write more code to process these results, and return the results back to a web page that is developed in JSP. There are many drawbacks to this solution. You have to handcode the solution while taking into account security, performance, reliability, governance, scalability, and service management. You also need to code and maintain low-level infrastructure software such as network protocol handling, data transformations, and a high-speed XML parsing and transformation engine. This chapter has hopefully shown you that Oracle offers a wide range of sophisticated application and process integration products and solutions that make this custom coding approach out dated.

Oracle AIA brings all the products in the Oracle SOA Suite umbrella into a framework to expedite application integration projects. Oracle BPEL is often the first choice when it comes to a complete application and the process integration solution. Oracle Service Bus is also used, but does not provide the completeness of a human workflow, process integration, complex event processes, and rules processes provided by Oracle BPEL. The introduction of Oracle SCA now makes it easy to integrate integration projects that use Oracle BPEL, OSB, a Perl program exposed as web service, JMS component, JCA service or a SOAP service into one course-grained composite service.

This chapter finalized the discussion of information and process integration. In the first nine chapters, we covered every conceivable Oracle database and Fusion Middleware tool, technology, and product that can be used to integrate applications and data. In the next chapter, we will cover in detail a topic that is just as important. This topic is how you manage and archive your ever-exploding data in your Oracle databases.

9
Information Lifecycle Management for Transactional Applications

According to industry analysts, data is growing at the rate of 60 to 80 percent per year, or in other words we are seeing exponential growth of data. While most data growth is perceived to be from unstructured data sources such as e-mails, file systems, and social media sources, what has been overlooked is the significant growth from structured data sources. Apart from this, relational databases like Oracle Database support **CRUD** (**Create**, **Replace**, **Update**, **Delete**) operations on all types of data, whether it is traditional structured or unstructured data types. More and more modern enterprise applications are linking structured data and unstructured content to provide a comprehensive insight into transactions like a new customer coming in or a new order being placed.

Most organizations run some kind of large-scale enterprise application system that manages customer, financial, product, supply chain, orders data, and so on. These could be pre-packaged applications such as Oracle Financials, PeopleSoft or Siebel.

E-Business Suite, PeopleSoft Enterprise, Siebel, JD Edwards or custom-built applications sit on top of a relational database. Using these applications, enterprises store massive amounts of data ranging from customers, credit card transactions to product inventories or data related to the business the enterprises are operating in. The data stored in applications drive supply chains, payrolls, customer interactions, and many internal and external web sites. In essence, we are looking at vast amounts of information which is fundamentally driven by enterprise applications, and managing the data assets or information in these applications is becoming far more important than ever to the **Chief Information Officer** (**CIO**).

In the next sections of this chapter, we will dive into details to understand why it is important to manage information or data in enterprise applications, and different techniques that can be used.

Data growth challenges

Growing data volumes have long been known to negatively impact application and reporting performance. General estimates by industry analysts have commonly seen that most enterprises have about 80 percent data from the enterprise which is historical and not accessed frequently or at all, providing little value to the business and production applications. Historical data is primarily used for reporting purposes or to analyze or mine intelligence from it and is kept in production databases, causing overheads and affecting application performance. This creates a significant impact on application performance, increased storage costs, and takes longer to complete a backup and recovery. End-of-month financial closings, inventory reporting, and manufacturing processes are often built around these systems, making any performance or availability issues a priority for senior IT and business managers. Application performance can have a serious impact on enterprise applications that sit on top of databases as they generate vital business information. More and more organizations are now looking at the total cost of data, including maintenance, storage, and more recently, energy consumption.

In some Oracle E-Business Suite modules such as General Ledger, there can be several thousand transactions added to a database in a day. After just a few months, running queries and reports on these large database instances can take a while to complete. To address this issue, organizations may run batch processing over the weekend or, in some cases, overnight. This way, the reports are finished when employees return to work and secondary jobs do not negatively impact application performance. With enterprise application usage on the rise and the amount of information generated and stored within a database increasing, organizations can no longer rely on off-hours processing to generate the reports needed to run the business. Additionally, with more global business operations requiring constant access to application data, there may never be a good time to run reports and batch processes. Further complicating matters are complex, integrated application environments where access equates to running regular queries to capture the latest manufacturing plan or other operations. These normal processes may be delayed because the size of the database prevents results from being returned in a reasonable period of time.

According to an **International Oracle Users Group (IOUG)** survey done on data growth, 86 percent of respondents claimed data growth caused application performance issues (refer to the following screenshot). In a nutshell, while all data is not equally used, all data is treated equally and kept in production databases.

Data Growth Create Application Performance Issues

Yes,all of the time	10%
Most of the time	20%
Some of the time	49%
Not at all	9%
Don't Know	5%

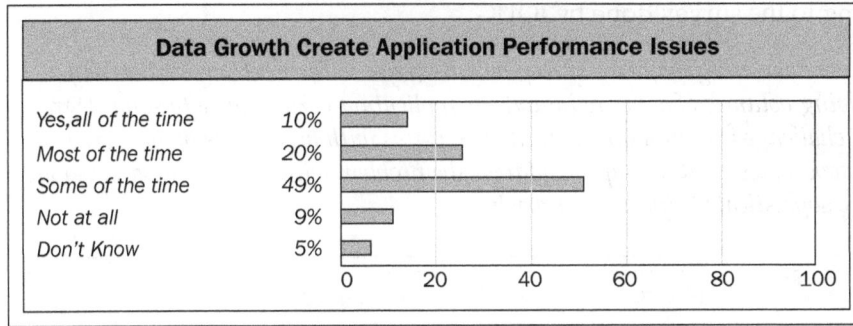

How enterprises try to solve data growth issues

In the next section, we will take a look at a few strategies that firms use to tackle these issues. The usual path is through hardware refreshes, tuning or data consolidation. We will look at each of these and complement that with data archiving.

Hardware refresh

Most enterprises try to deal with the issue by adding or throwing in more hardware resources. This includes adding more servers, or upgrading the number of CPUs, memory on existing servers, and adding expensive, fast Tier 0 or Tier 1 storage systems. As the data growth is not a one-time problem, organizations quickly tend to realize that hardware upgrades can only take them so far. Apart from hardware upgrades, just adding new hardware will not address the underlying issue of increasing backup and recovery windows putting pressure on the business continuity strategy deployed by IT. The continuous addition of hardware also has a significant impact on the maintenance costs of the applications, which include hardware, storage, and administration costs. Whether the enterprise provisions new hardware through IT or requests the outsourced or cloud provider to add hardware, it will have direct impact on **CapEX** or **OpEX**.

According to the survey done by IOUG,

> *An overwhelming majority of respondents (refer to the next screenshot) say growing volumes of data are inhibiting application performance to some degree. The challenge is even more acute at enterprises with high levels of data growth. However, most still attempt to address the problem with more hardware, versus more sophisticated/efficient approaches.*

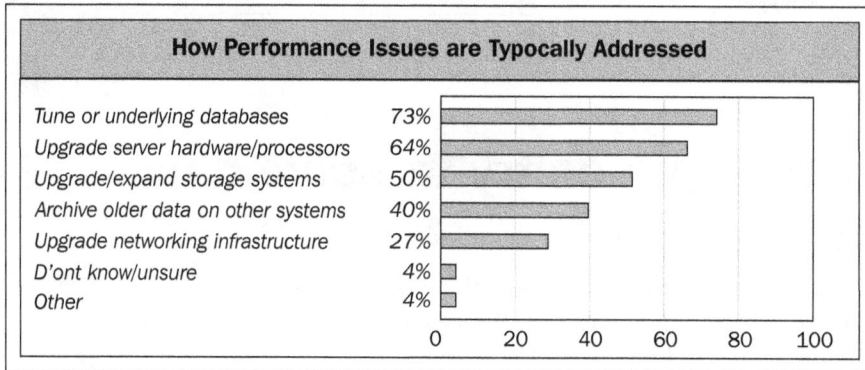

How Performance Issues are Typocally Addressed	
Tune or underlying databases	73%
Upgrade server hardware/processors	64%
Upgrade/expand storage systems	50%
Archive older data on other systems	40%
Upgrade networking infrastructure	27%
D'ont know/unsure	4%
Other	4%

SQL/DB tuning

The next strategy deployed by enterprises is requesting the database administrators to tune the SQL or database and see if application performance can be improved. Again, many organizations quickly come to the realization that this technique has limited success. As in the case of hardware upgrades, it still doesn't solve the problem of business continuity and also doesn't lower the storage costs.

Delete historical data

Earlier, we mentioned that approximately 80 percent of the application data is typically historical and infrequently accessed. Some organizations do consider the fact that they can potentially truncate the older or historical data to keep databases small. Unfortunately, this solution is far from reality as enterprises aren't sure which data needs to be kept and which data needs to be deleted. Apart from this, many industries have strict regulations on how long the data needs to be retained as per corporate and legal policies; historical data also has to be produced when a compliance or legal discovery request comes in.

According to the survey done by IOUG, many companies feel compelled to hold on to data for extended periods of time, forever in some cases, and are having difficulty making it accessible to end users. Refer to the following screenshot:

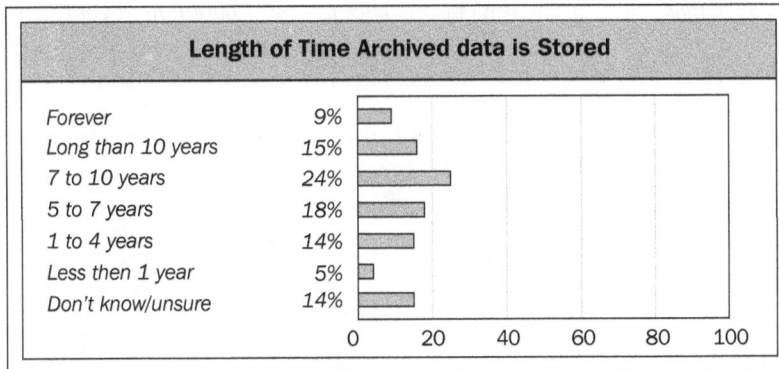

Length of Time Archived data is Stored

Forever	9%
Long than 10 years	15%
7 to 10 years	24%
5 to 7 years	18%
1 to 4 years	14%
Less then 1 year	5%
Don't know/unsure	14%

For the three reactive models of addressing the data growth issue, enterprises find that money is spent on operational issues rather than strategic initiatives which help the business grow. They don't address the increasing storage costs and business continuity requirements.

What is Information Lifecycle Management?

Information Lifecycle Management (ILM), is a set of policies and procedures that govern the lifecycle of all corporate data. These policies and procedures once created are typically enforced by software or storage systems. The policies for ILM are different for each organization and they depend on industry/country-specific regulations. ILM policies help organizations dictate the lifecycle of data for the entire lifespan of the information. For example, a Human Resource transaction could reside on a production system for the first two years, then on an archival system for the next seven years, and on a long-term archive for the next 15 years, after which it may be destroyed. The notion of implementing ILM for data is to properly manage the data growth and move it along different tiers based on usage, regulatory, compliance, and storage requirements and eventually destroy data that is no longer required by the enterprise.

According to the survey done by IOUG:

> *Two out of five companies recognize the value of information lifecycle management to better manage storage growth. However, these are the early stages for ILM strategies for most companies. ILM approaches are most common at companies with high levels of data growth, though the most common approach continues to be that of buying new hardware to address the problem.*

According to the survey, at least 47 percent of respondents (refer to the next screenshot) have at least a partial ILM strategy underway.

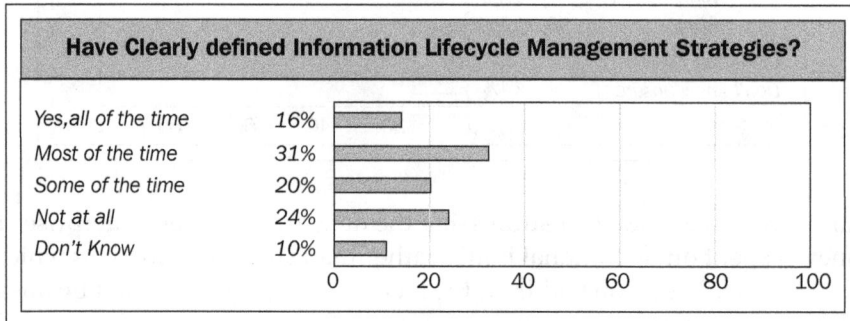

Have Clearly defined Information Lifecycle Management Strategies?

Yes, all of the time	16%
Most of the time	31%
Some of the time	20%
Not at all	24%
Don't Know	10%

What benefits can ILM offer?

ILM offers several benefits to enterprises, including:

- Controls data growth
- Risk mitigation, compliance with data retention regulations
- Storage cost reduction
- Use policy-based storage
- Increase application performance
- Reduce backup and disaster recovery cycles

ILM can be applied to all types of data, including unstructured data, semi-structured, and structured or transactional. As the focus of this book is on structured data, the next sections of this chapter will delve into details on how ILM can be applied to structured and transactional data. There are two classes of structured applications. The first is transactional production data. The second is considered legacy application data in which no new transactions are being entered into these systems, but enterprises are required to keep these applications up and running for policy, historical, or legal reasons. There are two different paradigms that help enterprises implement ILM for these two classes of structured applications. Pre-packaged, custom, legacy applications, and Data Warehouses can be classified into one of these two categories depending on their usage:

- Active Application Archiving
- Application Retirement/Application Sunsetting/Application or Legacy Decommissioning

Active Application Archiving

Active Application Archiving allows us to manage data growth in one or more enterprise application that could be mission critical and currently active with a significant amount of data growth. These structured applications typically sit on top of one of the standard relational databases such as the Oracle Database.

Prepackaged applications such as Oracle E-Business Suite, PeopleSoft, Siebel, and JD Edwards typically have data stored across several hundreds of tables, depending on the number of modules that are being used. Modules in these applications provide a set of functionality that can be interlinked with other modules. For example, a General Ledger (GL) is linked with Accounts Payable (AP) and Accounts Receivable (AR).

Custom applications built in Java or .NET can also be sitting on top of databases that are accumulating significant amounts of data. These custom applications could be capturing new customers, their orders, and line items.

Almost every application has metadata. Metadata is the data that describes the data structures and the application. It also captures the information about tables and their interconnected relationships with other tables, modules, and so on. Metadata can be at the database level using the functionality of database relationships. For example, a Customer can have many Orders and each Order can have many Line Items. In the following screenshot, for an Order Entry sample schema in Oracle Database, which is seen in many prepackaged applications like Oracle E-Business Suite, metadata can be captured at the application level. In next sections, we will see the very important role metadata plays in archiving application data.

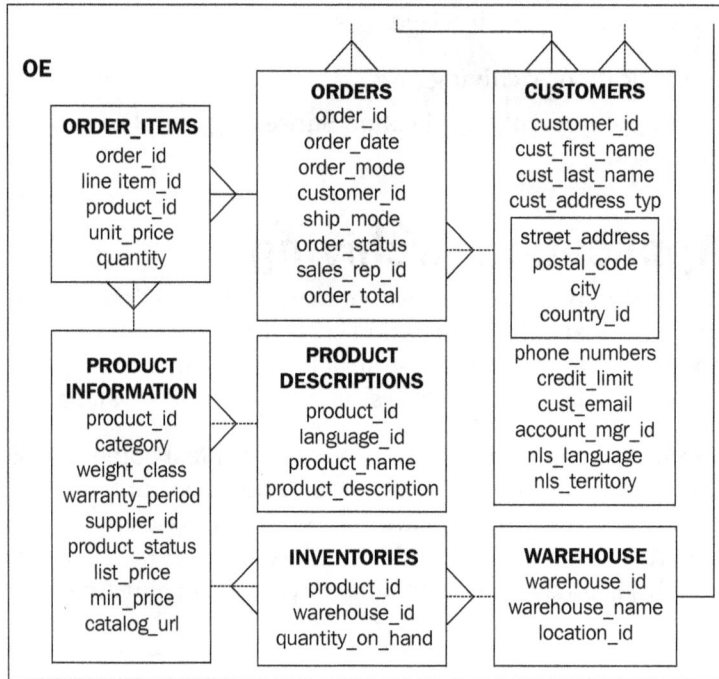

Enterprises want to have the flexibility of defining what data has to be archived and the data that needs to reside in the production database servers. This flexibility is achieved by creating a model that is driven by a set of business rules. The next screenshot defines which set of Purchase Order transactions should be archived in a JD Edwards environment.

TABLE NAME	DESCRIPTION
F4311	PO HEADER
F4301	PO DETAIL
F43121	PO RECEIPT
F43199	PO LEDGER
F4111	ITEM LEDGER

- ✓ The Purchase orders should be a status of 999. (Purchase receipts process is complete. F4301 & F4311 records can be processed.)
- ✓ The Purchase Order detail table F4311 has to be purged first before purging of PO header F4301
- ✓ Before the F4311, F4301, F43121 are purged ensure that Voucher match process is completed.
- ✓ PO test lines (F4311) to be moved to a status of 999 before they can be purged.
- ✓ Business should determine the way forward plan for purging, which is on the basis of Transaction date.
- ✓ Mode for archival process (Tape, diskette, etc) & timeframe for archive process should be decided.
- ✓ If there are other criteria for items to exclude, those criteria can be included by customizing the configuration.

Since transactions can be chained and a transactional business object can span across several tables, archiving just at a table or partition level without knowledge of the transactional status or comprehensive set of business rules doesn't help enterprises to implement ILM policies and enforce consistent data governance across data assets.

Using the metadata of the applications and constructing business rules that drive the archiving provides enterprises with the required flexibility. The metadata-driven approach for archiving provides several benefits, including:

- Ability to identify a transactional business object
- Ability to create a comprehensive set of business rules that can work with governing corporate policies for data retention
- Ability to be agnostic to underlying database
- Provides a fine-grained approach to drill-down to a specific set of transactions

The following screenshot shows how the transactional business objects Customer, Sales Order, Service Order, AR Receipts, Inventory, and GL Journals can be linked across tables, table spaces, and partitions:

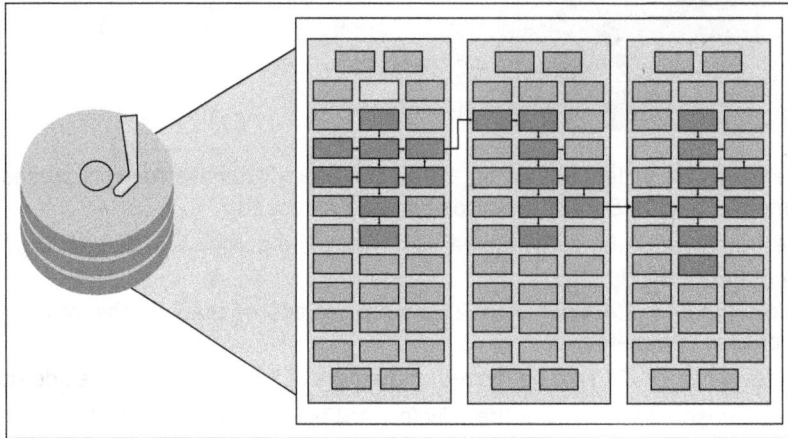

Now that we have seen how a metadata approach can help us to identify the transactional business objects, the next step would be to actually archive the transactional business objects or transactional data. Typical transactional archiving software solutions help to identify the transactional business objects that need to be archived. They do the job of archiving from production databases to archive databases.

Based on set ILM policies, the data would be kept in archive databases for a certain number of years, and as the data ages it could be destroyed or moved into a long-term or historical archive. While the data keeps moving to different stages, the transactional archiving software solutions purge the data that is archived from the previous store, to get the full benefit of storage cost savings. Once the data is moved into a long-term archive, it can be further managed with data retention policies and provisioned for search, reporting, and legal discovery functions.

In this chapter, we are going to use the Solix Enterprise Data Management Suite (Solix EDMS) software solution to illustrate the complete lifecycle for active application archiving. Solix EDMS is provided by the California-based software company Solix Technologies.

The following screenshot illustrates the lifecycle for typical prepackaged or structural applications. We will walk through the entire process in the next section.

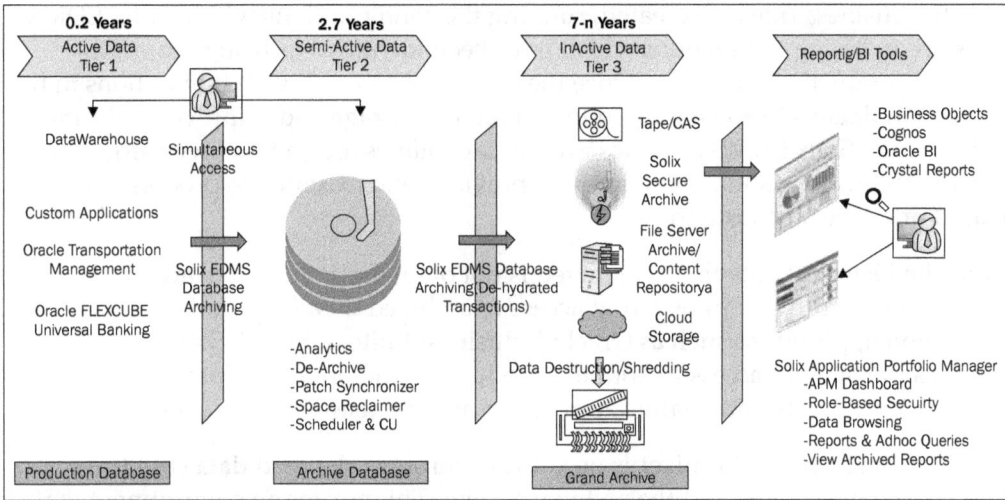

Solix EDMS comes with a metadata framework that is prepopulated with metadata for different prepackaged applications such as Oracle E-Business Suite, PeopleSoft, Siebel, JD Edwards etc. The same metadata framework can be extended to populate metadata from custom applications or Data Warehouses.

Using either the prepopulated metadata or the metadata that is extended with the customizations carried out for applications, a set of business rules that could include retention period information is created. The following figure was created using Solix EDMS Configurator:

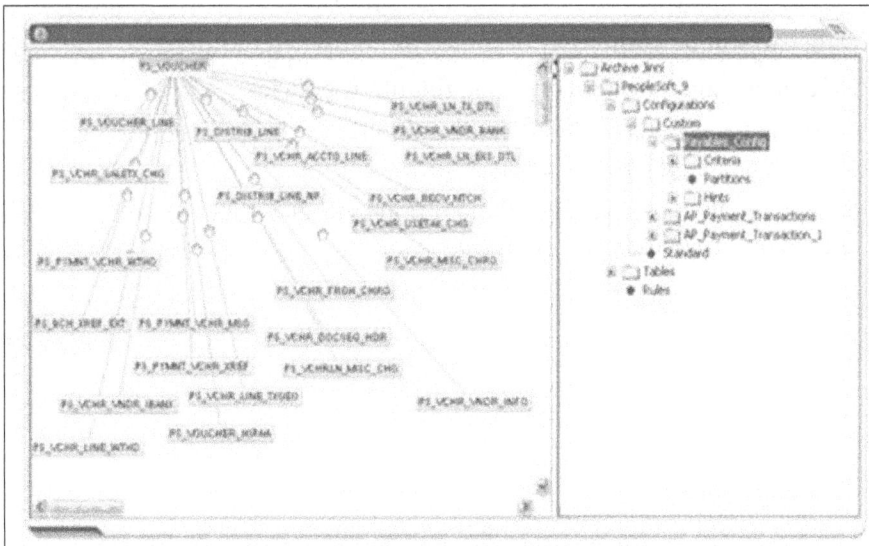

Once the business rules are created, running the configurations within Solix EDMS will start archiving transactions which have been identified as being required longer to production databases. Once the data has been archived, transactions in the production database can be purged to reclaim the storage and improve application performance. Solix EDMS provides unique capabilities around archive-purge cycles, with capabilities to simulate the process, preview, and execute the process in a phased or single-step fashion.

While the historical data that is archived is not often used, the active archived application can provide transparent access to archived data from native in-production applications such as Oracle E-Business Suite or Siebel. Solix EDMS provides transparent access to both the production and archived data, or a combination of both using native application and database security models.

Solix EDMS Patch Synchronizer is used to synchronize changed data structures between the production and the archival system. This creates an environment that is easy to maintain through production upgrade cycles.

The data resides in the archive database or Tier 2/Tier 3 for a certain period of time, based on ILM policies and thereafter the data can get destructed or moved into long-term archives. Solix EDMS provides capabilities to merge master data from the production database and transactions from the archive to provide complete context and move the data into a long-term archive, which could be tapes, file systems, content repositories, or highly compressed databases based on column-based technologies that could providing compression of up to 90 percent.

Once the pertinent data has been moved into long-term archives, we need to ensure:

1. Data can still be seamlessly accessed as and when required.
2. Data is managed under corporate retention policies.
3. Data can be searched, placed on legal holds, and produced for a legal discovery in case a request comes in.
4. Data is finally destroyed when retention expires with complete audit trial and chain-of-custody information.

Solix EDMS provides a comprehensive solution for a long-term archive with Solix Application Portfolio Manager (Solix APM). Once the data is in a long-term archive, Solix APM starts the management of data by applying relevant retention policies that can either be entered into the system or imported from the corporate retention schedule. While Solix APM is managing and monitoring the data, it also serves as an end/business user reporting tool where business users can create queries that are working against business views of data. These queries can be saved and scheduled for future runs as well. If a request comes for the legal or compliance department to produce a certain data subset, Solix APM can place legal holds on data objects and export the relevant data to a legal archive for further processing and culling. Finally, Solix APM sends notifications to data stewards when retention for data expires and processes the data for destruction once approval is received with complete audit-trail information.

Application Retirement

Application Retirement is part of ILM that holistically manages the enterprise application portfolio. With the recessionary economy and the consolidation of companies in 2009, large numbers of enterprises and data centers across a variety of industries are looking for ways to reduce IT expenditures. The mantra of 'doing more with less' has become much more pervasive in executive board meetings to small project meetings. This phenomenon along with Mergers & Acquisitions (M & A) activity across industries have been the driving factors for application retirement solutions. This allows companies to retire seldom-used applications to significantly cut hardware, storage, and software maintenance costs in addition to indirect expenditures such as power, space, and so on. Companies that successfully complete application retirement projects must adhere to compliance regulations that require them to retain large amounts of data for years, while preserving the application context and making the data accessible from standard reporting tools.

Eventually, every application reaches the end of its useful lifetime and needs to be retired. In some cases, the need to shut down a group of legacy systems is urgent and immediate, for instance:

* When migrating off mainframe hardware in favor of a less expensive hardware, SOA, or cloud-based infrastructure
* When migrating to newer functionality such as:
    ° From older departmental control systems to ERP
    ° From older Oracle applications to Oracle Fusion
    ° From in-house applications to Software-as-a-Service (SaaS)

- When the vendor withdraws support
- When the application only provides limited support for modules
- When older applications cannot support access by new mobile platforms or remote users
- When it becomes difficult to customize the application to meet changing business needs
- When the last programmer with the skills needed to maintain the application retires

Application retirement should be part of the plan for new application installation, with a retirement schedule set and funding allocated. Unfortunately, in many cases application retirement is not intrinsic to project completion. While hardware wears out, software does not, and as a result obsolescent applications do sometimes live on long past their useful lifetime. A variety of issues contribute to this:

- Many IT shops do not maintain complete software inventories, or if they do, they seldom review that software to identify applications that no longer contribute more business value than the cost.
- Pulling the plug on an obsolescent application always carries political and business risks. Users often resist change to new solutions, sometimes the application may still meet a legitimate business need not supported by a replacement, and IT is often hesitant to make the experiment.
- Even if the application is seldom used, the data is still important. In today's business, regulatory compliance, and legal environment, companies have to retain large amounts of data for years, and often that means the applications that generated them are also retained to ensure access to that data, which is often in proprietary formats no longer supported by more modern replacement systems.
- Multiple instances and versions of an application may hide in the inventory.
- Mergers and acquisitions often introduce applications that duplicate existing functionality but arrive with their own strong group of supporters, both in IT and among users, creating strong political pressure to maintain both.
- Application retirement has often been an expensive process, particularly when the data needs to be preserved in an accessible form to satisfy legal and business requirements. The result is that each application retirement often becomes an expensive consulting project.

- This practice of maintaining applications long past their obsolescence, however, creates a drain on company resources both in the form of direct and indirect costs, including:
    - ° The cost of license and maintenance renewals
    - ° The cost of staff time, and often of maintaining obsolete skills, required to run the applications
    - ° The cost of hardware required to run the software
    - ° The cost of power, cooling, and data center floor space
    - ° The added cost of backing up the application and its data and restoring it in the event of a hardware failure or larger disaster
    - ° The drag on business efficiency it creates when end users use obsolescent software, either through choice or necessity, to access data that is otherwise unavailable

Legacy applications also hamper agility. Today, more than ever, IT needs to directly align with business direction to support the organization's growth and, in today's economy, sometimes its survival. In order to achieve this, IT needs to:

- Provide more responsive systems
- Increase flexibility to respond to changing business needs
- Better support business processes (for example, decrease the need for work arounds)
- Evolve toward SOA and cloud computing
- Increase value to customers

Obsolescent or legacy systems interfere with all of these goals. Overall, applications need to be retired when the cost of supporting and maintaining them exceeds the business value they provide. The business cannot afford to carry obsolete software. Thus, the IT department in every organization, regardless of size, needs a systematic plan for identifying and retiring those applications that are no longer productive, while avoiding or minimizing business disruption and ensuring continued access to data that is no longer maintained in production systems.

Start with Application Portfolio Management

Managing the application inventory starts with establishing a portfolio approach to management. This requires an inventory of all applications running in the data center, but goes beyond a mere list to create a cross-reference portfolio organization that identifies key aspects of each application, such as:

- Its main functions and any important limitations in functionality

- Its licensing and maintenance costs

- Any important limitations in its license, particularly any that might create legal complications when decommissioning

- Who uses the application and how often

- The business needs for the application

- The product road map and level of vendor support

- Other applications from the same vendor, particularly those closely linked, either technically or legally

- Costs, benefits, and risks involved in continued use of the application

We discussed this at length in our earlier book *Oracle Modernization Solutions*, 2008 published by Packt. Applications can be cross-referenced by all of these criteria and any other that seem relevant. In a large enterprise this can be a lengthy process, but it is not necessary to complete the analysis of the full population of applications before starting to identify retirement candidates. For instance, if the organization has multiple instances of an application, merging them into a single instance is usually obvious. Obsolete applications that are no longer vendor supported and are no longer part of the production environment can also be retired early and inexpensively. If it has two different applications with essentially duplicate functionality, one of those should move to the early retirement portfolio, with adequate training and support to minimize business disruption. Overall, if 70 percent of the functionality of a legacy application is duplicated in more modern replacements, it should be considered for decommissioning.

Less obvious but vital questions are whether the application fits the strategic business direction of the organization, and even if it does, whether it provides an important competitive advantage. If the answer to either of these questions is no, IT should investigate replacing it with a modern technology-based alternative that can provide the functionality the organization needs at a lower overall cost, while freeing staff and IT resources to support higher value applications. This is not an automatic decision, of course, and the enterprise needs to investigate the modern technology-based alternatives like cloud candidates. To be sure, they provide adequate levels of service and data security, but as the cloud offerings mature, they will become increasingly attractive as alternatives to in-house applications. This may also prove to be true in areas central to business operations such as ERP and corporate financials, when they do not provide direct competitive advantages to the organization. In such cases, moving that functionality to the cloud can decrease capital and operating costs and increase flexibility, making it the smart strategy when linked to a plan for retiring the in-house application.

Retiring legacy applications should not be treated as a one-off or special activity. IT needs to partner with the business to create a formal review process designed to:

- Agree on which applications should be retired
- Establish funding for the de-installation
- Define and execute retirements without causing undue anxiety, risk, or inconvenience among either IT staff or business users

One major concern in any retirement plan is creating a strategy for handling the data from the application. This is complicated as technical, business, and legal requirements must all be considered. Questions that need to be answered include:

- Are the data sets still needed for the production environment, or are they candidates for archiving?
- What reports are run on this data, are they still needed, and if so how can they be provided once the legacy application is de-installed?
- If some data is still required in the business environment (such as, to support ongoing business processes), how can that data be identified and migrated to the new application?
- What long-term legal/compliance and/or decision support requirements apply to the data, and how can these needs be satisfied at the least cost once the application is de-installed?

Once the candidate applications have been identified through Application Portfolio Management then the actual application retirement process can be categorized into four broad sections:

- Classify legacy data to be migrated
- Migrate legacy data to an archive platform
- Provide access to migrated data
- Retention management and legal discovery

Application retirement is an important part of any Application Portfolio Management strategy. These four categories are critical to help enterprises better manage application retirement projects and also properly execute an ILM strategy. The following screenshot shows the process for application retirement projects:

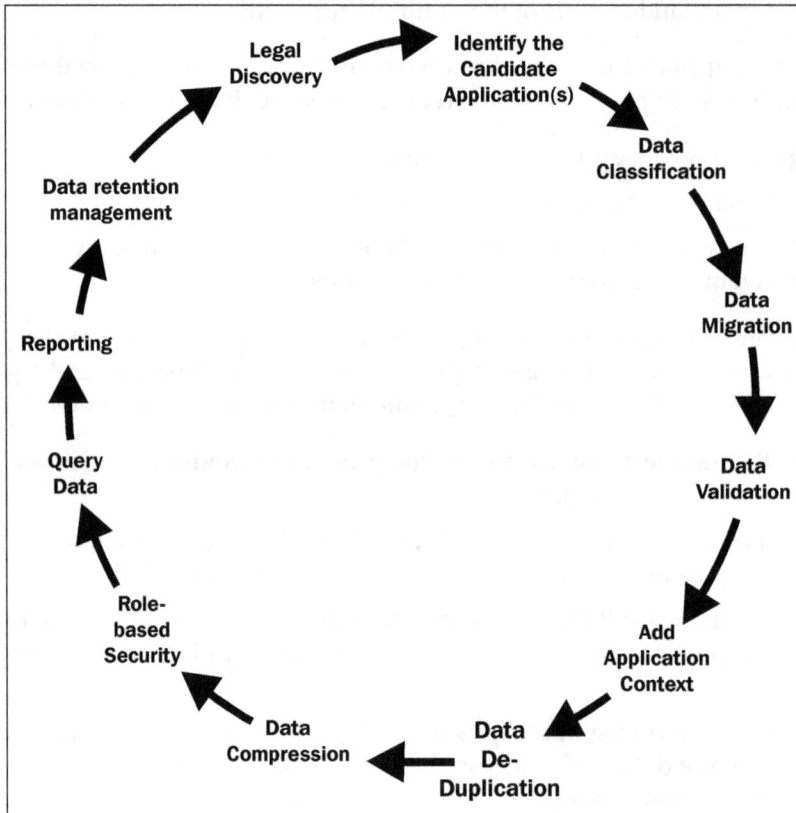

This process starts with the classification of applications. At this stage, enterprises have to determine which data needs to be put into a historical archive. One basic approach could be to move the entire dataset as is to a historical archive, the second approach could be migrating the data based on certain criteria such as data range, and a third approach could be migrating the top 10 percent of the data to the modern application that is replacing the legacy application and then migrating the remaining 90 percent to the historical archive.

Once the data has been classified, the next logical step is the actual data migration from legacy applications to a historical archive. Long-term or historical archives can be based on a relational database like Oracle Database or data can be ingested in CSV or XML format. The required **Service Level Agreements (SLAs)** for data retrieval will determine how enterprises will choose the target architecture. Once the choice for archiving platform is made, then data has to be migrated to the archive using the data classification model that has been performed previously.

What an organization needs to ensure during the application retirement process is that there is no loss of data or loss of precision for the data during the migration process. Loss of data can become a compliance or discovery nightmare. Data validation is the technique that would help to ensure that all the data is migrated from the legacy application database to the archive platform. Different data validation algorithms help to slice and dice the migrated data and ensure the migration of data has been completed successfully.

One of the benefits of the ILM process is reducing storage costs by tiering the data based on retention policies. When several applications are being retired, provisioning the same amount of storage in the archive platform doesn't reduce storage costs. Compression and deduplication of archived data help in reducing the storage requirements for the data that is migrated from legacy applications.

Once the data is stored in the archive and compressed, the application retirement process needs to ensure that seamless access is provided to the migrated data. Before this access is provided, enterprises typically want to make sure that the right people are accessing the right set of information. For example, Employees who have access to HR data might not have access to Customer or Product information. This is where role-based security needs to be set up for the archived data and enterprises are likely to already have an enterprise identity management solution with a single sign-on established. In this case, the role-based security of archived data needs to be integrated with either LDAP or Active Directory-based solutions that are already deployed in the enterprise.

Once the role-based security is provisioned, data can be accessed by end/business users to perform adhoc queries, save, and schedule queries with the ability to export the data if need be.

Executing retention policies or retention management of data allows the execution of over arching ILM policies. The data that has been migrated from legacy applications has to be assigned to predefined retention policies that will keep the data in different storage tiers for a particular period of time and eventually be destroyed when retention expires for a set of data objects.

Many organizations across industries face legal discovery requests where legal or compliance departments request data across several different sources, including archive platforms where structured or transactional data from legacy applications is stored. When a request comes in, the archive has to be able to support the search for a finite set of data which is relevant to that particular request. They then have to stop the retention execution on the data in case retention has expired and then place a legal hold on the requested data, so that the data under hold is not altered. Once the data is placed on hold, the archiving solution can export the relevant data for legal discovery processing and culling which can be finally produced in a court of law.

As discussed earlier, having an application retirement process helps enterprises manage the application portfolio with a proper process and execute ILM policies on structured applications that are prime candidates for retirement, but whose data has been managed under strict supervision.

Application Retirement solution from Solix Technologies and Oracle partner

Solix Technologies provides comprehensive solutions for application retirement through two products lines:

- Solix EDMS Application Retirement
- Solix ExAPPS — the industry's first application retirement appliance

Solix EDMS Application Retirement is an enterprise software that can be installed on-premise, where Solix ExAPPS is an integrated appliance that is a purpose-built solution for application retirement, where a highly compressed database, storage, server, and application retirement software (Solix EDMS Application Retirement) are prebuilt into the appliance so that enterprises can have the simplicity, a quick Return on Investment (ROI), and ease of use and manageability for maintaining data from legacy applications.

Both Solix solutions allow enterprises to follow the application retirement process that we have defined in the previous section of this chapter, where we started from data classification to legal discovery.

Solix EDMS and ExAPPS allow retirement for different categories of applications that could be on the mainframe, custom applications running on legacy or relational databases, or packaged applications like SAP, BaaN, MFG/Pro, and so on.

Some of the unique features are:

- Solix EDMS and ExAPPS provide comprehensive sets of data validation algorithms that have been defined in the previous sections. Full-fledged reporting and analytics on validation failures with pointers to specific column and row sets makes it easy to test, debug, and deploy the application retirement projects.

- Solix EDMS and ExAPPS allow either the import of the application context from the application data dictionary or create an application context using the tools built Solix EDMS. These features allows enterprises to create business views for data migrated from legacy applications so that the data makes and provides business sense when the legacy application is entirely decommissioned.

- Solix provides a highly compressed archive—Solix Secure Archive that provides 90 percent compression for transactional data objects to significantly reduce storage requirements and maintain the data in an immutable format.

- Solix Application Portfolio Manager (Solix APM) provides management of data in the archive. Solix APM can be tied with enterprise security with LDAP or Active Directory so that role-based security can be provisioned for users accessing data in the archive. Once the security is provisioned, Solix APM allows business users to simply select one or more data objects, select columns, and create reports that can be saved for future runs or scheduled to run at a predefined time. Solix APM also allows users to export queried data into CSV and XML if required, so that business users can do further analysis on legacy data.

- Solix EDMS and ExAPPS provide complete retention management and legal discovery functionality. A specific retention schedule can be assigned to different data objects and a notification framework keeps in sync with the internal clock to kick-off workflow notifications to data owners when retention expires. When the approval is received from data owners, Solix EDMS and ExAPPS can perform data destruction with complete audit trial and chain-of-custody. Apart from this, data requested by legal and compliance can be placed on hold until further notification, so that retention expired data is not destroyed and data is made immutable to prevent any tampering to the data on the hold.

Summary

Structured or transactional data in enterprises is growing at exponential rates, which is resulting in enterprises spending significant amounts of money to keep up with application performance, storage costs, risk mitigation from industry regulations, and so on. Traditional techniques like hardware and storage refresh are only taking enterprises so far. ILM allows enterprises to manage data growth consistently in adherence with corporate policies.

ILM policies allow enterprises to address the data movement from its creation to destruction, while improving the performance of applications by keeping the production databases at optimum levels and reducing the storage costs with the data being moved based on retention policies. The ILM strategy for structured applications helps both active applications as well legacy applications that are prime candidates for retirement but are kept running for the sake of their data.

Archiving solutions that enable ILM policies assist production applications to move identified transactional business objects from the production database to the archive database, while keeping the access to both the production and archive data transparent from a business user perspective. As the data for active applications keeps aging, this data can be migrated to a long-term archive where data is put under retention and made available for reporting and legal discovery.

For legacy applications, enterprises can combine a comprehensive application retirement process along with ILM policies to better manage their application portfolio. This can reduce significant IT costs for maintenance and mitigate the risk from legacy data by properly managing it under the retention and discovery process. ILM provides the benefits of controlling data growth, risk mitigation, and compliance with data retention regulations, storage cost reduction, increased application performance, and a better business continuity strategy for enterprises.

For more information refer to *Keeping Up With Ever-Expanding Enterprise Data – 2010 IOUG Database Growth Survey*.

Appendix

The appendix will look at some topics that are emerging in the market place such as integration in the cloud, and data application and process integration convergence. For some readers these topics may not be new, for others, these topics are not something they encounter in their day-to-day tasks. The idea is to discuss technology trends in the integration space and discuss the merits and drawbacks to some of these technologies. Web services will be discussed in terms of whether a web service-based approach for all your integration needs is the best solution.

Cloud integration

There are many components of your IT infrastructure that can be deployed to the cloud. With grid computing, driving data center consolidation and resource sharing, the need to further cut the cost of operating data centers filled with disparate systems led to an evolution known as **cloud computing**. The National Institute of Standards and Technology (NIST) define cloud computing as follows:

> "Cloud computing is a model for enabling convenient, on-demand network access to a shared pool of configurable computing resources (such as, networks, servers, storage, applications, and services) that can be rapidly provisioned and released with minimal management effort or service provider interaction."

The basic premise of cloud computing is that users can get access to any IT resource, including storage, CPU resources, memory, and software, over the Internet whenever they want. Users can pay for their actual use of the resource, rather than incurring capital and operational expenditures in order to own and operate the IT infrastructure. This computing scheme closely mimics the way households pay for utilities such as electricity and gas on metered usage.

The NIST cloud computing model is composed of five unique characteristics, three service models, and four deployment models. The five characteristics associated with this model mainly enable easier availability of metered, scalable, elastic computing resources that can be provisioned through self-service and can be accessed from any thin or thick client over the network.

The most well-known option is to run your applications in the cloud using **Software-as-a-Service (SaaS)**. It is also possible to run your database systems in the cloud using **Database-as-a-Service (DaaS)**. It is even possible to run your entire IT software and hardware infrastructure in the cloud using **Platform-as-a-Service (PaaS)**. It is also possible to deploy your integration architecture into the cloud, **Integration-as-a-Service (INaaS)**.

INaaS is defined and implemented using a variety of technologies. It all depends upon the IT vendor you are referring to. IT vendors are going to define and implement INaaS that most closely matches their current product offerings. Most INaaS offerings make use of web services, well-defined interfaces, and are loosely coupled. Some vendors offerings are nothing more than placing their current integration products, with some minor changes, in a PaaS environment and branding the solution as INaaS.

For SaaS providers, an INaaS solution is a necessity. As SaaS gains greater acceptance among companies of all size, there is a need to exchange data from in-house hosted applications and databases to the newer SaaS solutions and hosting facilities. However, there is also an increasing need for data integration solutions aimed at integrating a variety of SaaS solutions to support a company's internal processes and external interactions. This is because SaaS is not only being used within enterprises to facilitate various internal functions, it also enables companies to transact business with other companies over the Internet.

`Saleforce.com` is the leading independent SaaS provider. Looking at what `Salesforce.com` is doing in the INaaS space is a logical place to start when discussing INaaS and SaaS. `Salesforce.com`'s approach to INaaS is to offer rich web services APIs and a catalog of pre-integrated applications. The developer API-focused approach makes sense given `Salesforce.com`'s rich heritage of developing easy to use and extensible applications which are accessible over the Internet.

Workday is another pure-play SaaS provider to enterprise customers. The Workday cloud-based approach to integration is more extensive than what is offered by `Salesforce.com` as it includes these three core components:

- **Standards-based, web services APIs**: At the core of Workday are open, standards-based APIs that give complete programmatic access to business operations and processes

- **Integration Cloud Platform**: An INaaS platform for building, deploying, and managing integrations to and from Workday; where all integrations are deployed to and run in the Workday Cloud without the need for any on-premise integration software or application servers

- **Integration Cloud Connect**: Cloud Connect is a growing ecosystem of pre-built, packaged integrations and connectors to complementary solutions that are built, supported, and maintained by Workday

Traditional integration IT vendors are also starting to offer INaaS. Infomatica has been the most aggressive integration vendor when it comes to offering INaaS. Informatica has offered INaaS for over five years and continues to add capabilities, has a number of high profile references, and also continues to add out of the box cloud integration with major COTS and SaaS providers. Informatica Marketplace contains pre-packaged Informatica Cloud end-points and plugins. One such Marketplace solution, is integration with Oracle E-Business Suite using Informatica integration. The Informatica E-Business Suite INaaS offering includes automatic loading and extraction of data between the Salesforce CRM and on-premise systems, cloud-to-cloud, flat files, and the relational database. The entire Informatica Cloud integration solution runs in an Informatica-managed facility (PaaS). When running in a PaaS environment, Informatica offers an option to keep an exact copy of your cloud-based data on-premise for archival, compliance, and enterprise reporting requirements.

A new technology area like cloud computing always attracts new IT vendors that provide solutions specific to the new technology area. This is the case in cloud computing and new IT vendors that offer products specific to INaaS. Hubspan and Cordys are two such companies. Hubspan offers a multitenant integration platform that can handle all major enterprise applications, transports, and data formats, as well as core business processes such as procurement, logistics, payments, and human capital management. The Hubspan solution is offered in a SaaS model. Cordys offers a **Business Operations Platform (BOP)** suite as a PaaS enablement play for enterprises. Its vision is to become an enterprise application integration replacement by providing 'Tibco-like integration' in the cloud. Cordys BOP suite includes **Business Application Monitoring (BAM)**, BPM, master data management, and integration tools.

Implications of web services for all Integration

New business processes typically must be web service-ready, as they're expected to communicate in a bidirectional manner with service-orientated technologies such as BPEL and ESBs. Today, BPEL process managers using web service interfaces have become a core component for business process execution and integration in service-orientated infrastructures. Traditional ESBs have been messaging-based proprietary platforms, but are focused more on providing integration through web service interfaces. In both the BPEL and ESB cases, web services are being positioned by IT vendors and industry experts as the 'holy grail' of **Enterprise Information Integration (EII)**. The IT vendor's answer is to make your applications, data, and processes web service-enabled, and your EII and EAI woes will all be addressed. However, there are some potential issues with using web services for all integration needs:

- **Performance**: The XML-based messages that are exchanged when using web services can lead to performance problems on several fronts. The first area is that the XML message must be built using expensive CPU cycles and memory on the source machine. On the receiving end, due to web services using XML to exchange information, these documents require marshaling of the request or the message being sent, and de-marshaling (essentially reading the message that was sent). Processing the XML message requires more CPU resources, and potentially larger data storage than a typical integration approach would consume.

- **Network**: XML is an ASCII-based (human-readable text in a document) and contains the data definition tags inside the XML document along with the data payload. This can cause the internal network to become saturated with web service XML-based integration traffic. For external web service network interaction, the situation is worse because you may have a slow network where bulky XML-based communication can perform very poorly. Even if the network is fast and can support a lot of bandwidth, the XML documents travel over HTTP, which is not optimized to work with the underlying network protocol which is TCP/IP. In addition to the current integration solutions, you may just use TCP/IP, by introducing web services into the current architecture where you have two communication protocol layers (HTTP and TCP/IP) as opposed to one (TCP/IP).

- **Not everything can be made a web service**: DOS Windows-based application or C applications are two examples of applications that don't have web service capabilities built into them. You can use products from companies like Seagull Software to make these applications web service-enabled; however this entails purchasing, learning, and maintaining a new product. Technologies and languages that are not easily web service-enabled may be better served by keeping the current custom-built application point-to-point integration solution, using message-based products, simple flat file transfer using FTP, or some other product like an ETL/ELT solution.

- **Current integration solutions**: It is safe to say that your company currently uses a number of custom and vendor-based integration solutions. These solutions are not going to disappear from the corporate landscape any time soon. Some of these solutions may not even support web services. These current solutions still need to be leveraged for years to come as you migrate to a web services approach to integration.

These potential issues may not be a concern, based upon the hardware are you using, the types of languages your applications are written, in the network bandwidth at your company, and the number of legacy integration solutions.

It is always important to learn from past lessons. Remember **Enterprise Java Beans (EJBs)**, built for remote invocation of Java objects across the network? The EJB standard was intended to solve the issues related to application integration by making it easy for Java modules to integrate. 'Easy' is a relative term as learning and implementing EJB technology was not necessarily easy. EJB interfaces and communication implementation assumed that EJBs would be calling other EJBs in other locations; remote application integration. The issue was, that when most companies deployed EJBs they discovered that in a majority of cases EJBs were communicating with EJBs on the same machine or at least within the same company. EJBs incurred a lot of internal processing and communication overhead was required for remote invocation when in most cases this overhead was not necessary. So, Plain Old Java Objects (POJOs) came along which did not have the overhead of remote communication and building remote interfaces. POJOs are built to use Inter-Process Communication (IPC) and assume that both Java objects will reside locally in the same hardware infrastructure.

The authors are not implying that web services are going the way of EJBs. Web services are here to stay and continue to gain momentum as the leading EII and EAI technology. However, you should be aware of the four potential issues, listed previously, with web services and watch what leading IT infrastructure vendors do to address these issues.

Data, process, and application integration convergence

Data integration is typically the domain of the organization and people that manage the databases. The products used to integrate data in these organizations are a combination of custom data transfer and load scripts, ETL, and ELT products, and in some cases database stored procedures. Application integration, on the other hand, is often done by the application developers using custom-written applications, message brokers or an enterprise service bus. Process integration is often done by developers, but can also be done by business analysts, or even business users. Process integration uses a workflow engine, BPEL product, or a proprietary orchestration engine like Microsoft BizTalk to orchestrate a set of processes into one business flow. Each of these technologies have offered solutions focused in their own domain:

- **Data integration**: Used to unload, move, transfer, and load data from one database engine to another database engine from the same or different vendor. Also used to load flat files received from outside or within the company, and extract flat files from the database.

- **Application integration**: Focused on applications communicating with each other to complete a business transaction, or exchanging data and messages between two or more applications. Many times it is used instead of data integration, so that application business logic can be applied to the data before, after or during processing.

- **Process integration**: Process integration combines a set of standalone processes into one end-to-end business process. Process integration usually involves integrating with many different applications, data sources, or web services in order to fulfill the business flow such as a purchase order.

What is happening is that each of these integration technologies is adding capabilities of the other two technologies:

- **Data integration**: Data integration products all have web services support. This has not always been the case. Web services exposed in data integration products can be consumed by applications or business processes. This makes integrating data integration products with applications or business processes very easy. ELT and ETL products have always had robust workflow engines that are very similar in functionality to a process integration product such as a BPEL Process Manager.

- **Application integration**: Application integration products now all have data adapters for the major relational databases, content management repositories, XML files, and flat files. This opens up the option of doing both application and data integration at the application tier.

- **Process integration**: Process integration products, like Oracle BPEL Process Manager, have a number of adapters from message, to flat file, and relational databases. BPEL Process Managers were built from the ground up to support web services, so they obviously can communicate with any application, data, or another process that is exposed as a web service.

Each of these products will probably continue to be sold separately by IT vendors. However, the focus on orchestrating business processing using a BPEL Process Manager, exposing applications, processes, and data as web services will cause these separate products to act and look more like one product than separate products. The adoption of SCA is expediting the convergence of data, application, and process integration.

Job scheduling, ETL/ELT and BPEL product convergence

Any time you buy something with a credit card, make a phone call, pay for a doctor's visit, or pay your mortgage, there's a high probability that the transaction was processed in a nightly batch cycle using flat file FTP-based integration. The transaction is typically flat file FTP'd to your company's data center. This flat file FTP-based solution is data integration at its core, and the processing of these flat files is part of your overall business EII architecture. These batch processing information integration components can be part of a job scheduler, a BPEL flow, a workflow engine, or an ETL/ELT product. The information integration could also be custom coded using COBOL, Perl, Java, Oracle PL/SQL, and OS scripts that make database SQL calls.

As more companies adopt an enterprise approach to information integration and define SOA strategies, a fundamental question asked is: *Do I put my current flat file batch processing into a job scheduler, an ETL/ELT tool, a workflow engine, or in BPEL? Is there a single product or tool that can manage both the business processing and information integration solutions that are required? If not, how can the various products and tools integrate?* Legacy mainframe systems are typically straightforward, as business processing is typically achieved in batches through a job scheduler, and the remaining workflow and business processes will be part of the COBOL, PL/1, or Assembler application. On distributed systems, the question becomes even more complicated. Part of the processing may happen in a job scheduler, some in a business process manager, some in an ETL/ELT tool, and some in a workflow engine.

There's some industry discussion that BPEL engines can provide the same type of functionality as a job scheduler. Fundamentally, job schedulers and BPEL Process Managers are machine and human workflow engines. However, this greatly simplifies the number of duties job schedulers perform to provide you with enterprise-wide batch load scheduling and management. Job schedulers provide functionality that isn't core to BPEL:

- **Platform support**: The ability to execute jobs on any popular hardware or operating system platform. This also includes integrated scheduling of z/OS, Linux on mainframe System z, iSeries, Tandem, Unix, Windows, and Linux workloads.

- **Job priority**: Service classes (job priority) are built into mainframe Job Entry Subsystems (JES) from the outset to provide a mechanism for prioritizing batch processing, based on resource requirements and job priority.

- **Calendaring**: This isn't just a simple system that starts a job at a specific time or date. This is a complex calendaring system with the ability to change dependencies and view daily, monthly, quarterly, and yearly job schedules. It offers easy configuration and maintenance of even the most complex schedules, letting users maintain a single job schedule calendar across the enterprise.

- **Proactive critical path analysis**: Job schedulers automatically calculate and display job dependencies and analyze the critical path. Proactive notification, in the event it appears, means the critical path is in jeopardy of completing on time. Also, the ability to analyze the impact of a change in the job schedule, or a new job being added before it's put into production, are tasks the job scheduler performs automatically.

- **Interface to hardware devices**: The job scheduler is proactive and can check the availability of peripheral devices, such as storage and printers, before it executes a job that's dependent on a device that's offline or not functioning properly.

Job scheduling systems served legacy systems well, when most of the processing happened in batches at night using flat file integration. New business processes must typically be web service-ready, because they're expected to communicate in a bidirectional manner with service-orientated technologies such as BPEL and ESBs. Today, BPEL Process Managers have become a core component for business process execution in service-orientated infrastructures on distributed systems and are taking the place of job scheduling products.

ETL/ELT products have both the capabilities of a BPEL Process Manager and job scheduler:

- **Workflow**: The ability to graphically design the flow of information through the ETL/ELT process and then deploy this workflow to an integrated workflow engine. The workflows in ETL/ELT products are typically as 'smart' as job schedulers. Job schedulers have the built in capability to determine the best path to use.

- **Human interaction**: ETL/ELT workflows offer the ability to add human intervention at any point in the processing of data.

- **Basic job scheduling**: Basic job scheduling to including starting a ETL/ELT workflow at a specific time, looking for input files and then starting processing, and process dependencies are all part of ETL/ELT products.

- **Web services integration**: The ability to expose any component or workflow as a web service (publish web services) and also the ability to consume web services.

Distributed systems job schedulers are available from several job scheduling companies, including ORSYP (Dollar Universe), UC4 (AppWorx), and ActiveBatch (Advanced Systems Concept, Inc). Oracle also has a free job scheduler that is part of the Oracle Database. As it is built into the Oracle Database, it is multi-platform and has all the reliability, availability, scalability, and performance that are part of the Oracle Database. Open systems business automation processing is typically achieved through BPEL Process Manager products. BPEL Process Managers let you orchestrate Web service implementations, human interaction, and system workflow quickly and easily using graphical, drag-and-drop techniques. The tools are end user-focused, allowing users to orchestrate their own systems. The execution language for orchestration is BPEL, and the runtime engine is Java EE. BPEL supports human and automated orchestration. Enterprises typically use BPEL Process Managers to streamline and rethink existing business processes.

The business information processing and information integration solution of the future will most likely be business service automation through the grid, cloud computing, dynamic workload automation, and job management as a service. This means workflow products, including job schedulers and BPEL Process Managers, will probably play an important role in batch-based information integration. Job schedulers, BPEL engines, and ETL/ELT products can be combined, leveraging the strengths of each to implement a batch-based information integration solution. ETL/ELT products will most likely continue to form the basis for the initial processing of flat files, data transformation, and database loading and extract flat files to and from relational databases.

Middle tier integration appliances

A dedicated and integrated software and hardware stack has taken the industry by storm, Netezza as one of the first out with an appliance for data warehousing. Oracle introduced the Exadata product that is an integrated software and hardware stack for both data warehouses and OLTP systems. Oracle then introduced an integrated application server hardware and software stack called Exalogic. So why not use an appliance for integration? Cast Iron Systems already offers 'integration as an appliance' with a product called the Cast Iron Integration Appliance.

Although new to the market, the Oracle Exalogic platform is already being viewed as a potential integration appliance. This is because the Exalogic machine runs the Oracle SOA Suite which has the OSB and Oracle BPEL Process Manager for integration. As the capacity of the smallest Exalogic configuration (96 cores in a quarter rack), Exalogic as an integration appliance only makes sense in high volume environments that require millisecond processing time. This is because Exalogic is not an inexpensive machine. The minimum configuration, called a quarter rack, has eight compute nodes (96 cores), 768 GB of RAM, 256 GB of FlashFire SSD and 40 TB of disk storage

How Exalogic and Cast Iron mature as integration appliances will be interesting to watch. It will also be interesting to see if other pure-play integration appliances emerge in the market place. Or perhaps other major IT vendors such as HP and Microsoft will introduce integration appliances.

Security

As data volumes grow and more data is moving over the network because of cloud computing, security of data is becoming more important. The two major aspects of data security are data at rest and data in transit.

One solution for data at rest is to encrypt the sensitive data in the database and store the encryption keys in a separate location; without the keys, any stolen data is worthless. However, you must strike a balance between two contradictory concepts: the convenience by which applications can access encryption keys and the security required to prevent the key theft. To comply with company and federal regulations, you need a solution immediately, without any complex coding. You can declare a column as encrypted without writing a single line of code. When users insert the data, the database transparently encrypts it and stores it in the column. Similarly, when users select the column, the database automatically decrypts it. This is done transparently without any change to the application code. Transparent data encryption of data at rest is becoming the norm in most relational database solutions.

Encryption of entire data devices or database storage units is another approach being taken. In the latest release of the Oracle Database (11*g*), it is possible to encrypt entire tablespaces. Tablespace encryption makes stored data encryption easier, without any storage increase, define a tablespace as 'encrypted' and use it to store your sensitive data. All major storage vendors including EMC, NetApp, IBM, Hitachi, and Oracle/Sun offer storage solutions that offer full disk encryption.

Although most companies take measures to encrypt and secure their production data, often the developer, quality assurance, and performance testing groups have unencrypted versions of the production data. Data masking allows for selected columns or all columns in the database table to have functionally equivalent data that is not the actual customer production data. Data masking allows for production data to be copied to test environments while not impacting the ability to perform proper application and system testing.

Most companies do an adequate job of securing data at rest from outside forces and internal IT users. However, some of the most recent high profile data breaches have been performed by IT personnel. This is why Oracle introduced the Oracle Database Vault. Oracle Database Vault addresses common regulatory compliance requirements and reduces the risk of insider threats by:

- Preventing highly privileged users (DBA) from accessing application data
- Enforcing separation of duty—providing controls over who, when, where and how applications, data, and databases can be accessed

Another product from Oracle, Oracle Audit Vault, transparently collects and consolidates audit data, providing valuable insight into 'who did what to which data and when', including privileged users who have direct access to the database. With Oracle Audit Vault reports, alert notifications, and centralized audit policy management, the risks from internal threat and the cost of compliance are greatly reduced. This type of tracking can identify when a DBA performs suspicious activity on sensitive data such as credit card numbers or customer bank account balances.

Data in transit is typically secured using SSL or Virtual Private Networks (VPN). Major IT vendors are providing their own product offerings that provide end-to-end security; from the client to the database server. Oracle application and database servers support major security standards and specifications in the areas of Java, JEE, web services, and so on. Oracle provides a Security Framework that is standards-based, and any third-party or custom-developed security product can be plugged in as a Service Provider. Also the Oracle framework ships with default out of the box Service Providers.

Data at rest and in transit solutions from leading IT vendors will continue to be integrated into their hardware, software, database, network, and storage solutions. The more security is embedded in your IT infrastructure, as opposed to being separate software components, the more transparent and performant it will be.

Mobile data and collective intelligence

There are a few obvious trends in the way we will be delivering new information that is a result of better integration strategies. For example, we are seeing more applications like BAM, OBIEE, and data from Oracle E-Business Suite being delivered through mobile devices and web browsers. This type of trend will only continue as salespeople continue to adopt mobile platforms (IE, Tablets) and employees that traditionally work at the office work from home or even at a coffee shop.

New releases of the Java platform combined with better computing power on devices is allowing for a return to fatter clients. We feel that there will be a growing trend in this area with the deployment of Java ME and Java FX. However, there are some bigger trends emerging today that may have integration at the core.

When we think about emerging technology and trends, we think about this in terms of disruptive technology. Disruptive technologies are those things that change the face of competition, buyer patterns or open up totally new industries. Consider Verizon. It was not that many years ago that Verizon provided mostly hardline phone systems. Undoubtedly, their management was building a strategy on how to lower costs and improve pricing schemes to attract more long distance customers. Today cloud computing and mobile platforms have become a genuine game changer for Verizon. Now they have added the Apple iPhone and have purchased TerraData, a cloud computing platform.

So, when we look to the future of technology and potential disruptions, we have to think about how emerging technologies are going to change the face of business. The need for realtime data integration and analysis is a critical factor for a company's success. Tim O'Reilly and John Battelle recently published a paper called *Web Squared: Web 2.0 Five Years On*. Look at the following quote, from their 2009 report:

> *Real time is not limited to social media or mobile. Much as Google realized that a link is a vote, Wal-Mart realized that a customer purchasing an item is a vote, and the cash register is a sensor counting that vote. Real-time feedback loops drive inventory. Wal-Mart may not be a Web 2.0 company, but they are without doubt a Web Squared company: one whose operations are so infused with IT, so innately driven by data from their customers, that it provides them immense competitive advantage. One of the great Web Squared opportunities is providing this kind of real-time intelligence to smaller retailers without monolithic supply chains.*

The concept of real-time intelligence will be taken to an entirely new level. As O'Reilly and Battelle point out, there will be a merging of traditional transaction data points along with social intelligence taken from different sensor points, like swarming twitter posts and photos. We will be able to merge pictures of reality based on analyses brought about from the community. We will be looking at a larger issue of data integration as we take in more than just multiple RDMS engines, but also ASCII twitter feeds and JPEG pixel images. This notion is considered the movement of the collective mind. The world continues to add sensors. As this becomes more prevalent we will be able to extract new ways to add value. Again from the O'Reilly paper, it has been discovered with the introduction of the smart meter, that each device connected emits a unique energy signature, down to the model and make of the appliance or home device. Information integration will be a key enabler here to unlock limitless possibilities.

Summary

The future is impossible to predict. In *Oracle Modernization Solutions*, written by two of the authors of this book, the book talked about the emergence of the Amazon cloud and data grids with respect to legacy modernization strategies. Some of these trends have continued to grow, but others stymied, such is the case with any predictions of emerging technologies. We have taken a look at several key developments that we are seeing within our customers and the industry as a whole.

There is no doubt that cloud computing is being adopted at a rapid rate by both large and small companies. We are seeing it happen all around us today. This is not possible without serious considerations to integration, consolidation, and migration. Cloud computing is all about shared resources. Shared resources are centralized resources that typically involve consolidation and migration projects in order to get to the shared resource, cloud model. Web services and the convergence in data, application, and process integration are not so much the future but are happening today. The future aspect of the trend toward web services for all integration needs, and process, application and data integration is whether these current trends will become de facto standards in the industry. We also looked at the current growth in mobile computing and how new information is being deployed to more powerful and ubiquitous devices. We merged this with the notion that mobile computing has enabled a new swarm of sensor data coming in for processing and analyses. Only time will tell how this will affect our very day-to-day life, but we do know for certain that it needs to be tightly integrated and consolidated for consumption.

Index

metadata 166
Meta-Data Services. *See* MDS
middle tier integration appliances 290
migration workbench 58
Millions of Instructions Per Second (MIPS)
    177
mobile data 292, 293
MQSeries 237

N

National Institute of Standards and Tech-
    nology (NIST) 281
New York Stock Exchange (NYSE) 239
NLSSORT clause 153
NLS_UPPER() function 153
NULL value
  handling 152
NUMBER subtype 145
numeric data
  about 145
  BINARY_FLOAT 145

O

OA adapter 235
OBI EE 58
Object Management Group (OMG) 221, 222
object names
  case-sensitive object names 143, 144
  length 144
  reserved words, using 142
OBR 237
ODI Suite 59
off-line mode 114-119
on-line capture 114
Online Transaction Processing (OLTP) sys-
    tem 35, 183
online transactions 75
open interfaces 228
open interface tables 228
Operational Data Store (ODS) 35
operator navigator 211
Oracle
  as service 180
Oracle ADF 247
Oracle Advanced Queuing. *See* AQ
Oracle Advanced Queuing (AQ) Adapter.

See AQ
Oracle Application Adapter. *See* OA adapter
Oracle Application and Process Integration
    Software Stack 230, 231
Oracle Application Developer Framework.
    See Oracle ADF
Oracle Application Framework (OAF) 254
Oracle Application Information Architec-
    ture (AIA)
  about 56, 60, 220
  data source 57
Oracle Application Server 11g Release 1
    (10.3.3)
  URL 72
Oracle AQ 60
Oracle as a Service (OaaS) 179, 180
Oracle B2B 240, 250
Oracle BI Enterprise Edition (OBIEE)
  about 42
  data source 42
Oracle BPA
  about 231, 250
  components 231
Oracle BPEL
  process manager 238
Oracle BPEL and database
  technical advantges, over mainframe batch
    processing 65, 66
Oracle BPM
  about 233, 250
  components 232, 233
  Enterprise Business Objects (EBOs) 243
  Meta-Data Services (MDS) 241
  Oracle AIA Foundation 247
  Oracle BPEL 237
  Oracle Business Rules (OBR) 237
  Oracle Business-to-Business (B2B) 240
  Oracle Complex Events Processing (CEP)
    239
  Oracle Service Component Architecture
    (SCA) 240
  Oracle Web Services Manager (WSM) 241
  Oracle Web Services Registry 241
  SOA adapters 233-237
Oracle BPM, components
  about 232
  Oracle BPM Dashboard 232

Q

R

S

[PACKT] enterprise
professional expertise distilled
PUBLISHING

Thank you for buying
Oracle Information Integration, Migration, and Consolidation

About Packt Publishing

Packt, pronounced 'packed', published its first book "Mastering phpMyAdmin for Effective MySQL Management" in April 2004 and subsequently continued to specialize in publishing highly focused books on specific technologies and solutions.

Our books and publications share the experiences of your fellow IT professionals in adapting and customizing today's systems, applications, and frameworks. Our solution based books give you the knowledge and power to customize the software and technologies you're using to get the job done. Packt books are more specific and less general than the IT books you have seen in the past. Our unique business model allows us to bring you more focused information, giving you more of what you need to know, and less of what you don't.

Packt is a modern, yet unique publishing company, which focuses on producing quality, cutting-edge books for communities of developers, administrators, and newbies alike. For more information, please visit our website: www.packtpub.com.

About Packt Enterprise

In 2010, Packt launched two new brands, Packt Enterprise and Packt Open Source, in order to continue its focus on specialization. This book is part of the Packt Enterprise brand, home to books published on enterprise software – software created by major vendors, including (but not limited to) IBM, Microsoft and Oracle, often for use in other corporations. Its titles will offer information relevant to a range of users of this software, including administrators, developers, architects, and end users.

Writing for Packt

We welcome all inquiries from people who are interested in authoring. Book proposals should be sent to author@packtpub.com. If your book idea is still at an early stage and you would like to discuss it first before writing a formal book proposal, contact us; one of our commissioning editors will get in touch with you.

We're not just looking for published authors; if you have strong technical skills but no writing experience, our experienced editors can help you develop a writing career, or simply get some additional reward for your expertise.

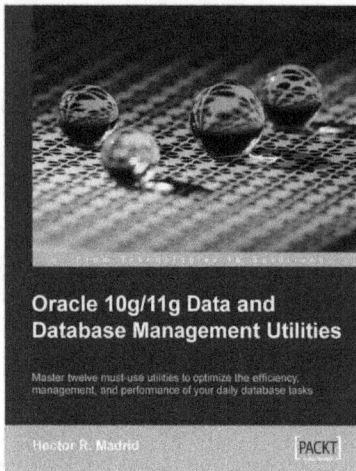

Oracle 10g/11g Data and Database Management Utilities

ISBN: 978-1-847196-28-6   Paperback: 432 pages

Master twelve must-use utilities to optimize the efficiency, management, and performance of your daily database tasks

1. Optimize time-consuming tasks efficiently using the Oracle database utilities

2. Perform data loads on the fly and replace the functionality of the old export and import utilities using Data Pump or SQL*Loader

3. Boost database defenses with Oracle Wallet Manager and Security

4. A handbook with lots of practical content with real-life scenarios

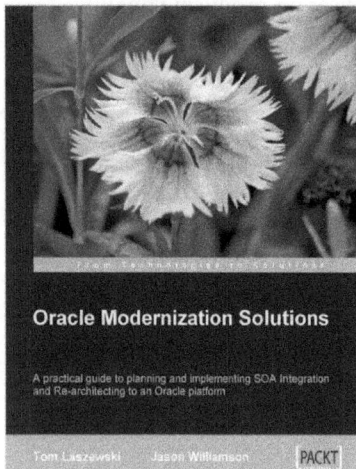

Oracle Modernization Solutions

ISBN: 978-1-847194-64-0   Paperback: 432 pages

A practical guide to planning and implementing SOA Integration and Re-architecting to an Oracle platform

1. Complete, practical guide to legacy modernization using SOA Integration and Re-architecture

2. Understand when and why to choose the non-invasive SOA Integration approach to reuse and integrate legacy components quickly and safely

3. Covers real-life scenarios with detailed hands-on examples

Please check **www.PacktPub.com** for information on our titles

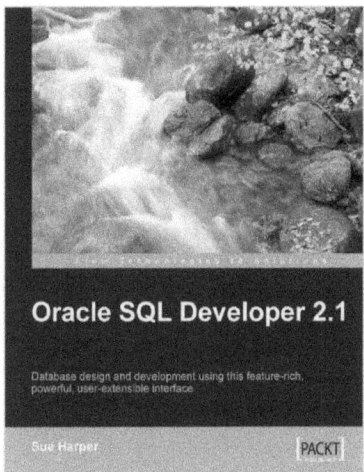

Oracle SQL Developer 2.1

ISBN: 978-1-847196-26-2   Paperback: 496 pages

Database design and development using this
feature-rich, powerful user-extensible interface

1. Install, configure, customize, and manage your
    SQL Developer environment

2. Includes the latest features to enhance
    productivity and simplify database
    development

3. Covers reporting, testing, and debugging
    concepts

4. Meet the new powerful Data Modeling tool –
    Oracle SQL Developer Data Modeler

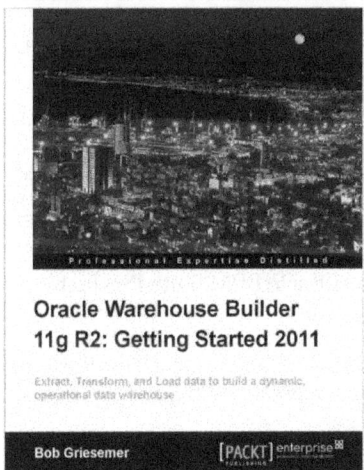

Oracle Warehouse Builder 11g R2: Getting Started 2011

ISBN: 978-1-84968-344-9   Paperback: 424 pages

Extract, Transform, and Load data to build a
dynamic, operational data warehouse

1. Build a working data warehouse from scratch
    with Oracle Warehouse Builder

2. Cover techniques in Extracting, Transforming,
    and Loading data into your data warehouse

3. Use a multi-dimensional design with an
    underlying relational star schema

Please check **www.PacktPub.com** for information on our titles

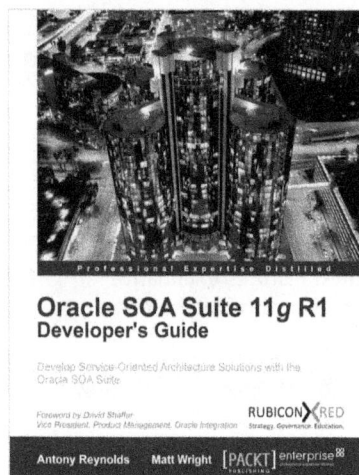

Oracle SOA Suite 11g R1 Developer's Guide

ISBN: 978-1-84968-018-9   Paperback: 720 pages

Develop Service-Oriented Architecture Solutions with the Oracle SOA Suite

1. A hands-on, best-practice guide to using and applying the Oracle SOA Suite in the delivery of real-world SOA applications

2. Detailed coverage of the Oracle Service Bus, BPEL PM, Rules, Human Workflow, Event Delivery Network, and Business Activity Monitoring

3. Master the best way to use and combine each of these different components in the implementation of a SOA solution

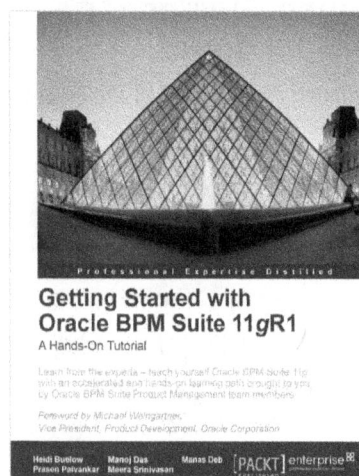

Getting Started with Oracle BPM Suite 11gR1 – A Hands-On Tutorial

ISBN: 978-1-84968-168-1   Paperback: 536 pages

Learn from the experts – teach yourself Oracle BPM Suite 11g with an accelerated and hands-on learning path brought to you by Oracle BPM Suite Product Management team members

1. Offers an accelerated learning path for the much-anticipated Oracle BPM Suite 11g release

2. Set the stage for your BPM learning experience with a discussion into the evolution of BPM, and a comprehensive overview of the Oracle BPM Suite 11g Product Architecture

3. Discover BPMN 2.0 modeling, simulation, and implementation

Please check **www.PacktPub.com** for information on our titles

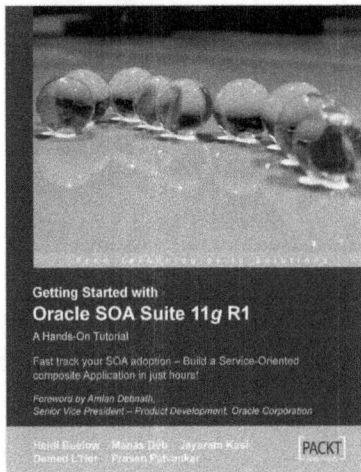

Getting Started With Oracle SOA Suite 11g R1 – A Hands-On Tutorial

ISBN: 978-1-847199-78-2   Paperback: 482 pages

Fast track your SOA adoption – Build a service-oriented composite application in just hours!

1. Offers an accelerated learning path for the much anticipated Oracle SOA Suite 11g release

2. Beginning with a discussion of the evolution of SOA, this book sets the stage for your SOA learning experience

3. Includes a comprehensive overview of the Oracle SOA Suite 11g Product Architecture

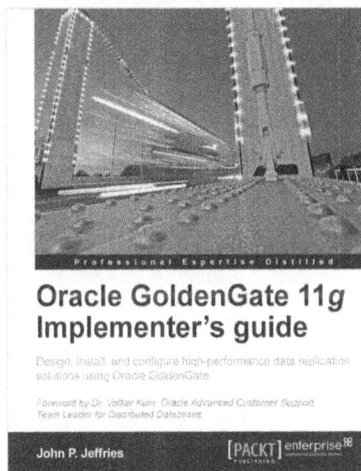

Oracle GoldenGate 11g Implementer's guide

ISBN: 978-1-84968-200-8   Paperback: 280 pages

Design, install, and configure high-performance data replication solutions using Oracle GoldenGate

1. The very first book on GoldenGate, focused on design and performance tuning in enterprise-wide environments

2. Exhaustive coverage and analysis of all aspects of the GoldenGate software implementation, including design, installation, and advanced configuration

3. Migrate your data replication solution from Oracle Streams to GoldenGate

Please check **www.PacktPub.com** for information on our titles

www.ingramcontent.com/pod-product-compliance
Lightning Source LLC
Chambersburg PA
CBHW080923220326
41598CB00034B/5661